Tools of the Trade
Modern Marketing for Construction Brands

by Neil M. Brown

Published by RB Communications, Inc., Aurora, IL.

Printed in the United States of America

Tools of the Trade: Modern Marketing for Construction Brands / Neil M. Brown

FOURTH EDITION
Includes bibliographical references.

ISBN 978-0-9849319-0-3
1. Marketing Construction Products and Services. 2. Marketing Strategy. 3. Branding. 4. Marketing Measurement. 5. Internet Marketing. 6. Social Media Marketing. 7. Channel Marketing. 8. Retail Home Improvement Marketing. 9. A/E/C Marketing.

To my partners, associates, contributors and clients —
thank you for all your help and encouragement.

///CMA

Table of Contents

Preface

WHAT IS CONSTRUCTION MARKETING?

In the broadest sense, construction marketing encompasses the variety of activities, programs and projects that support revenue generation. Similar to marketing in other categories, construction marketing is about developing and/or promoting products or services that serve customer needs. "Marketing 101" college textbooks defined marketing via the marketing mix and the **Four P's: Product, Promotion, Place and Price.** No question, these are still important. However, marketing has changed significantly in just the last few years. And a growing list of pundits voice that traditional marketing is obsolete, or that marketing is being replaced by new and interactive media.

TOOLS OF THE TRADE: MODERN MARKETING FOR CONSTRUCTION BRANDS addresses new media, traditional marketing, and the integration of both for measurable results. The objective of TOOLS OF THE TRADE is to identify and describe all aspects of a modern marketing program, and then to detail how each element of this new and different marketing mix can be implemented. To reinforce this learning, TOOLS OF THE TRADE provides visual examples and numerous case studies from our beloved construction industry (not billion dollar consumer brands that are not relevant).

To deliver on these objectives, TOOLS OF THE TRADE is organized in five units: Strategic Marketing, Tactical Marketing, Specialized Channels and Market Segments, Practical Marketing Considerations, and Construction Marketing Resources.

Strategic Marketing describes the foundational marketing initiatives that drive all downstream marketing implementation like planning, research, strategic tools, branding and how to measure marketing results. Tactical marketing describes functional activities including content, Internet, social media, advertising, publicity, new product development and much more.

Next, TOOLS OF THE TRADE identifies Specialized Channels and Market Segments including Distributor Channel Marketing, Retail Channel Marketing, and marketing to architectural, engineering or construction services or A/E/C marketing. Each of these channels or segments require vastly different marketing approaches than the others. Rather than being too general, we identify the specific marketing requirements of each.

The Practical Marketing Considerations unit provides insight into three areas deemed important by Construction Marketing Association members: hiring marketing talent, selecting marketing partners, and marketing automation.

///CMA

Please note that TOOLS OF THE TRADE is intended for experienced marketers, not beginners. Indeed, the book serves as the advanced marketing training guide for the Construction Marketing Association's certification program, the Certified Construction Marketing Professional (CCMP) designation. In fact, much of the content for the book is from ongoing training, webcasts and whitepapers from the Construction Marketing Association.

Some content for the book is provided by contributors and subject matter experts, duly noted in the respective chapters. Special thanks to the Construction Marketing Association Board of Directors for their ideas, support and volunteerism. Kevin Enke of Bosch Power Tools, Deborah Hodges, Executive Director of the Construction Writers Association, Jim Scarlata of Emerson Electric, Paul Deffenbaugh of DeepBrook Media, Tim O'Brien of CNH Construction Equipment. More special thanks to Lindsay Brown, my associate and manager of the CMA blog and social media program. Together we can achieve great things!

With marketing changing so rapidly, updates will be required. To this end, your comments and suggestions are appreciated. Contact information is listed at the end of the book. Please check back periodically for updates.

WHY IS CONSTRUCTION MARKETING IMPORTANT?

The construction industry has been one of the hardest hit in the recent recession. All sectors of construction—commercial, homebuilding and remodeling—have declined significantly. Some reports as high as 40%. Unlike prior recessions, construction is not expected to recover or return to the "exuberant" levels prior to 2007.

As a result of this economic turmoil, construction firms and the manufacturers that sell to them have undergone restructuring, layoffs and certainly, marketing budget cuts. This raises the question – how can you achieve marketing results with fewer resources? Less staff? A smaller budget?

The answer is more effective marketing. Doing more with less. Fortunately, some of the new marketing tactics are more cost efficient and measurable than traditional marketing. And when new marketing is integrated with traditional marketing, we have realized excellent results. Measurable results. So marketing is not just a cost center in a soft economic environment, but a growth engine. TOOLS OF THE TRADE will show you how!

Unit I: Strategic Marketing

Marketing implementation without a sound strategic foundation is risky, and potentially expensive to fix. Ideally, all downstream marketing implementation is guided by a plan, by an agreed upon strategic framework, and by customer or market insights that eliminate guesswork.

Our Strategic Marketing unit covers a broad range of topics. From the modern marketing mix, to branding considerations including naming and identity, marketing planning and budgeting best practices, market research that provides insight into marketing decisions, strategic marketing tools that support analysis and planning, and finally, the all-important measurement of marketing.

The Modern Marketing Mix

In 1960, marketing professor and college textbook author E. Jerome McCarthy coined the infamous terms, the "Four P's of marketing" and the "marketing mix." Henceforth, marketing has been defined as Product, Promotion, Price and Place. As recent as 1973, Webster's dictionary defined marketing as the advertising of products and services.

Long before the Internet, network TV and advertising dominated marketing. But now, mass media is highly fragmented—not to mention the ability to record television programs without advertising commercials. Today, for all but the biggest brands, advertising is a secondary tactic.

The modern marketing mix is evolving, in a good way. There are many reasons for this metamorphosis. First, construction and business-to-business buyers (like consumers) increasingly use the Internet for sourcing and selecting products and services. More specifically, buyers use search engines like Google, Yahoo and Bing. Consequently, search engine results have become a top marketing priority, and a new marketing discipline is born: search engine optimization or SEO.

Second, traditional marketing tactics like advertising and trade shows are expensive, and are being cut back and often replaced with less expensive tactics such as Internet and social media. This trend is reinforced by annual outlook surveys from the American Marketing Association, *BtoB* magazine and the Construction Marketing Association 2011 Outlook survey (below) identifies budgets increasing for Internet, social media and publicity, and declining for advertising, printing and tradeshows.

Marketing Tactic Increases/Decreases

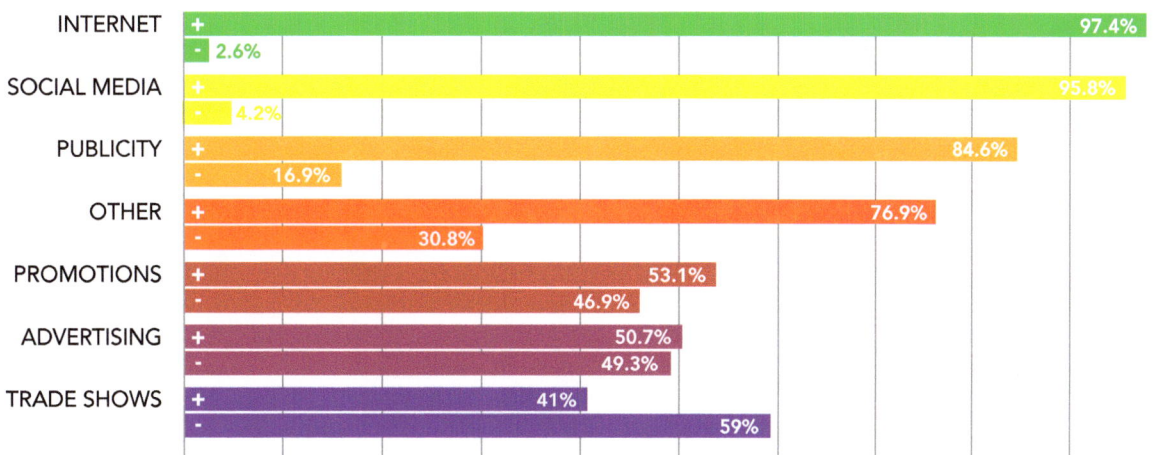

Tactic	+	−
INTERNET	97.4%	2.6%
SOCIAL MEDIA	95.8%	4.2%
PUBLICITY	84.6%	16.9%
OTHER	76.9%	30.8%
PROMOTIONS	53.1%	46.9%
ADVERTISING	50.7%	49.3%
TRADE SHOWS	41%	59%

Third, Internet-based marketing (including social media) can be more measurable than traditional marketing. Fourth, a focus on lead generation can be facilitated by website registration pages, and communicated via social media and integrated with traditional marketing.

In sum, the new marketing mix still requires a strategic marketing foundation to ensure all downstream marketing supports brand strategy and positioning. The new marketing mix "buckets" many traditional marketing tactics as Outbound Marketing, and many Internet and social media activities as Inbound Marketing, a term popularized by a leading internet consultant, Hubspot. Marketing measurement is integrated with both Inbound and Outbound and feeds back to planning and budgeting via reporting as a closed-loop system. See the modern marketing mix diagram on the next page.

The Modern Marketing Mix

Strategic Marketing

RESEARCH
primary research
secondary research
syndicated research
focus groups
competitive intel

PLANNING
strategic plans
media plans
forecasting
budgets
sales analysis
metrics
dashboard

STRATEGY
product
market
channel
content
positioning
segmentation

BRANDING
naming
logos
graphic identity
id standards
packaging
merchandising

PRICING

Outbound Marketing

ADVERTISING
print
broadcast
online
direct response
brand ads

PUBLICITY
news releases
news distribution
articles
media relations
press events

EVENTS
trade shows
webcasts
training
seminars
demos

SALES
sales tools
brochures
catalogs
promotion
channel programs
automation/crm

DIRECT
mail/email
list management
database
telemarketing

Inbound Marketing

INTERNET
web 2.0
seo
paid/ppc
microsites
mobile/apps
analytics

SOCIAL
blogs
linkedin
youtube
facebook
twitter
google+
pinterest
sharing
bookmarking

CONTENT
case studies
white papers
newsletters
research
surveys
ebooks
video
webinars

Marketing Measurement

TRADITIONAL
inbound telephone
customer acquisition
advertising inquiries
PR clips
database/CRM
market research
lead generation/
management
ESP dashboard

INTERNET
web stats/analytics
pay-per-click
SEO tools
registrations
PR dashboard
google alerts
UTM's

SOCIAL
linkedin
youtube
facebook
twitter
monitoring
(e.g. radian6)
google alerts
google+

Branding: Your Most Important Marketing Decision

Branding is often thought of as developing a name or a logo for a company or product (service). However, branding is much broader and includes brand strategy, brand identity, brand management and the brand experience.

1. *Brand strategy relates to customer and market insight, positioning, product definition, brand hierarchy, and platform; brand strategy serves as the foundation to brand identity, management and experience.*

2. *Brand identity is all visual (and verbal) elements including name (trademarks), logo, messaging, graphic themes (including color), taglines and messages, and standards or guidelines.*

3. *Brand management is the planning and administration of all aspects of brand marketing including launch, training, assets and tools, monitoring brand usage, and assessing brand (awareness, equity, preference).*

4. *Brand experience is all communications, interactions with your company or product, from advertising to telephone messages, signage to websites.*

Branding is one of the most critical marketing decisions you can make, and a decision that effects all other marketing. Why is branding important? A customer's brand perception is the sum of all brand experiences; positive perceptions lead to brand preference, commanding premiums, and driving financial success.

Brand strategy, implementation and management differ for established versus new brands or new products. For established construction brands, the brand name and visual identity of your company or product is your most valuable marketing asset. Corporate brands like Caterpillar (CAT), or product brands like SAWZALL® (Milwaukee Tool) come to mind.

Along with these names or trademarks are visual identities. For example, color palettes like Caterpillar yellow or Milwaukee red, logos and various graphic elements. Other branding elements include taglines and messaging.

Established brand identities are carefully managed by identity standards or usage guidelines. Brand names or trademarks are protected legally by trademark registrations and proper trademark usage.

New brands or new products should go through a strategic brand development process. Like established brands, the elements of a brand identity are the name or trademark, along with the visual identity including colors, logos and graphic elements.

Whether an established or new brand, using market research and various tools like perceptual maps can identify positioning strategy options.

Our chapter on branding will detail a proprietary brand name development process developed by author Neil M. Brown, along with information on taglines, trademarks and domain names. Next, visual elements of a brand will be considered including logos, brand architectures, and graphic identities.

To demonstrate how branding is being used by your construction category peers, the results of a 2011 survey on branding practices conducted by the Construction Marketing Association are shared below.

Survey Questions

1. *Are you responsible for brand development at your company?*
2. *Does your company have a single brand name, or multiple sub-brands and/or product brands?*
3. *What types of brand activities do you undertake?*

Brand Development Responsibility

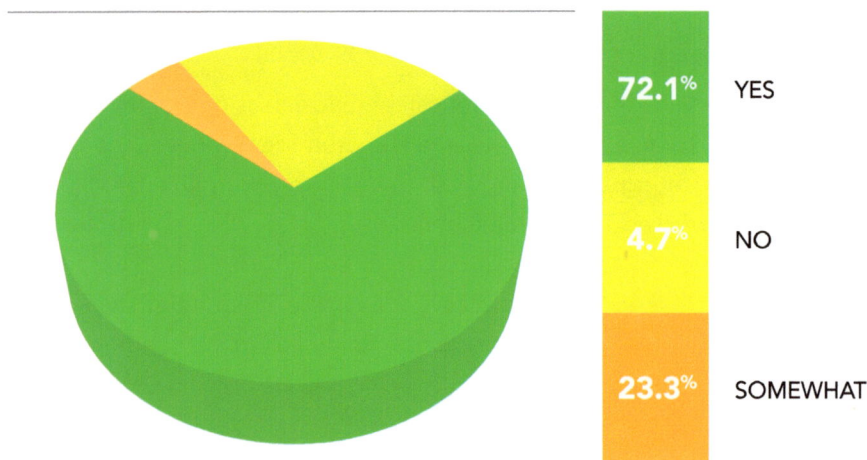

72.1%	YES
4.7%	NO
23.3%	SOMEWHAT

Single or Multiple Brand Names

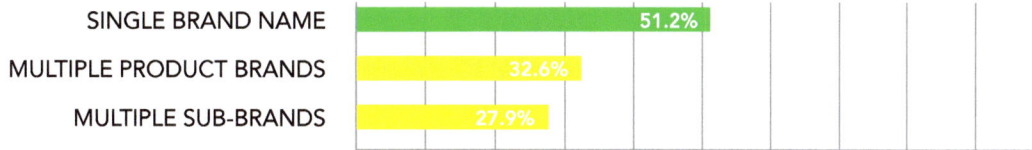

SINGLE BRAND NAME	51.2%
MULTIPLE PRODUCT BRANDS	32.6%
MULTIPLE SUB-BRANDS	27.9%

Types of Brand Activities

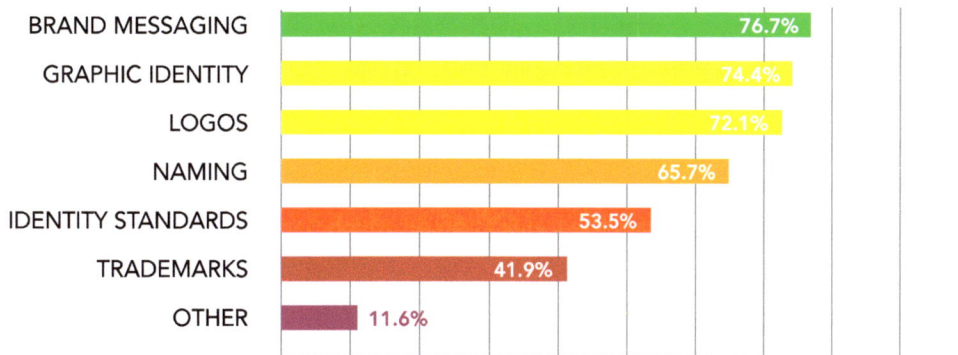

BRAND MESSAGING	76.7%
GRAPHIC IDENTITY	74.4%
LOGOS	72.1%
NAMING	65.7%
IDENTITY STANDARDS	53.5%
TRADEMARKS	41.9%
OTHER	11.6%

NAME THAT BRAND

Naming a company, a start-up, or a product or service is hard work, complex and often rife with mistakes. Billion dollar companies screw this up every year, while under-funded start-ups launch into the stratosphere with a name that seems brilliant and full of meaning, with little or no advertising.

Intuitively, your brand name is the foundation of all that is marketing. A great name is an advertisement in itself. A name can do more for achieving desired positioning than a large advertising budget. The best names tell a story, and make marketing easier. A breakthrough name can garner free publicity, just because of the name.

What if Google launched with its original name BackRub? Would it be as successful? We know the product is great, but is the invented word, Google much more memorable and interesting? Of course.

The best names become synonymous with the product. Kleenex tissue is an example. In construction, SHEETROCK or SAWZALL come to mind.

Creating the ideal name for your company, product or service will have great influence on its successful launch and staying power in the marketplace.

How important is a name? First, there is great power behind successful company or product naming. While not even the best name can save a bad product or idea, the ideal name can have tremendous impact on its success. It is the foundation on which the brand can grow and thrive.

Brand name development is certainly one of the first, and very likely, most important steps in marketing as it can dictate success or failure. Consider that many marketing experts estimate new product failure rates averaging 90%. And while campaigns change often, naming is likely the most permanent element in the marketing mix, if not the most costly to change.

The importance of naming is growing. Why? Many of the best names are already taken, if not trademarked. In some categories, trademark conflicts during a name development exercise can approach 80-90%. Consider that in 2007, 33 million domain names were registered, with total domains now over 153 million. Also in 2007, a record 298,796 trademarks were filed with the United States Patent and Trademark Office (USPTO), and another record 39,945 international trademark applications were received by the World Intellectual Property Organization (WIPO).

Yet despite these trends, too often naming is subjective or poorly executed, without the disciplined processes that are applied in other business areas. While other departments employ statistical process control and black-belt initiatives, marketing may coordinate a naming contest in which the "favorite" name is voted on by employees. Or the CEO's secretary weighs in. Or the top marketer campaigns his or her pet name. You know how ugly this can get.

Given the trends in brand failures and name saturation, a more thorough and disciplined process should be used. But how? An internal task force? A contest? Certainly you can hire a boutique branding consultancy, or the branding agency division of a major advertising holding company.

Internal committees are more often than not, ineffective, while hiring naming consultants is most often very expensive. Typical fees will start at $10,000 for a boutique to develop a brand name, and rise to millions for a corporate name from a branding division of a large advertising network.

WHAT'S YOUR NAME TYPE?

Understanding the different types of names is essential to effective name development. Why? Because without this knowledge, there is a tendency to only consider certain types of names which, depending on the category, may be less than differentiated. Also, managers may tend toward naming fads, even if out-dated and ineffective. Finally, mapping competitors' names by name type is a very worthwhile exercise, demonstrating naming opportunities that will be unique and differentiated in the category. Therefore, before jumping into brand name development, give careful consideration to the different types of names.

In 2009, Neil M. Brown authored the book *Branding Best Practices: A Guide to Effective Business and Product Naming* (ISBN 978-0-6152-2146-5). In the book, Neil states that names should be categorized by four (4) basic types—**Literal, Synthesized, Metaphorical and Hybrids**.

Most names fall into literal or descriptive name types. There are several sub-categories of literal names. Most often, literal names describe a company or product with key words or terms common to the category. Another type of literal name is an acronym based on key words or terms. And yet another type of literal name is when companies use the founder's name or geographic reference.

Examples of literal names include Computer Associates, IBM and (Michael) Dell respectively. Positives of literal names include ease of understanding, and in the case of a founder's name, trademark and domain name availability. Negatives are lack of differentiation (common keywords), and lack of depth or meaning.

The next naming type—synthesized names—are made-up words, most often the combination of two words or key words, sometimes called coined names. Alternatively, synthesized names can be derived from Latin or Greek roots, often as prefixes or suffixes. Finally, synthesized names can be made-up words that are based on alliteration (repeated sounds) or rhyming. Examples of synthesized names include Microsoft (combo), Oracle (Greek roots) and Google (alliteration/rhyming).

Synthesized names can sound important or intelligent, and usually obtain trademark and domain name availability. Significant negatives include difficulty in understanding and, often, a lack of meaning or emotion. As a result, synthesized names may require significant marketing spending to be successful.

The next naming type, metaphorical names, create an association, or ideally, an emotional response that somehow relates to the company or product in an intuitive or relevant way. While literal names describe the company, product or service, effective metaphorical names relate to the desired positioning, and are aggressively different than most competitors in any given category. When mapping competitive names for a given category, you will inevitably find that metaphorical names are rare. Therefore, by definition, metaphorical names are unique and differentiated—a key to effective positioning.

Indeed, of the four name types, metaphorical names offer the opportunity to change whole business categories or industries, sometimes with the name itself generating publicity far greater than paid media exposure. The negative of metaphorical names is when no perceived meaning or relation to positioning exists, the name can seem random or wacky.

Examples of effective metaphorical names include: Virgin Airlines, Apple computer and Yahoo.com. Considering these examples, metaphorical names can sometimes sound silly or have potentially negative connotations. But with contextual support, these effective metaphorical names reinforce positioning, and are highly memorable, even industry-changing (examples: Virgin= new, Apple= simple or different, and Yahoo= exuberant).

The last type of name—hybrid—is a combination of name types, often literal and metaphorical, as a Case Study in the next chapter will demonstrate. But hybrids can also be both literal and synthesized, or synthesized and metaphorical.

The type of name you choose will vary vastly depending on the product or service and market. No two product categories or market segments are alike. Each is unique, with its own competitive landscape and name types. More often than not, competitor names will cluster around one or two name types. Mapping competitor names by type will expose opportunities for differentiation—a tenet of effective marketing.

THE NAMING PROCESS

With an understanding of naming types, name generation can commence. Brown's branding book defines a comprehensive 10-Step process to "optimize" name development. The steps include category understanding, customer analysis, competitive analysis, keyword generation, alternative positioning definitions, name generation, name scoring and ranking, trademark and domain screening and review, final evaluation and testing, and of course, name selection.

The first step in any naming project is researching and understanding the category in which the business, product or service competes. Review all company or product information, industry publications, websites and research. Locate secondary or syndicated market research, and even primary research, if possible.

Even if you are a client that works in this category daily, step back and grind through this step to uncover new information or insights in a dynamic environment. The category read-in step will provide a great deal of input for the next two steps.

With category background, step two includes identification of customers, customer profiles or segments. This step is quite different for consumer versus business-to-business (B2B) markets. For consumer markets, identifying target audience demographics (age, gender, education, market area) and psychographics—personality, interests, attitudes, lifestyles—are important. For B2B markets, we often classify customers by industry or market segment, job title, purchase decision process, needs and benefits derived, or other attributes.

Certainly the third step, identifying and analyzing competitors, is critical. Understanding relative competitive positioning allows you to define a market position that is unique and differentiated—not redundant and "me-too". Mapping competitor names by name type is a great exercise. Again, you will find that most competitors tend to use literal name types. Some categories like pharmaceuticals and technology will have a high concentration of synthesized names. Surprisingly, most internal name development projects neglect even basic competitive analysis.

Fourth, brainstorm and generate as many keywords as possible that relate to your product, service, market, customer benefits, applications or uses. Review category, customer and competitor insights for more key word possibilities. Use a thesaurus to generate additional keywords. Next, group or consolidate these keywords into similar categories, ideally no more than five or six.

Here's where an experienced naming strategist can help. Based on insights from category research, customer and competitive analysis and keyword generation, step five entails identifying alternative positioning platforms using one or more keywords to describe each platform. Next, rank the viability of each platform.

Criteria for ranking positioning platforms include importance to customers, unique/differentiated and defendable. Defendable means this position is more relevant to your product or company than a competitors', or your product or company would be perceived as the most likely owner of this position.

Finally, we're ready for the fun part, step six. With keywords grouped by positioning platforms, you can start generating names that relate to each platform. Use a thesaurus and a dictionary to identify synonyms, definitions and meanings. Attempt to generate names in each of the naming type categories—Literal, Synthesized, Metaphorical or Hybrids.

Some positioning platforms will be easy to generate names, others not so easy. Try to generate 50-100 names, as internal screening, trademark screening and domain name screening will eliminate a high percentage (up to 90% in certain categories) of names.

Step seven is the time to eliminate names from this long list. To add objectivity to the process, Brown employs a proprietary technique that assigns scores to several criteria including distinctiveness, relevance, depth of meaning, trademark/domain availability, buzz potential, appearance, sound and others. The scores are then ranked highest to lowest, and the top ten or so are selected for the next step: trademark and/or domain name screening.

The eighth step, trademark and domain screening can be accomplished using the United States Patent and Trademark Office (USPTO) database at www.uspto.gov (see the trademark chapter for more details). In some very competitive categories, trademark screening can eliminate up to 90% of generated names.

Domain names are even less available but nevertheless, should be screened using the Internic "WhoIs" database at www.internic.com. If any potential trademark conflicts exist, engage trademark legal counsel to conduct a legal opinion.

Name development, step nine, involves a thorough evaluation and comparison of the final few names that are available after trademark or domain review. If possible, test the finalists with customers and stakeholders to support final name selection.

Step ten, final name selection, should be based on name scores, trademark and/or domain availability, customer and stakeholder feedback and your best judgment or strongest gut feeling.

Some of the tools used in Neil M. Brown's proprietary brand name development process, Naming Optimization™, include competitor name mapping, name ranking and scoring, trademark and domain name screening. (Source: Branding Best Practices: A Guide to Effective Business and Product Naming

Competitor Name Mapping

Literal	Synthesized	Metaphorical	Hybrid
Klein	Power Blade	Journeyman	Sir Nickless
Greenlee	WireMan	Terminator	Ideal
Close Quarters	Stripmaster	Ridgid	IMP
Rothenberger	Grip-N-Strip	Great White	
Conduit Cutter	Smart-Grip	Dead-On	
Commercial Electric (HomeDepot)	Flex Splitter		
	KwikCut		

Name Ranking and Scoring

Name	Distinctive	Positioning	Depth	Trademark	Buzz	Appearance	Humanity	Sound	TOTAL	RANK TOP 10
RocketKut	9	6	5	9	6	7	5	6	53	
SafetyCut	7	8	7	7	7	7	7	7	57	
ScoreNSnap	9	8	7	9	7	8	6	9	63	
Service360	9	6	6	8	5	7	6	7	54	
Swifty's	8	7	7	7	6	7	7	8	57	
SteelTough	7	6	7	6	6	7	8	8	55	
Symmetric	9	5	6	8	5	7	5	6	51	
Threshold	6	6	6	7	6	7	5	6	49	
Union Grade	7	8	7	6	7	8	7	7	57	
UnionPro	7	8	7	6	7	7	8	8	58	
Verity	6	7	6	6	6	7	8	6	52	
Volt	7	6	6	6	5	8	5	5	48	
VoltEDGE	10	8	8	10	8	9	7	8	68	5

Trademark and Domain Name Screening

Name	Trademark	Domain
Ground Control	Available	Available*
Ground Force	Available/Review	Available*
King KiloWatt	Available	Available*
Electrician's Choice	Available	Available*
VoltEDGE	Available	Available*
Code Safe	Available	Available*

*Available as a variation

TIPS ON TAGLINES

Developing effective taglines is a disciplined process that melds insight with positioning strategy and creativity. So what is a tagline, and how can tagline development deliver a breakthrough? Sometimes called tags, positioning taglines, slogans, jingles, unique selling propositions or descriptors, taglines distill your corporate or brand position to a few simple and memorable words—ideally from one to five words, and never more than seven words.

Taglines are flexible, persuasive, differentiating, extendable and very often, more memorable than the corporate and brand names they modify. Why? Many names are legacy names, likely descriptive and sometimes over time, less relevant to positioning due to changing markets. With years of equity, it can be difficult to change names, but taglines can change with new campaigns, or to target different audiences.

Similar to names, there are different types of taglines. With metaphorical names that have highly provocative meanings, sometimes simple, descriptive taglines can add clarity and anchor aggressive branding.

Like their name counterparts, metaphorical taglines deliver meanings (ideally double meanings) or associations that reinforce desired positioning, often when names by themselves cannot. Metaphorical taglines can be particularly effective when paired with descriptive names to reinforce a position and improve memorability.

A great example of a metaphorical tagline is Chevy Trucks', "Like a Rock", communicating durability, and leveraging memorability by virtue of the popular (Bob Seger) hit song. On the corporate front, GE's "Imagination at Work" delivers the double meaning.

Consumer product brands and corporate America are enamored with aspirational taglines. And why not? Consumers often buy products based on a desire for self-improvement, and corporations always want to be perceived as benevolent. One of the most famous taglines in history, "Nike, Just Do It", is clearly aspirational with a meaning of achievement and athletic performance. In the corporate arena, examples abound, from HP's "Invent", to Apple's "Think Different".

When a secondary competitor seeks to take on the category leader, a comparative tagline can quickly and effectively deliver differentiation. Consider Taco Bell's, "Think Outside the Bun," or "Pork, The Other White Meat," or the poster child for comparative taglines, "Avis, We Try Harder."

Jingles are most often associated with catchy tunes for consumer products with big advertising budgets. Brown's Branding Best Practices book states that jingles also describe tagline types that use slogans that employ rhythm, rhyming or alliteration. Examples include Bounty, "the quicker picker-upper," or "Don't get mad, get Glad".

ALREADY SPOKEN FOR: TRADEMARKS

One of the biggest difficulties, indeed roadblocks, to name development is the high likelihood that the brilliant name that came to you in your sleep last night is already trademarked.

In saturated categories like consumer products, healthcare and technology, trademark "knock-outs", or eliminations from consideration due to existing trademark conflicts can approach 90%! What's more, in the United States, even if the trademark does not show up in the United States Patent and Trademark Office (USPTO) database, a trademark conflict can still exist. Finally, if the trademark will be used internationally, various trademark laws must be considered.

So what are the considerations for trademarks? Often the intended geographic scope of your trademark use, and who the owners of existing trademarks are will determine whether you can use a brand name that is already trademarked. Consider whether trademarks are local or national, business-to-business or consumer, domestic or international.

Large consumer product corporations are sophisticated in trademark law and will vigorously defend their trademarks. Local businesses typically do not even register trademarks, but can prove first usage and legally defend a trademark.

If you are marketing your company or product nationally (within the U.S.), screen trademarks using the United States Patent and Trademark Office (USPTO) website at www.uspto.gov. Select the trademarks link or: www.uspto.gov/main/trademarks.htm. Click on search, and enter your name or tagline (trademark) candidate.

The database will show all trademark registrations, along with words close to the search term(s). Importantly, the database will also display whether the trademark is Live or Dead. Obviously, dead or non-active trademarks are not a conflict. Click on live trademarks that are an exact match to your candidate and evaluate whether the description of "Goods and Services" represents a conflict.

As an example with a recent tagline project, we searched the trademark database for the term "Smart Cookie". The search returned 48 results, of which only 14 were "Live", and of these, four with exact name matches, none of which were related to edible cookies (mostly education). Only one potential conflict existed, Jimmy Schmidt's SmartCookie.

The Jimmy Schmidt's SmartCookie may or may not be a conflict, as the name was also part of the registered trademark. If you intend to use the trademark nationally or internationally, do undertake a legal review and opinion using professional legal counsel. Otherwise, you risk losing trademark application fees, and often more importantly, time.

For international trademarks, the World Intellectual Property Organization (WIPO), based in Geneva, Switzerland, is the administrative body. Per the WIPO website: "The WIPO-administered Madrid System for the international registration of trademarks offers a trademark owner the possibility of having a mark protected in up to 80 countries by filing one application, in one language (English, French or Spanish), with one set of fees, in one currency (Swiss Francs)."

Applicants wishing to use the Madrid system must apply for trademark protection in a relevant national or regional trademark office before seeking international protection. An international registration under the Madrid system produces the same effects as an application for registration of the mark in each of the contracting parties designated by the applicant.

If protection is not refused by the trademark office of a designated contracting party, the status of the mark is the same as if it had been registered by that office. Thereafter, the international registration can be maintained and renewed through a single procedure. Thus, the system provides a cost-effective and efficient way for trademark holders to secure and maintain protection for their marks in multiple countries.

Per the WIPO website, "The system is governed by two international treaties, namely the Madrid Agreement and the Madrid Protocol. The grouping of both agreements is referred to as the Madrid system. The Madrid Protocol which became operational in 1996 introduced several features including the ability to submit applications in English and to extend the period for notification of a refusal. Spanish was introduced as a working language in 2004. These features made the system more flexible and attractive to a larger number of countries. The total number of countries party to the Protocol is 75 and the overall current membership of the Madrid system is 82 (81 countries plus the EC)."

GENERIC TRADEMARKS

A primer on trademarks would be incomplete without considering those names that have become synonymous with the entire product category. A "genericized" trademark, also known as a generic trademark, is a trademark or brand name that has become the colloquial or generic description for (or synonymous with) a particular class of product or service.

A trademark typically becomes "genericized" when the products or services with which it is associated have acquired substantial market dominance or mind share. The term is legally significant in that unless a company works sufficiently to prevent such broad use of its trademark, its intellectual property rights in the trademark may be lost. Specifically, a company must always use the trademark as an adjective modifying a noun that describes the product.

With trademark legal search and opinions completed, you can confidently select your final name, and complete the trademark registration process. For U.S.-based trademarks, you can prepare and submit your trademark application electronically, at a standard fee charged by the USPTO.

Often-cited Generic Trademarks in the Construction Category

Formica®	Has become a trade name for countertop laminate.	A registered trademark of Formica Corporation.
Jacuzzi®	Has become the generic name for whirlpools.	A registered trademark of Jacuzzi.
SheetRock®	Synonymous with gypsum board or drywall used in construction.	A registered trademark of USG Corporation.
Spackle®	Has become the verb for repairing drywall.	A registered trademark of the Muralo Company.
Wing-Nut®	Has become the generic name for screw-on wire connectors.	A registered trademark of the Ideal Industries.

If you utilize an attorney, application fees range from $500 to $5000. Typical trademark services, including those provided by Construction Marketing Advisors include:

- *Legal review using national and international databases*
- *Trademark opinion summary report and recommendations*
- *Trademark registration application completion*
- *Communication of registration results*

THE DOMAIN NAME GAME

Depending on the type of business or product, the availability of a domain name (also called URL or Uniform Resource Locator or website address) may be critical to the name selection. However, most common names, acronyms and interesting domain names are already registered. Why? Because each year over 10 million domain names are registered, with total domains now over 255 million. *(Source: VeriSign)*

Certainly, there are tips and strategies for working around this lack of available domains. Before we get into domain name strategies, you will have to consider trademark availability, as well as domain name impact on search engine results. For those of you new to domain names, consider some background information.

A domain name is basically a numeric map to your website that has been encoded into a recognizable "name" to provide users (read: potential customers) with a simple way to find your company's information on the web.

The "top" domain, also known as the domain extension, is where the domain is registered. The most recognizable are commercial (.com), network services (.net), non-profit (.org), government (.gov), school and university related (.edu), and even country-specific such as United Kingdom (.uk) and Italy (.it).

The three most widely used are: ".com," ".net," and ".org." All of these domain name extensions can be accessed by anyone, without restrictions, and are recognized throughout the world. Every domain name is registered under each of these domains to avoid duplication—in other words, every name must be unique.

Businesses or companies ideally will want ".com," as this is the most common domain because it is the most recognizable, memorable and easily accessed domain for companies.

You will create a unique sub-domain and register this name with a domain registrar (e.g. GoDaddy.com). Together, the sub-domain and extension or top domain makes up your domain name. The simplest way to see if a domain name has already been purchased is by entering the address in the URL bar to see what pops up.

In the United States, the Department of Commerce manages a central database of domains called InterNIC, where you can search registrations through the website: www.internic.com. Other countries maintain their own NICs (network information centers).

On this site resides the WhoIs database that lists whether the domain is available, and if not, who the owner is in case you want to contact and consider bidding on a domain name if it has been registered. Otherwise, there are many options for domain names, many of which a registrar will identify if your first choice was registered. For example, if CoolName.com is taken, the registrar will suggest:

- *coolname.net, .biz or .org*
- *coolnames.com*
- *coolnameweb.com*
- *coolnameonline.com*

If your name is a common or literal business or company name, you can add key words to differentiate your name.

During name generation, consider the fact that synthesized names and metaphorical names will have a higher chance of domain availability versus literal and common names. It's unlikely a name like UltraHyperFizzyWhiz.com would be taken versus Wizard.com.

Following are some tips for domain name selection. Most generic names are taken, if not by competitors, so use a memorable name that relates to your product or service. Keep it short and simple. Long names are difficult to spell and remember. Hard to spell names are a big problem. Avoid hyphens unless is can deliver a really great name otherwise not available. Avoid plurals if your competitor owns the singular. Find a name that you can own both the singular and plural versions to avoid competitors. And be sure the name conveys your product or service's message.

VISUAL BRAND IDENTITY

A company or product visual brand identity is comprised of logos, typefaces, color palettes and graphic identities.

Logos are visual identifiers for companies, brands and products. Not all brands require a logo. Some brands are named with simple typefaces.

Following are several logos for construction brands developed by Construction Marketing Association's agency partner, Construction Marketing Advisors.

Brand architecture or brand hierarchy is the relationship between master brands and sub-brands, or corporate brands and product sub-brands. Typically this relationship is defined in corporate identity standards or identity usage guidelines.

To illustrate a brand architecture, following is a print ad for Weather Guard (product brand), with Emerson (corporate brand) appearing in the signature, or bottom right position.

Print Ad with Product and Corporate Brand Architecture

A company or brand's graphic identity encompasses all visual elements including logo treatments, color palettes, and graphic elements. Ideally, a brand's graphic identity is unified across all marketing elements to reinforce a consistent brand image.

To illustrate a complete graphic identity, following are examples of FC Lighting, a manufacturer of architectural lighting, including corporate and product brand identities, stationary system, and integrated marketing elements. (Program developed by Construction Marketing Advisors)

Corporate and Product Brand Identities

Stationery System

Visual Identity with Integrated Elements

To illustrate a typical corporate identity standard, following are examples for Emerson Electric and Knaack.

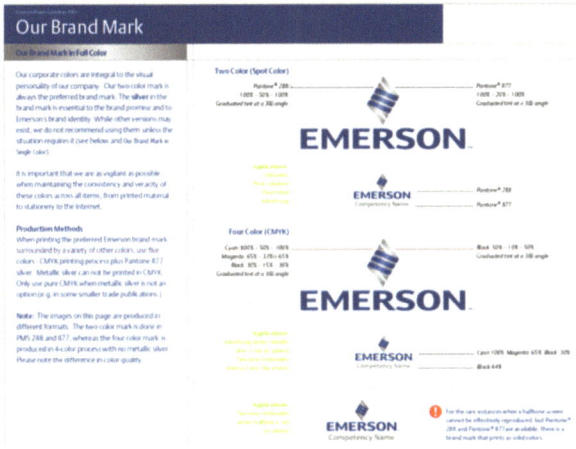

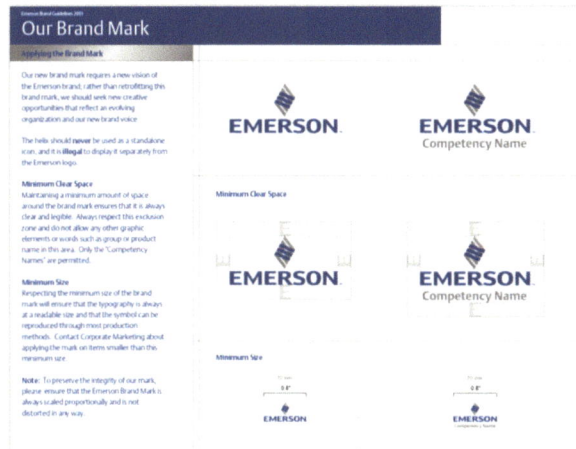

Sample Identity Guidelines (Emerson)

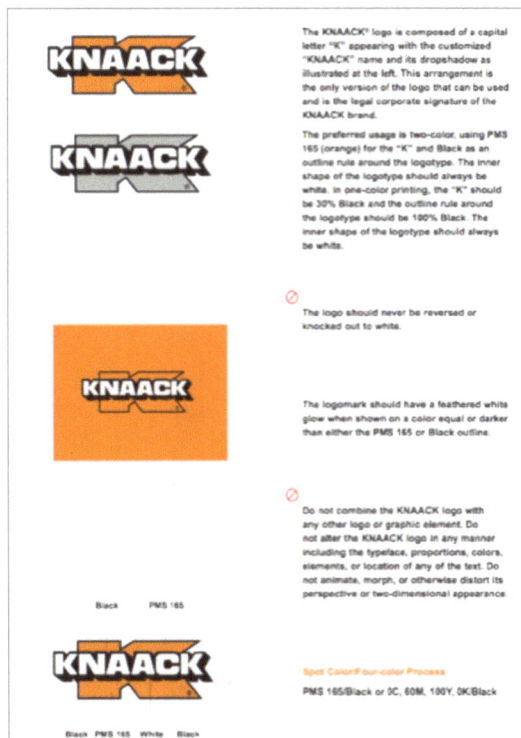

Sample Identity Guidelines (Knaack)

Marketing Planning Best Practices

In the midst of this severe construction market recession, results-oriented marketing is more important than ever before. Marketing budgets are increasingly being scrutinized more than ever before. Surely, the skill and quality of marketing planning can support both the effectiveness and efficiency of marketing. Likewise, understanding marketing planning best practices can aid marketers at all levels in realizing their potential.

This chapter will consider the different types of marketing plans, how to establish marketing budgets, and how much some top construction brands spend on marketing. Finally, a marketing planning checklist is provided.

TYPES OF MARKETING PLANS

There are several varieties of marketing plans from tactical marketing plans, specific project or functional plans, to strategic marketing plans. The most common type of marketing plan is the tactical marketing plan, which often is in the form of an annual marketing activity plan, along with corresponding budgets and schedules. This plan is used by construction brands and corporate America to efficiently coordinate and implement the multitude of marketing activities.

The tactical plan doesn't focus on strategic issues like market segmentation, or competitive intelligence; but instead focuses on identifying the specific details of all known marketing programs, campaigns or initiatives. An example of a specific tactical plan line item: vertical email campaign to plumbers, electricians and HVAC pros; monthly frequency; content themes include frequently asked questions, installation tips, and testimonials; budget $1800 per month; goal of 2000 leads.

Depending on company size or budget, project or functional plans can be part of the tactical plan, or separate. Examples of project plans might include the plan for a new website development, or a new sales training program. Whereas functional plans might include advertising/media plans, trade show plans, and publicity plans.

Strategic marketing plans are the most rigorous of plans. What differentiates a strategic marketing plan from a tactical marketing plan is the longer time frame (typically 3-5 years), the analysis and research aspects of a strategic marketing plan, the potential financial aspects of a strategic marketing plan, and the consideration of new business or marketing initiatives that may be quite different from your existing business.

Strategic marketing plans are most often used by large brands or corporations, or when a new marketing regime or executive team takes over. Often, the strategic marketing plan is updated on an annual basis to include new research, or changing economics. The strategic marketing plan might include one or more of the following:

- *Company or brand financials (historical/projections/forecasts, revenue, units, margin, ROI, payback, break-even)*
- *Market analysis, sizing, segmentation*
- *Secondary research (Internet, association studies, publications*
- *Syndicated research (Dodge Reports, Reed Construction Data, EDA, other)*
- *Primary research results (surveys, interviews, focus groups; awareness, preference, purchase intention)*
- *SWOT analysis (strengths, weaknesses, opportunities, threats)*
- *Competitive analysis (share, positioning, intelligence)*

MARKETING BUDGETING

A very important aspect of market planning, whether tactical, project or strategic is the budgeting of marketing expenditures. Inevitably, marketers must get approval for marketing budgets from executive management. Construction brands and corporate America develop budgets based on one of three approaches: a percentage increase (or decrease) over last years budget, task and objective budgeting, or a percentage of (forecasted) sales based on industry or competitive benchmarking. Often budgets are developed using a combination of these approaches.

In good times, management is inclined to simply increase budgets gradually based on prior budgets. Given the economic turmoil of the past few years, I suggest that budgets are no longer "rubber-stamped", but rather closely scrutinized.

With detailed tactical, project and functional planning, task and objective budgeting becomes more feasible, and is intuitively appealing for relating directly to planned activities. Sometimes called zero-based budgeting, task and objective budgeting involves a detailed build-up of anticipated marketing expenditures, often prioritized to allow for elimination of budget items and programs.

Percent of sales is more often a vestige of times when advertising was the largest expense, and also when advertising expense was widely reported through information service providers. The author suggests the use of the Schonfeld report, (www.schonfeldassociates.com/adv.html) one of the remaining resources that tracks advertising and marketing expenditures of public companies. The report lists expenditures as a percentage of sales, allowing for some benchmarking which can be useful, for example, when requesting budget increases. As a reference, the following are marketing expenditures for several leading construction brands.

Marketing Expenditures

Company Name	Ad Spend 2009 (Mill)	Ad/Sales % 2009
Newell Rubbermaid	358.2	5.4
Sherwin-Williams	233.4	2.9
Deere & Co	199.7	0.6
Black & Decker	162.3	2.7
WW Grainger	130.5	1.8
Makita Corp	99.2	2.7
Pulte Homes	82.9	0.02
Stanley Works	77.0	1.6
Lennox Intl	69.7	2.0
Ingersoll-Rand	66.3	0.5
Caterpillar	66.2	0.1
Komatsu	57.3	0.2
Cooper Industries	48.1	0.7
USG Corp	24.5	0.6
Owens Corning	22.8	0.4
Thomas & Betts	22.7	0.8
Bldg Materials Corp Amer	20.8	0.7
Hubbel Inc	18.5	0.7
Gardner Denver	11.3	0.5
Coleman Cable	2.1	0.2

A MARKETING PLANNING CHECKLIST

As discussed, marketing plans come in a number of "shapes and sizes", from the annual tactical plan, project or functional plans, to the detailed strategic marketing plan. A Marketing Planning Checklist can be a useful tool to help identify a broad range of items to be considered for typical marketing plans.

A given marketing program may range in complexity, budget and requirements. Different markets and products likely require vastly different marketing strategies and tactics. So a Marketing Planning Checklist will allow for a range of marketing scenarios. This checklist is based on a typical construction and/or business-to-business marketing scenario.

///CMA

I. BACKGROUND

A. Company or brand
    i. Historical sales, margins, volume
    ii. Economic drivers (macro)
    iii. SWOT analysis

B. Market Analysis targets
    i. Market sizing
    ii. Market segmentation
    iii. Customer identification (incl. demographics)
    iv. Channels of distribution
    v. Sales process (incl. cycle)

C. Market Research
    i. Secondary research (internet, associations, publications)
    ii. Syndicated research (Dodge Reports, Reed Construction Data, EDA, other)
    iii. Primary research (surveys, interviews, focus groups)

D. Competitors
    i. Market share
    ii. Branding/positioning
    iii. Key marketing initiatives
    iv. Intelligence

E. Prior Marketing Programs and Results
    i. Sales
    ii. Inquiries/sales leads/new customers
    iii. Website traffic statistics (Google analytics, host stats)
    iv. Other measures

II. OBJECTIVES (quantify)

A. Sales (Revenue, Volume, Margin)

B. Market share

C. Other measures (ROI, payback, breakeven)

III. STRATEGIES

A. How to achieve objectives, not specific tactics
    i. New products
    ii. New markets
    iii. Promotions
    iv. New Programs
    v. Customer initiatives

IV. TACTICS

A. Branding
    i. Re-branding
    ii. Naming
    iii. Identity
    iv. Sub-branding, trademark registration, identity standards

B. Internet
  i. Website development, re-development, microsites, landing pages
  ii. Search engine optimization (SEO), search engine marketing (SEM)
  iii. Social media (profiles, content, blog and forum posts)
  iv. Email campaigns (landing pages, registration forms)
  v. Webcasts, webinars, web conferences

C. Advertising
  i. Media (research, planning, placement, traffic)
  ii. Print (trade publications)
  iii. Online (banners, directories, Google AdWords)
  iv. Broadcast (TV, radio)

D. Publicity
  i. News releases
  ii. Press list
  iii. Press kit
  iv. Press events
  v. Article (writing and placement)
  vi. Media relations
  vii. Distribution (internet, wire service)

E. Sales Promotion
  i. Programs
  ii. Training
  iii. Contests, coupons, sweepstakes

F. Collateral
  i. Brochures, product sheets, flyers
  ii. Catalogs, manuals, instructions, installation
  iii. Educational pieces (white papers, guides, how-tos)

G. Trade shows and Events (national, international, regional shows, dealer open houses)
  i. Exhibit design
  ii. Booth graphics
  iii. Pre-show promotion

H. Channel marketing
  i. Dealer or distributor programs
  ii. Promotions
  iii. Merchandising support, POP, packaging
  iv. Training programs
  v. Launch kits
  vi. MDF and Co-Op programs

I. Direct marketing
  i. Direct mail
  ii. Database marketing
  iii. List procurement, email, webcasts

J. Photography and video (supports all tactics above)

GETTING STARTED ON PLANNING

It's that time of the year to develop annual tactical marketing plans, functional plans and strategic marketing plans. If you have undertaken any of these in the past, the new planning cycle should entail updates and modifications. If not, starting from scratch can be daunting. A number of marketing planning templates are available on the Internet. (See American Marketing Association website, Resources). For tactical or functional plans, we prefer a spreadsheet with grouped projects, monthly columns, and budgets that can be modified easily.

To help you get started, it often helps to do some benchmarking. What are other construction brands planning for 2011? To this end, please share the results of the recent survey, 2011 Marketing Planning Outlook. Construction Marketing Association members will receive the report via email, including updates. You can receive this report free, for a limited time, by simply completing the quick and easy survey at: http://constructionmarketingblog.org/survey-says/#more-859

Wait, there's more help! The association's Construction Marketing Advisors partner will provide a Marketing Plan Review, complete with analysis and recommendations, under non-disclosure, for the modest fee of $500. For questions or to request, please use the association's contact form and reference Marketing Plan Review.

Happy planning!

Market Research

Market Research is the process of gathering information about your customers, competitors, markets, trends and related. There are many types of market research, often categorized as primary vs. secondary research, quantitative or qualitative research, and syndicated research.

Secondary research is the most common, defined as published, publicly available and free information from websites, magazines and publications, trade associations, government, and of course search engine results.

Primary research is information collected directly from the source, often custom to the project and typically includes surveys, interviews, and focus groups.

1. *Qualitative research uses open-ended responses typically with interviews or focus groups.*

2. *Quantitative research employs statistically significant sampling and closed-end questions typically with surveys.*

3. *Syndicated research is conducted by a research firm and sold to several users on a fee or subscription basis; Dodge Reports and Reed Construction Data are examples of syndicated research (note that our A/E/C marketing chapter has a complete summary of construction lead services).*

4. *Other types of research include competitive intelligence, customer satisfaction, brand awareness/equity/preference, positioning, segmentation and more.*

Why is Market Research important? Market research is used to support planning, budgeting, and decision-making for new products, market-entry, marketing communications, customer initiatives and more.

Marketing without research, customer or market insight is guesswork, with high risk of failure. To reinforce this point, new product failure rates are reported in excess of 90%. Insights from market research promise to reduce the risk of failure. Niche markets likely do not have available secondary research, thus requiring primary research.

/// CMA

MARKET RESEARCH SURVEY RESULTS

CMA conducted a national survey in 2011 to identify market research practices.

Survey Questions

1. *How often do you conduct Market Research?*
2. *What types of Market Research have you employed in the last 24 months?*
3. *What types of information are you seeking with Market Research?*

Market Research Frequency

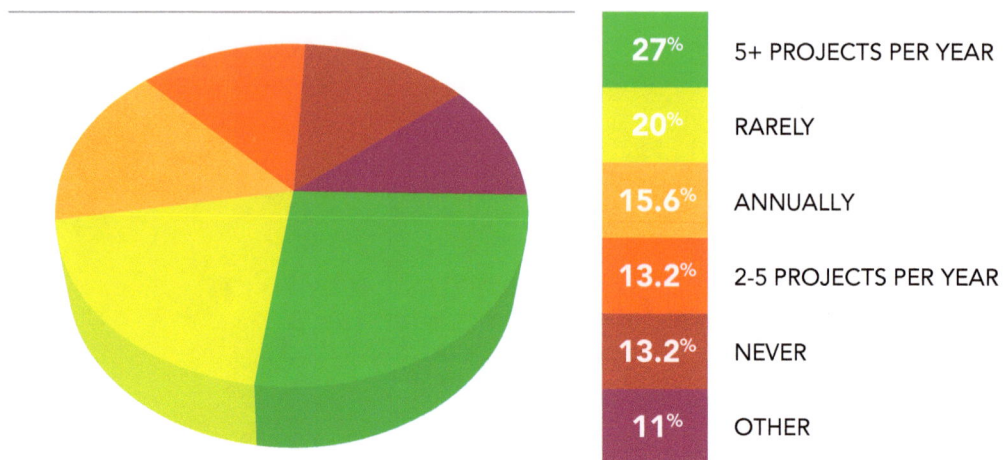

%	Category
27%	5+ PROJECTS PER YEAR
20%	RARELY
15.6%	ANNUALLY
13.2%	2-5 PROJECTS PER YEAR
13.2%	NEVER
11%	OTHER

Types of Market Research Used

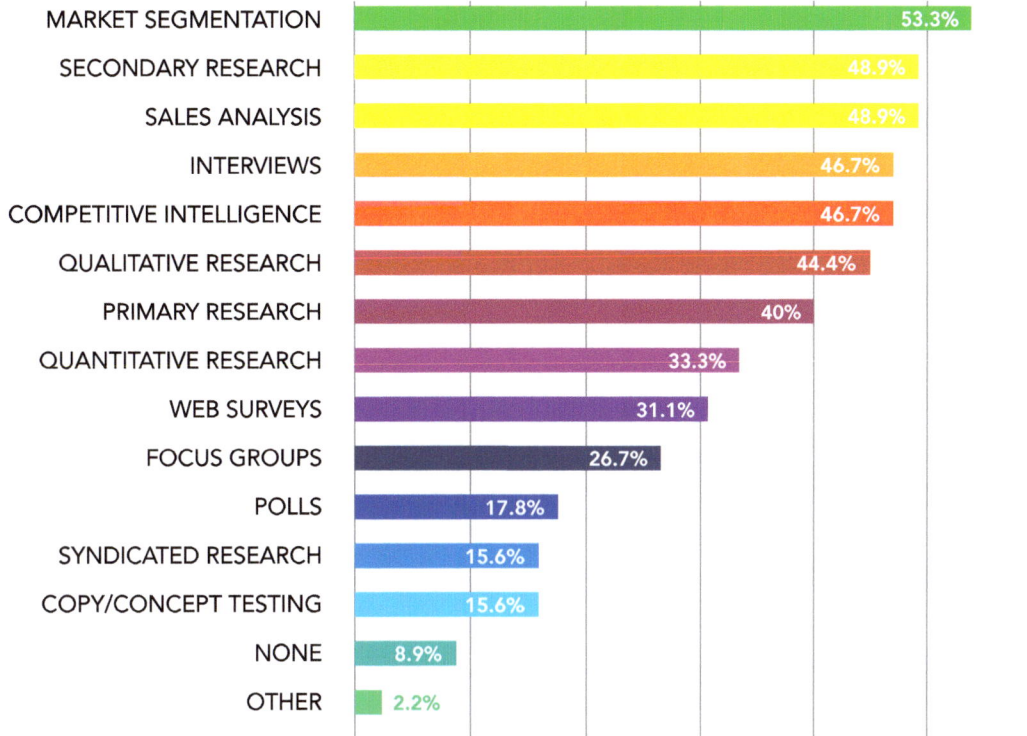

MARKET SEGMENTATION	53.3%
SECONDARY RESEARCH	48.9%
SALES ANALYSIS	48.9%
INTERVIEWS	46.7%
COMPETITIVE INTELLIGENCE	46.7%
QUALITATIVE RESEARCH	44.4%
PRIMARY RESEARCH	40%
QUANTITATIVE RESEARCH	33.3%
WEB SURVEYS	31.1%
FOCUS GROUPS	26.7%
POLLS	17.8%
SYNDICATED RESEARCH	15.6%
COPY/CONCEPT TESTING	15.6%
NONE	8.9%
OTHER	2.2%

Types of Information Sought

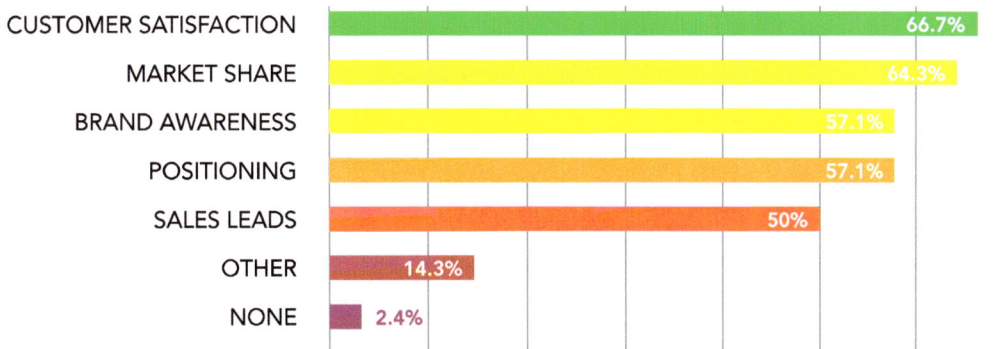

CUSTOMER SATISFACTION	66.7%
MARKET SHARE	64.3%
BRAND AWARENESS	57.1%
POSITIONING	57.1%
SALES LEADS	50%
OTHER	14.3%
NONE	2.4%

///CMA

Tools of the Trade: Modern Marketing for Construction Brands

Strategic Marketing Tools

Per our last chapter on market research, there are several options for gathering information about customers and their buying preferences and purchase intentions. But what are some of the strategic tools that can be employed to assist in marketing decision-making?

Below are several popular strategic marketing tools including internet-based competitive intelligence, market segmentation, perceptual maps, the growth-share matrix, and product life cycle analysis.

Certainly some of the measures covered in the upcoming Marketing Measurement chapter are possible tools, for example, Google Analytics. We use Google Adwords daily to identify keyword search volume, and competitive keyword analysis. Some related keyword analysis tools include SEMRush, SpyFu and Compete. The free Marketing.Grader.com tool identifies competitor search engine optimization with a detailed report.

Internet tracking tools range from simple Google Alerts for competitor brands, keywords and topics, to social media monitoring tools like Radian6 or Sysomos that identify keyword mentions in blogs, Tweets and other social posts.

Market segmentation for construction and business-to-business categories can be accomplished via assigning Standard Industrial Classifications (SIC), or the North American Industry Classification System (NAICS). As an example, categorize each of your customers by SIC code, and conduct some basic sales analysis to determine your top-ranked market segments.

When analyzing your brands and/or competitor's advantages or relative positioning, use a perceptual map to quickly visualize points of differentiation, with two-dimensional, numeric scales. See a perceptual map for the plumbing category below.

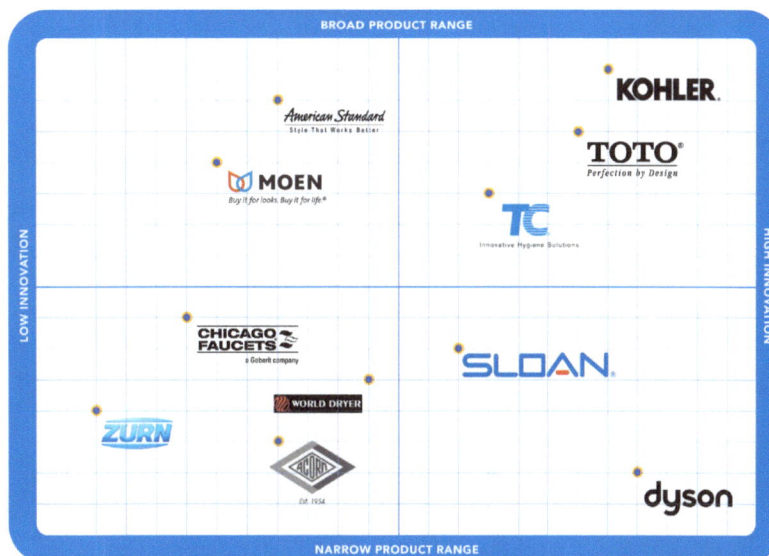

Tools of the Trade: Modern Marketing for Construction Brands

///CMA

Another strategic marketing tool that assists in competitive comparisons and positioning analysis is SWOT analysis (Strengths, Weaknesses, Opportunities and Threats). This simple appearing grid is based on a company's analysis of itself and its competition.

SWOT ANALYSIS

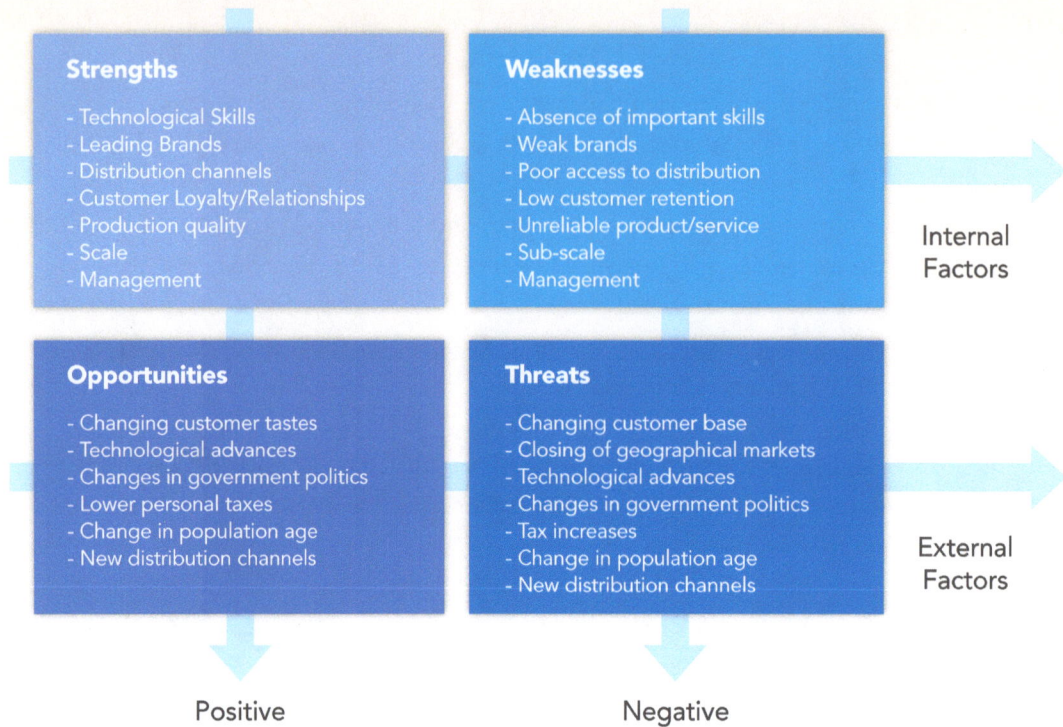

Strengths

- Technological Skills
- Leading Brands
- Distribution channels
- Customer Loyalty/Relationships
- Production quality
- Scale
- Management

Weaknesses

- Absence of important skills
- Weak brands
- Poor access to distribution
- Low customer retention
- Unreliable product/service
- Sub-scale
- Management

Internal Factors

Opportunities

- Changing customer tastes
- Technological advances
- Changes in government politics
- Lower personal taxes
- Change in population age
- New distribution channels

Threats

- Changing customer base
- Closing of geographical markets
- Technological advances
- Changes in government politics
- Tax increases
- Change in population age
- New distribution channels

External Factors

Positive   Negative

The Growth-Share Matrix was coined by the Boston Consulting group, and helps analyze business units or product lines to allocate resources. Based on evaluations of relative market share and market growth rate, a scatter graph is formulated that breaks down items under consideration into categories of cash cows, dogs, question marks, and stars. This matrix helps users quickly sort through the available financing options.

Growth Share Matrix

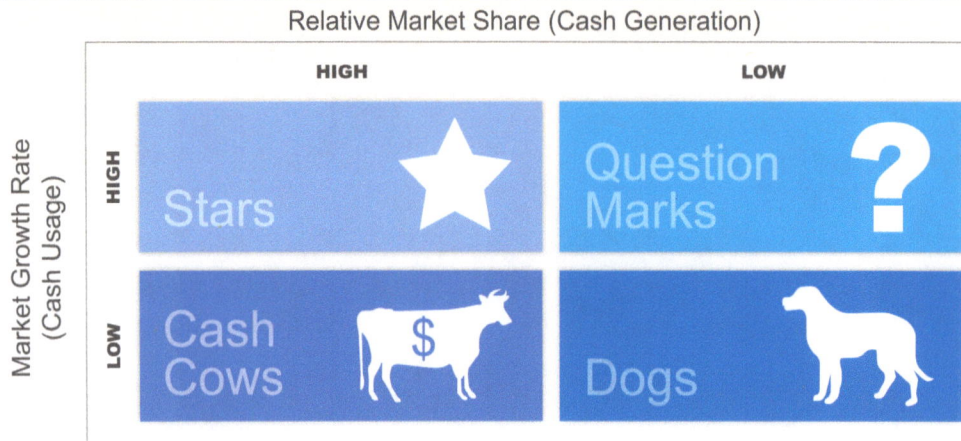

Relative Market Share (Cash Generation)

	HIGH	LOW
Market Growth Rate (Cash Usage) — HIGH	Stars ★	Question Marks ?
Market Growth Rate (Cash Usage) — LOW	Cash Cows $	Dogs

The product lifecycle diagram helps you understand what stage your product is in - introduction, growth, maturity, or decline - and how that compares to your competitors. This is one of the strategic marketing tools that can affect the decisions you make on how much emphasis to place on marketing your product or service.

PRODUCT LIFECYCLE

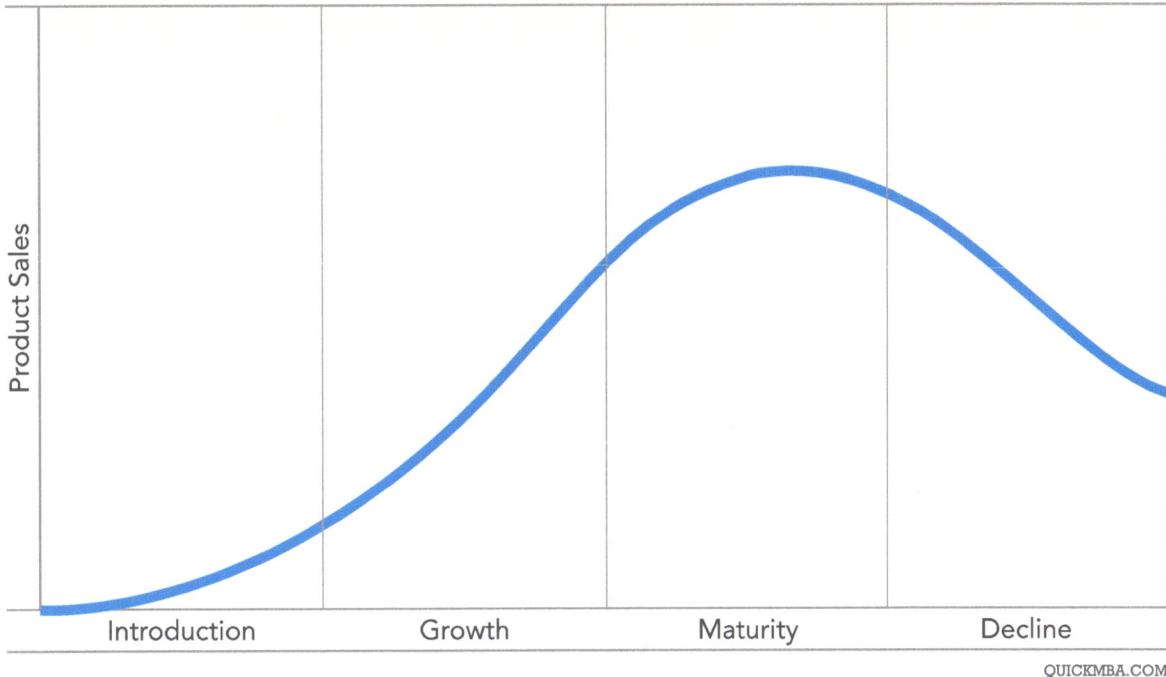

Product Sales

Introduction   Growth   Maturity   Decline

QUICKMBA.COM

Despite all of the sophisticated new methods of gathering information, strategic marketing still goes back to making decisions about product, price, promotion and placement. What these strategic marketing tools do provide is the ability to gather sound information and analyze it in a way that will support solid decision-making.

///CMA

Tools of the Trade: Modern Marketing for Construction Brands

How to Measure Marketing Results: New Rules

In a recent survey sponsored by the Construction Marketing Association, 21% of construction marketers ranked Measuring Marketing Results as their top priority for 2011, beating all other priorities including Internet and Social Media. Clearly in a difficult market, marketing is under increased scrutiny to prove results and justify budgets.

Frequently called marketing metrics, depending on the scale of your company or program, measuring marketing results can range from simple to a variety of complex methods and approaches. Today marketers must consider three broad types of measures, with multiple individual tools, 1) traditional methods of measuring including research, 2) the use of internet-based measures, 3) along with new tools for social media monitoring.

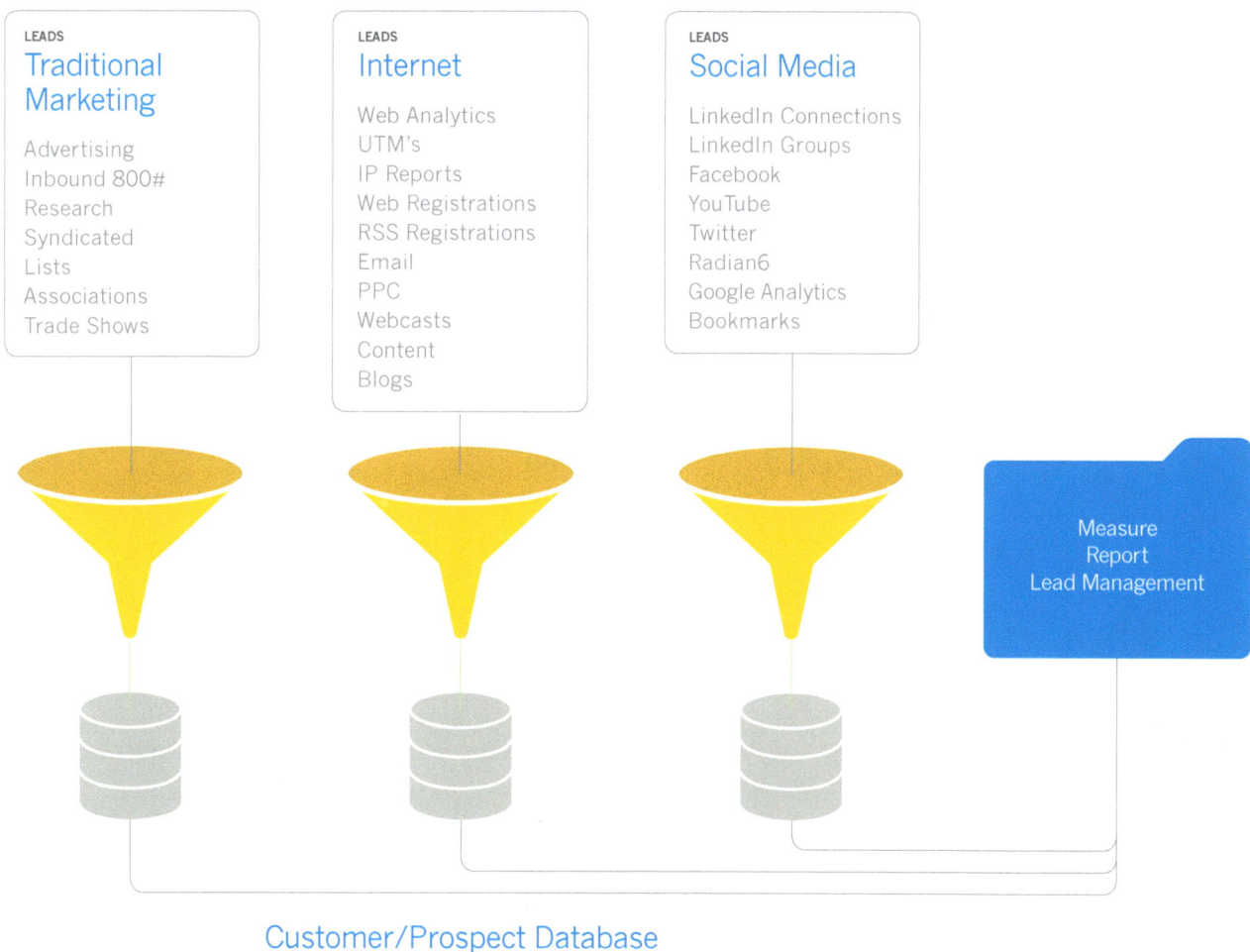

LEADS
Traditional Marketing
Advertising
Inbound 800#
Research
Syndicated
Lists
Associations
Trade Shows

LEADS
Internet
Web Analytics
UTM's
IP Reports
Web Registrations
RSS Registrations
Email
PPC
Webcasts
Content
Blogs

LEADS
Social Media
LinkedIn Connections
LinkedIn Groups
Facebook
YouTube
Twitter
Radian6
Google Analytics
Bookmarks

Measure
Report
Lead Management

Customer/Prospect Database

///CMA

TRADITIONAL MEASURES

Some of the traditional methods of measuring results are still some of the most important. Financial measures like sales revenue, unit volumes or profit margins are not only important, but also closely tied to company or brand success.

Other traditional approaches might include identifying new customers, and having sales, service or telemarketing personnel ask (and document) how they found out about your product or company (source of exposure). Inbound telephone calls and inquiries can likewise be qualified, as can trade show and/or event inquiries. At one time trade print advertising supplied reader response cards and reports, which are now less used, if at all. In the PR area, clipping services provided "hard copy" clips of publicity placements, most of which have been replaced with electronic distribution and reporting.

Tracking measures can be facilitated by a customer or prospect database, or for smaller scale marketing programs, a spreadsheet. If and when the database is integrated with corporate information systems, CRM systems or sales force automation, these customer records can help manage reporting, as well as identify such customer or marketing scenarios as new customer acquisition, retention, dormant and lost customers.

Another traditional approach to measuring marketing results is the use of marketing research, which can be a variety of types and methods. Marketing research types include secondary research, primary research or syndicated research. Secondary research is already published, and may include information publicly available on the Internet, or published by industry publications or associations. Primary research is undertaken by brand owners and could include surveys, focus groups or interviews. Syndicated research is undertaken by research firms, analysts or other independent firms and sold to any interested users (Forrester, Frost & Sullivan).

Regardless of research type, often the information reported by marketing research can be useful in measuring marketing results. Examples include market size, market share, brand awareness, brand preference, customer satisfaction, market trends and more. For specialized markets, such intelligence can prove the most useful in measuring results of marketing.

One of the challenges for traditional measures is relating back to specific marketing campaigns or initiatives. To measure specific, traditional marketing campaigns or initiatives effectively, always use direct response offers and promotional codes for all initiatives and campaigns. In addition, most construction products sell through channels of distribution, or through retailers to consumers. In these cases, end user insights must be provided by channel partners, or retail POS data (syndicated research data).

Certainly, traditional marketing can be integrated with Internet marketing with its own set of measurement tools and options.

INTERNET MEASURES

With construction marketing increasingly moving toward Internet programs, it's no surprise that the Internet will offer many of the tools for results measurement. Foremost among Internet measures, are website statistics, and/or analytics. In addition, marketers can measure Internet marketing with pay-per-click dashboards, and a variety of search engine optimization (SEO) tools, website registrations, email campaign metrics, electronic news distribution services, Google Alerts, and a new technology called UTMs. All website hosting providers offer website statistics for a website domain.

Other advanced statistics are available, however, this author prefers Google Analytics, which provides site and page level traffic information, along with such useful measures such as Visits and Page Views, Pages/Visit, Bounce Rate, Average Time on Site (stickiness), Traffic Source, Geographic and more. Below is a typical Google Analytics dashboard.

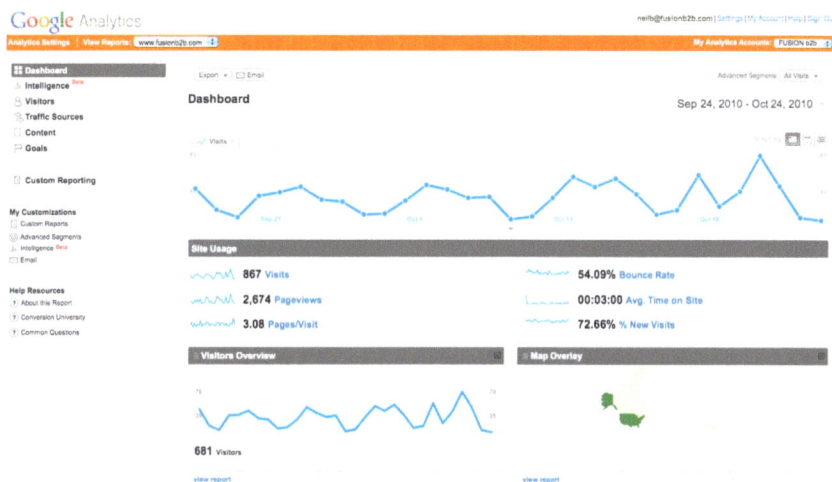

Another common Internet measure is Pay-Per-Click (PPC) advertising, where companies pay for sponsored advertisements on search engine results pages, or other (usually topic-related) web pages that have sponsored advertising. This model is typical on search engines like Google, Bing, & Yahoo.

Google Adwords is one of the most robust and user friendly PPC dashboards that can be found. Below is a sample of a Google Adwords dashboard for a recent campaign which lists the titles of each advertisement, along with several measures including Max Cost-Per-Click (CPC), Total Clicks, Total Impressions, Click-through Rate (CTR), Average CPC, Total Cost, and Average Position.

Certainly website statistics and Google Analytics are useful in measuring search engine optimization (SEO), however a number of more specific tools are now available. For example, Hubspot's free Website Grader tool (www.WebsiteGrader.com) provides an overall grade of Internet presence based on proper meta coding, indexed pages and links, RSS and conversion forms, and social media integration (Twitter and Blogs).

///CMA

Website registrations can come from a number of offers, registration pages or conversion forms. Marketers may have such electronic forms for subscriptions (newsletters, updates, warranties), white papers, catalogs, training material downloads, promotions and events; or RSS registrations for blogpost updates and news items. Also, email addresses from LinkedIn Connections, and LinkedIn group members can be used to build the prospect database.

When utilizing an Email Service Provider (ESP) to develop and distribute email campaigns, most provide robust campaign reporting and metrics including deliverability, bounces (bad email addresses), open rates, click-through rates (CTR), and Opt-Outs. Examples of ESPs include iContact, Benchmark, Constant Contact or MailChimp. Comparing rates to average benchmarks is a useful exercise. Some email rules-of-thumb: open rates average 5-20%; click-through rates average 10%.

When utilizing electronic news release distribution services like PRNewswire, BusinessWire or PRWeb, each provides a useful dashboard for measuring news placements. As mentioned, traditional press clipping services are still available.

Another Internet measurement tool, Google Alerts, is equally useful in monitoring social media, and will be covered below. Finally, a new technology called Urchin Tracking Units or UTMs offer powerful measurement opportunities. UTMs are used to add extra information to a URL to allow significant website traffic monitoring. UTMs are specifically designed to provide the most accurate measurements of unique website visitors. For businesses looking to gain a deeper understanding of their online visitor behavior, the UTM is an extremely valuable technology. UTM combines with Google Analytics to showcase exactly where website traffic is being generated from. UTMs can be used to track all forms of advertising, including print and electronic (e.g. banner ads). UTMs are a powerful combination with social media because you can track what content is generating traffic to a website.

MEASURING SOCIAL MEDIA

Recent surveys of marketing executives and managers reveal that measuring marketing is becoming increasingly important and a top priority as marketers are under increased budget scrutiny and pressure for results. Social media is no exception, so we are pleased to share some of the features and tools for measurement that are now available, and extremely useful. This section will identify those tools for each of the top social networks (YouTube, Facebook, Twitter, LinkedIn), as well as social bookmarking and monitoring tools independent of platform. But first, please consider the illustration below that demonstrates a modern marketing program with marketing measurement via traditional, Internet and social media.

Measuring YouTube

All YouTube pages include a profile with total channel views and upload views, launch (join) date, and subscribers. In addition, YouTube has an impressive metrics system called YouTube INSIGHT. The dashboard includes total views of all videos on your channel, as well as percentages of views. YouTube INSIGHT also provides demographics including age, gender, geographic locations, and more. A typical YouTube dashboard appears below.

1. YouTube Administrative Navigation
2. InSight Dashboard Navigation
3. Total Video Views
4. Video Views by Date
5. Percentage View of Videos and Attention
6. Demographics
7. Popularity of Video

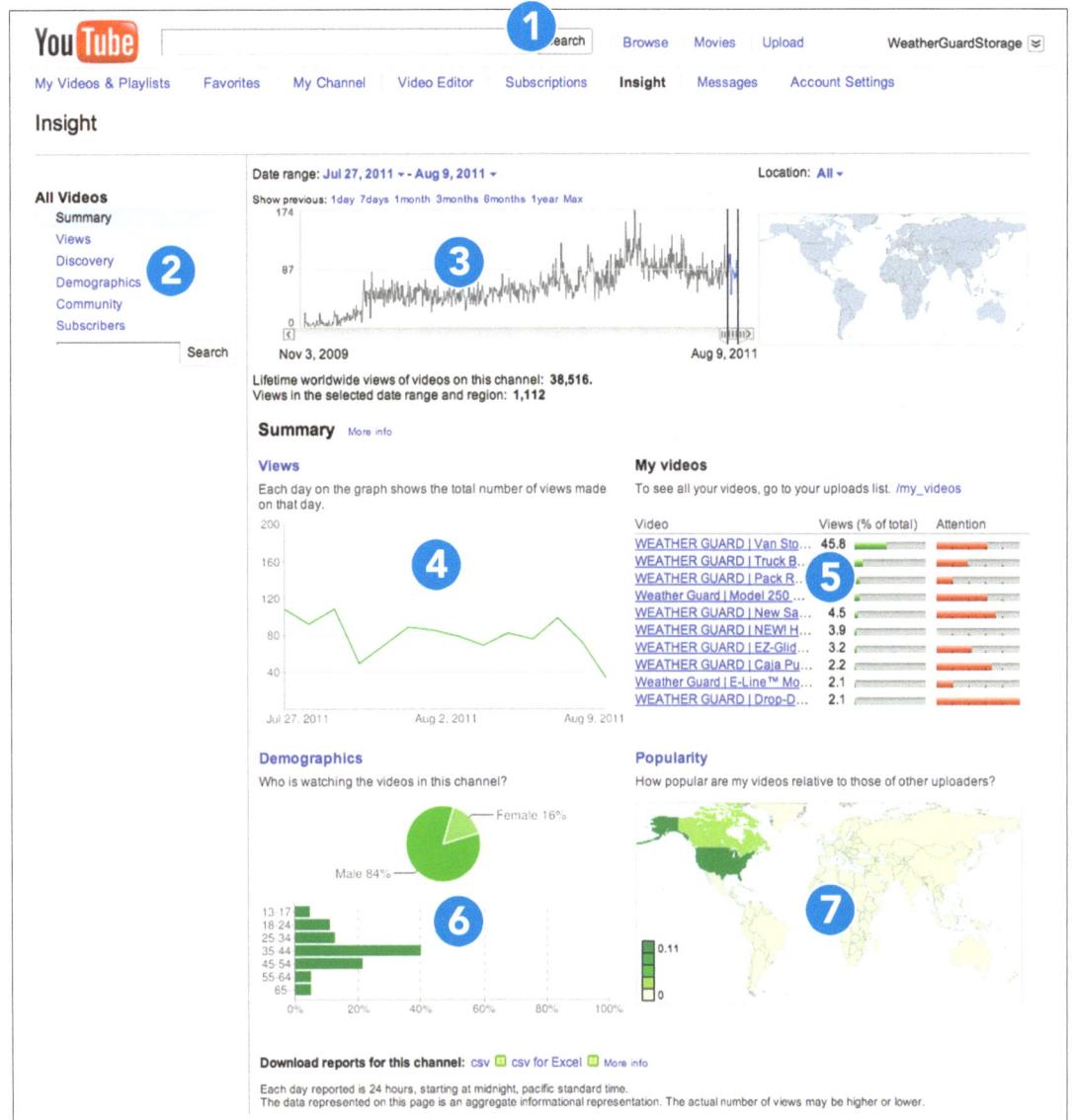

///CMA

Measuring Facebook

Facebook has made great strides to become more business friendly. Businesses now have the ability to create their own fan page. Fan pages allow you to post relevant articles, photos, pictures, and recently added custom 'tabs'. The "Like" button was introduced to allow users to become fans of content, or business/company/brand fan pages.

Similar to YouTube, Facebook has extensive built in metrics, called INSIGHTS (plural). The amount of 'Likes' a given business page has on Facebook is an important measure. Total 'Likes' give a glimpse of how popular a page has become over time. Facebook INSIGHTS also shows the number of interactions within a Facebook page. The peaks in interactions can be linked to content generated which induced an individual to Like the page. Demographic information is also collected by Facebook INSIGHTS to identify who is interacting with a fan page. A typical Facebook dashboard appears below.

1. *InSights Dashboard Navigation*
2. *Aggregated Important Metrics*
3. *Page User Breakdown*
4. *Daily User Breakdown*
5. *New Likes and Total Lifetime*
6. *Demographics*

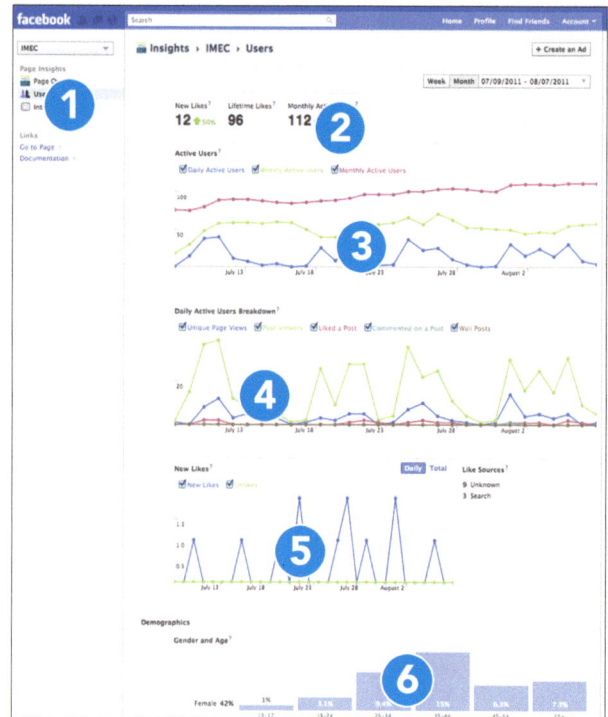

Measuring Twitter

Twitter does not have any significant metrics, but there are still ways to track engagement. The most obvious metric is 'Followers' which defines how many people are viewing information that you Tweet. Another important metric to understand is influence in the Twittersphere. The WeFollow.com directory rates influence for a specific keyword(s). Certain Twitter profiles gain credibility based off the amount of Tweets written, amount of times listed by other users, or the amount of times Retweeted (RT).

The effectiveness of any Tweet can be measured in two ways; 1) the amount of times a Tweet is Retweeted, or 2) Link click-through rates. Klout is a free service that will rank your Twitter profile based off several craiteria.

Twitter does not have built in click-through measurement tools so utilizing a link-shortening tool is crucial. www.Bit.ly is a great metric for link click-through, while shortening the length of a link so you can be more efficient with your 140 characters per Tweet.

While Twitter does not offer a dashboard, TweetDeck and HootSuite are applications that help manage your Twitter profiles, and provide dashboards with some metrics. Both are freeware with the option to upgrade for more features. Twitter recently acquired TweetDeck, so we've reason to believe this application will add features. Below are sample dashboards of each. Each dashboard also offers link shortening.

TweetDeck Dashboard

TweetDeck is a desktop application, which means you have to download the software in order to use it on your computer. TweetDeck's dashboard offers no analytics, and can really become cumbersome when you manage more than 4-5 accounts. As you can see below, you get a new column on your TweetDeck dashboard for each account, so it can become overwhelming once 5+ social media accounts are added. There is no cost to TweetDeck and you can add an unlimited amount of profiles. As previously stated, TweedDeck was acquired by Twitter, so it will surely become highly integrated as time progresses and Twitter finalizes their business plans to utilize TweetDeck efficiently.

1. TweetDeck Dashboard
2. Type a Post Here
3. Accounts Managed

Sample HootSuite Dashboard

Hootsuite has a much "cleaner", organized feel to its dashboard that allows for easy navigation. Each Account added gets a dedicated profile tab which allows you to keep searches, sent tweets, direct messages, and home feed organized. Hootsuite limits you to five profiles for free, but to receive an unlimited amount of accounts it costs $5.99 a month. Hootsuite also acts as collaboration software, which is useful when working with a social media team. Tasks can be scheduled and users can be given to-do-lists to ensure all tasks are completed.

Hootsuite also gives you analytics for your social media profiles in customizable reports (see image 5.1.) Each account receives one free report a month, but unlimited once you sign up for the premium account.

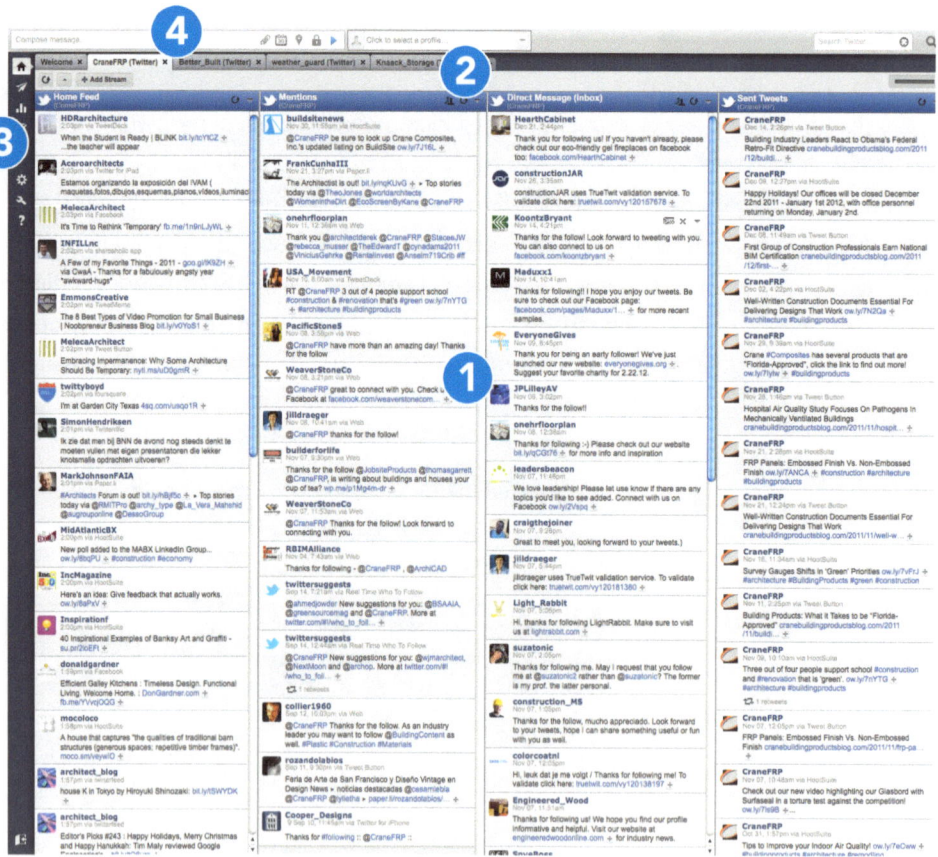

1. Main HootSuite Dashboard
2. "Tabbed" Organization for easy Management
3. Main HootSuite Navigation
4. Type a "Tweet/Post" here

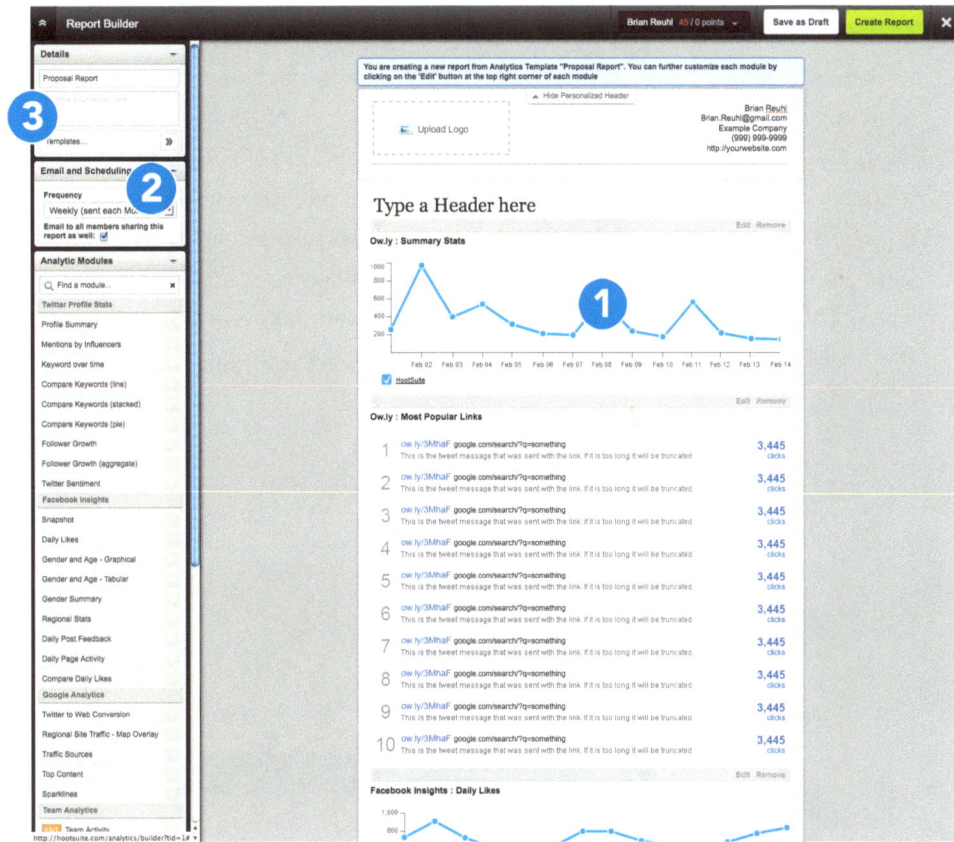

1. Custom Analytics Report
2. Analytics Report
   Navigation
3. Hootsuite Navigation

Measuring LinkedIn

An intriguing way to measure your LinkedIn network is your amount of connections. LinkedIn displays how many 1st degree connections, 2nd degree connections, and 3rd degree connections you have. The level of connections at each degree exponentially increases based on the strength of your network within LinkedIn.

As with Twitter, LinkedIn can be strengthened by the use of link shortening. Using a tool such as www.bit.ly will shorten the horrendous look of a long link, while providing click-through metrics demanded by marketers. LinkedIn offers a minimal amount of metrics for your company page. It allows you to measure how many page visitors you've had click on products or services, and LinkedIn members following your company.

Finally, LinkedIn company pages allow hyperlinks to websites, including the registration pages that can be measured via analytics.

Measuring Social Media Bookmarking

Social Bookmarking has also become an integral approach for increasing social media presence. Tracking the amount of times your content has been bookmarked, or shared is an important metric to understand. The most popular bookmarking tools include Digg, Delicious and StumbleUpon. As an example, Digg allows users to identify how many times an article has been shared. As content gains more views, or more "Diggs," it gains a significant amount of credibility with users and search engines because it has been verified by the many, instead of the few. It allows social media users to decide what content is worthy for their peers. Below is a sample page from Digg that presents the analytics that are available from social bookmarking sites.

1. *Main Navigation*
2. *Primary Analytics*
3. *Top Ranking Stories*
4. *Submit Article Here*

Tools of the Trade: Modern Marketing for Construction Brands

Beside the measurement features of top social platforms, there are a number of social monitoring tools available. Radian6 is just one example of such a monitoring tool, and is one of the most user-friendly and powerful. Radian6 allows monitoring of the entire Internet, and any posts that are going on about a topic, brand or company. This tool shows exact posts instead of just a numerical overview of engagement. The ability to track how many posts are going on about your brand or keyword topics is a powerful glimpse into why social media is the future of marketing. Radian6 is available on a (reasonable) subscription basis.

A typical Radian6 dashboard appears below.

1. *Total # of Mentions by Brand/ Topic*
2. *"River of News" All Mentions of Brand or Topic*
3. *Industry Search Volume*
4. *Word Cloud Surrounding your Brand*
5. *Brand Mentions Bar Chart by # of Conversations*

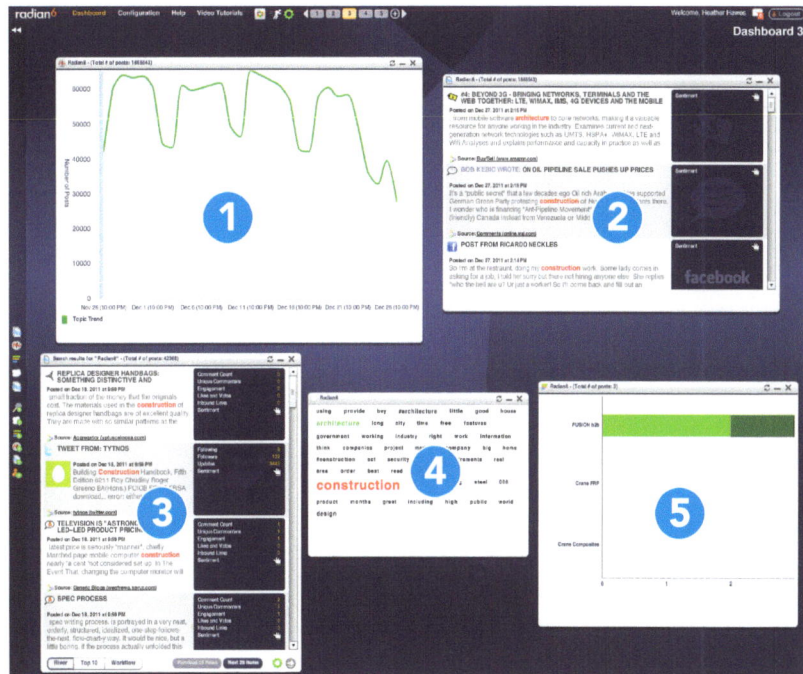

Google

Another monitoring tool that is important to your marketing efforts is Google Alerts. This tool is very powerful, yet simple enough that anyone can be alerted via email when Google finds a topic of his or her choice. Alerts can be for a single keyword, or combination of keywords. This is a free tool that can be combined with all of the above metrics to completely grasp the posts and interactions revolving around your brand, company or keyword topics on the Internet. Keep in mind that Google offers several free services that help to track and monitor your social media efforts. Google analytics will list refferal social media traffic within their robust dashboard. This will give you a perspective of how much website traffic is coming directly from social media websites, and more importantly which sites are most successful for your campaigns.

Measuring social media, like other marketing programs, is a top priority for marketers. Identifying results is key to justifying resources and budgets. Thankfully, the top social media networks (YouTube, Facebook, Twitter and LinkedIn) continue to add tools and features that support measurement. Social bookmarking sites also provide measures including Digg, Delicious and StumbleUpon. Radian6 is a robust monitoring tool that identifies social mentions by keyword(s). Also, Google Alerts is a simple but powerful tool to deliver all keyword mentions to your email.

Unit II: Tactical Marketing

While some of the chapters in this unit require strategy or a strategic foundation, we included such items as Content, Advertising, and Product Development in the Tactical Marketing Unit as most require numerous activities, and therefore are more about marketing implementation than just strategy.

The order of marketing tactics is based on both chronology and likelihood of using the tactic. For example, Content Marketing is the first chapter as most downstream marketing implementation requires it. Internet Marketing is the second chapter, as all construction brands, whether products or services require a website.

Remember, this is the modern marketing mix, so we follow with fast growing blogging and social media that is often integrated with Internet marketing.

Next, traditional marketing tactics such as advertising, publicity, trade shows and events, and direct marketing are explained. These chapters are followed by marketing tactics that may or may not be used by all marketers in the construction category including new product development and pricing.

Content is King!

Content is covered first because it is the driving force of nearly all tactical marketing initiatives, from websites to sales training programs. Marketing departments and marketers are transforming into authors and publishers. Content marketing is the creation and distribution of educational and/or compelling content in multiple formats to attract and/or retain customers. Content marketing is becoming a critical part of the marketing mix, supporting brand awareness, customer retention, and lead generation.

Content types include web and print, social media, articles, events, eNewsletters, case studies, blogs, whitepapers, webcasts, magazines, videos, microsites, print newsletters, research reports, eBooks and more.

Content planning requires a publication calendar, developing content categories and subcategories, and using multiple formats, e.g., Interviews, Q&As, opinion pieces, "charticles", lists, serial pieces, case studies and more.

An unprecedented 2012 study sheds light on content marketing (2013 B2B Content Marketing, Content Marketing Institute)

1. *Nine out of 10 B2B marketers are using content marketing*

2. *Adoption rates by industries range from 78% (low) to 94% (high)*

3. *Goals include brand awareness (78%), customer retention (69%), and lead generation (63%)*

4. *Most marketers (51%) plan to spend more on content marketing in 2011*

5. *Content challenges include producing engaging content (36%), producing enough content (21%), and content budgets (20%)*

CONTENT MARKETING USAGE (BY TACTIC)

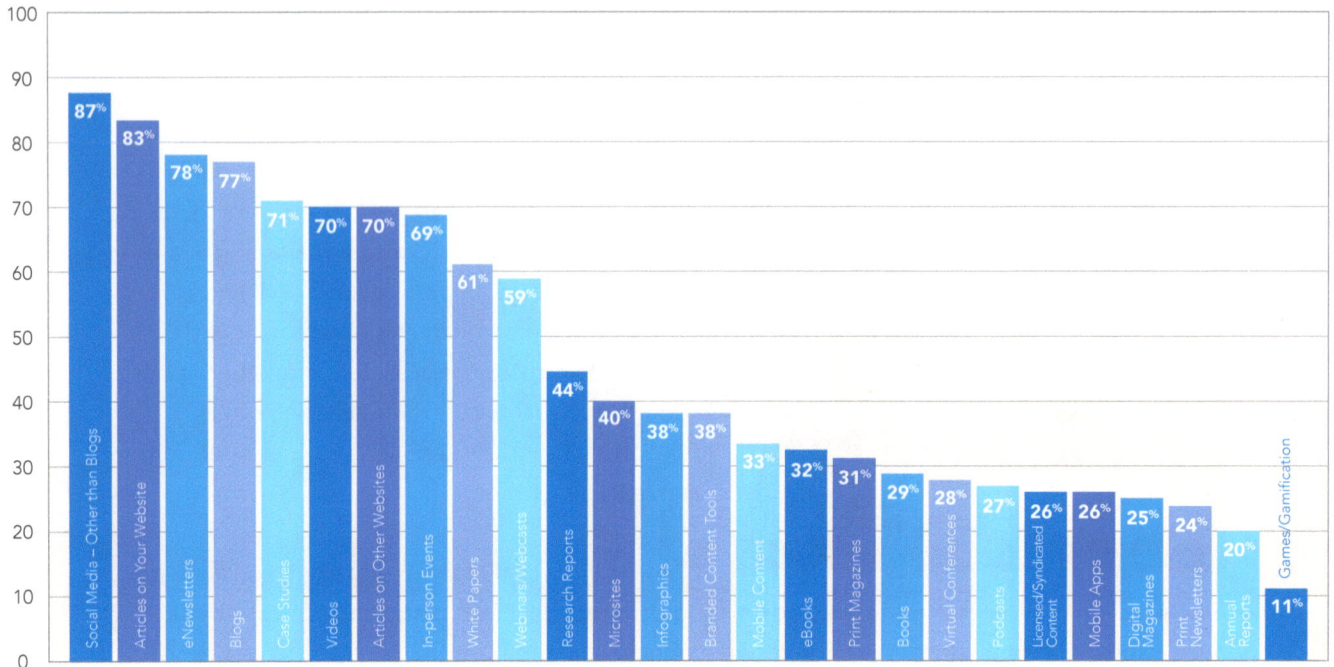

Social Media – Other than Blogs — 87%
Articles on Your Website — 83%
eNewsletters — 78%
Blogs — 77%
Case Studies — 71%
Videos — 70%
Articles on Other Websites — 70%
In-person Events — 69%
White Papers — 61%
Webinars/Webcasts — 59%
Research Reports — 44%
Microsites — 40%
Infographics — 38%
Branded Content Tools — 38%
Mobile Content — 33%
eBooks — 32%
Print Magazines — 31%
Books — 29%
Virtual Conferences — 28%
Podcasts — 27%
Licensed/Syndicated Content — 26%
Mobile Apps — 26%
Digital Magazines — 25%
Print Newsletters — 24%
Annual Reports — 20%
Games/Gamification — 11%

Figure 1 – 2013 B2B Content Marketing Benchmarks - North America: CMI/MarketingProfs

CHALLENGES THAT B2B CONTENT MARKETERS FACE

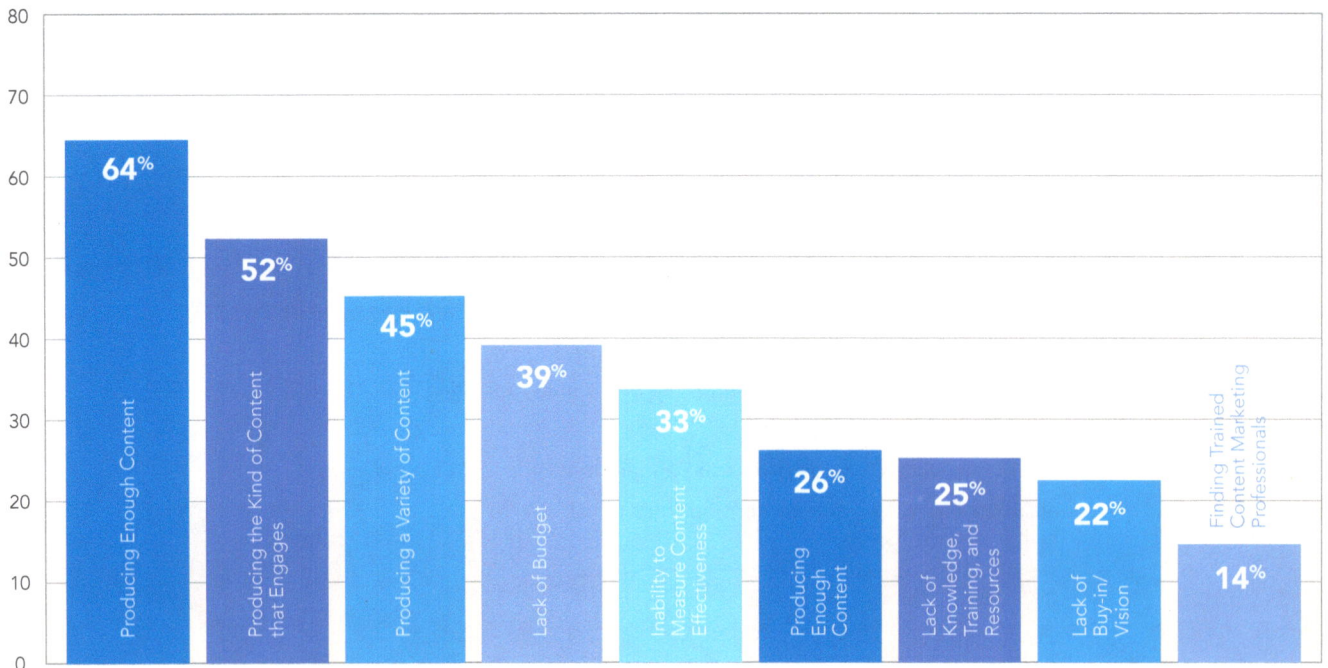

Producing Enough Content — 64%
Producing the Kind of Content that Engages — 52%
Producing a Variety of Content — 45%
Lack of Budget — 39%
Inability to Measure Content Effectiveness — 33%
Producing Enough Content — 26%
Lack of Knowledge, Training, and Resources — 25%
Lack of Buy-in/ Vision — 22%
Finding Trained Content Marketing Professionals — 14%

Figure 2 – 2013 B2B Content Marketing Benchmarks - North America: CMI/MarketingProfs

In 2011, the Construction Marketing Association conducted a national survey regarding content marketing practices. Following are the results.

1. Do you develop/manage content internally, outsource or both?

    a) Internally (63%)

    b) Outsource (0%)

    c) Both (37%)

2. What percentage of your time is devoted to content development or management?

    a) None (19%)

    b) Up to 20% (38%)

    c) Up to 50% (38%)

    d) Up to 100% (6%)

3. What is your approximate ratio of content that is print vs. digital?

    a) 100% Print (0%)

    b) 50/50 Print/Digital (28%)

    c) 75/25 Print/Digital (11%)

    d) 25/75 Print/Digital (44%)

    e) 100% Digital (17%)

CREATING GREAT CONTENT: HOW GENEROUS INFORMATION-SHARING BUILDS YOUR CONTENT-BASED MARKETING PROGRAM

by Eric Gagnon

Wherever I go, I try to stay on the lookout for ideas and how-to-do-it lessons for making better products, and for ways to market and sell products and services more effectively.

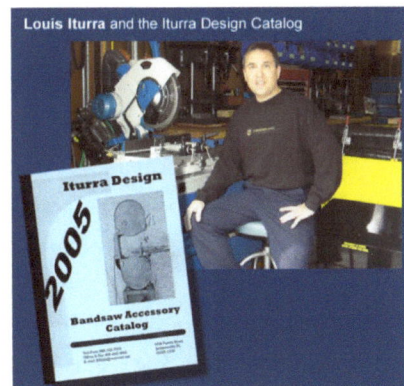

Louis Iturra and the Iturra Design Catalog

Awhile back, I encountered a great company run by a guy who makes great products, and who really knows how to communicate with his prospects and customers. As marketing pros, there's much we can learn from his company that can be applied to any B2B marketing program or project.

Louis Iturra is the founder of Iturra Designs, a supplier of band saw parts and accessories in Jacksonville, FL. If you've just bought a band saw and start "Googling" around for information, Iturra's name comes up everywhere—even though he's never had a website, and is too busy to spend much time online.

Iturra manufactures and sells parts to help you rebuild, improve, and optimize the performance of your band saw. Owners of the venerable old made-in-U.S.A. Delta band saws, as well as the new, Chinese-built clones of these machines come to Louis for parts and accessories to help them cut straighter, thicker, faster, and more smoothly.

In addition to sales made to retailers and catalog companies, 70% of Iturra's business is generated by his massive 230-page free catalog—more like a book than a catalog, actually.

A plain, black-and-white piece run on a half-dozen laser printers in Louis' shop, the Iturra Designs catalog is packed with useful information on every aspect of buying, rebuilding, modifying and using band saws. And whether you're selling high-end industrial machining products in Chicago, shop floor automation systems in San Jose, or Web design services in Denver, there are lessons to be learned in the way Louis does business for every B2B marketer.

Your Readers Want Honesty

Many of Louis' loyal customers are owners of classic American-made woodworking machines, such as those made by Delta from the 1930s until recently, when they outsourced their manufacturing to China. Owners of these old U.S.-made band saws have a dedication to solid American engineering rivaling that of Harley-Davidson owners. Louis helps owners of these old saws restore, rebuild, and modernize them so they run better than new.

Other Iturra customers include recent owners of Chinese-made clones of Delta band saws, cheaper machines of lower quality than the older, American-built saws. Louis helps these owners upgrade the weak points of these machines with ingeniously designed products, most of which Louis designs and makes himself.

Louis begins his catalog with a two-page editorial on the decline of American manufacturing and product quality, pointing the finger at greedy, disconnected, number-crunching CEOs for wrecking the quality and dominance of many of America's leading manufacturing brands. Strong words, but true: An unorthodox way to lead off a product catalog, but it honesty strikes a chord with Louis' prospects and customers, and sets the tone for his approach to product development and marketing.

The first lesson we learn from Louis is that honesty and truth are the most important things in marketing: Say what you believe and speak the truth, and you'll be a standout. This is a good thing.

Branding=Reputation: Selling Great Products Builds Your Brand

By now you can probably sense that Louis doesn't care anything about fancy marketing concepts like "branding," yet, if you want to use this term, he's created one of the strongest brands in his business.

How does he do it? Since branding is another name for a company's reputation, Louis has a great brand because, first and foremost, he makes and sells great products. In the old days they used to call this a reputation; now they call it branding.

Louis started out nine years ago with a single product —a 3-inch high-tension steel spring. A favorable article in Fine Woodworking magazine led to a flood of orders lasting months, which gave Louis the cash flow to design and manufacture other products he's added to his lineup. Each product is of the highest quality, built much better and stronger than it needs to be.

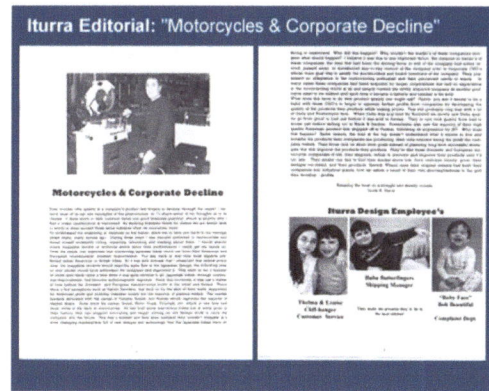

Iturra Editorial: "Motorcycles & Corporate Decline"

When you buy any of his products, you get a beautifully machined part that's better than its stock Chinese-made replacement, featuring design elements that make it work better or more precisely than the stock part it replaces. The hallmark of American design and product character are the generous use of materials that serve product function, design that serves functionality, and rock-solid reliability. Louis is right: this was how we made things in America before the finance geeks took over our best companies.

"Show What You Know" with Honest, Comprehensive, Helpful Product Info and Advice

In addition to selling great products, Louis is obsessive about providing intensely detailed and informative descriptions and instructions for every product in his catalog.

The most important part of the Iturra catalog are its product listings, which read more like mini-tutorials for installing and using each product. Many product listings span a page or more, and give out far more information than the typical catalog sales copy you'd see in his competitors' product catalogs.

Read through the Iturra catalog and you'll not only see the range of products Louis offers, you'll get a near-complete education on the operation, restoration, and use of band saws and related accessories.

Louis doesn't hold anything back here—there are plenty of photos, diagrams where needed, and copious amounts of text for each product. With Louis, it's not so much a case of "show what you know," as it is "share what you know," since much of the information contained in his catalog is a result of his direct experience, and this is the knowledge he shares freely with his customers and prospects.

This comprehensive information-sharing also extends to the instruction sheets Louis includes with every one of his products, large and small; they're loaded with detailed, concise, understandable photos and text covering every step involved in installing and using each one of his products.

Louis also spends hours on the phone each week with prospects and customers who call in with questions about his products. I've called him a few times and am impressed with the range of knowledge he will freely share with his customers, and by how much additional information he provides that's way beyond basic product details—and I'm sure his other callers feel the same way.

Ask Louis about putting a more powerful motor on your band saw and he'll not only give you every detail on doing this, he'll also tell you how to run a 220-volt line into your basement, if you also need to know this (I did).

Louis could easily cut his catalog by half and sell like everyone else, and he could delegate his customer service to an order-taker, but by sharing what he knows, he's created a standout position in his field, and gains an almost cult-like loyalty from his customers.

And remember, he's doing it all with crude, laser-printed, hand-made catalogs and tiny ads in woodworking magazines. No Web site. No fancy ad campaigns. No monthly PR firm retainer.

A better catalog design and clever copy wouldn't make Louis any better off. When you know what you know and share what you know, all you need to do is put this information out there and make it clear to your reader; do this well and you're more than halfway there to persuading your reader to buy your product.

How Can You Show, and Share, What You Know?

While the way Iturra communicates with his customers and prospects is unique to him and his business, there are some very useful underlying lessons we can draw from his approach.

First, there is no such thing as providing too much helpful information. Louis errs on the side of providing too much helpful information to his readers, and that's a good thing. His prospects want all the information they can get so they can make an informed purchase decision. Don't your prospects want the same thing?

Think about your products from your prospect's viewpoint: Is there anything—and anything else —your prospect should know about your product? If so, it probably belongs in your marketing deliverables. You can't lose by providing too much useful information.

For example, would the presentation of your next product catalog be more effective if you introduced a mini-tutorial on using one of your products? Would readers gain a more favorable impression of your product if you provided a description of your manufacturing process, and described how your process makes your product better than the other guy's product?

How else can your product or service be used by your customer? Are there complex or unique applications for your product that would not be readily understood by your prospects? If so, would your reader benefit by knowing these ways? And if so, then how?

Are there other ways your customers use your products that other prospects and customers would find interesting, useful, productive, or profitable in their business? A real-life profile of current customers who use your products adds truth and character to the way you present your company and its products to the rest of your customers and prospects.

It's not only true that "the more you tell the more you sell," but by your willingness to provide extreme detail on the uses, issues, and applications involved with your company's products or services, you also position your company (or client) as more knowledgeable than your competitors. The more you do this, and the longer you do it, the higher the chance your company becomes recognized as the go-to supplier for the product or service you're selling. You also mitigate against the risk of leaving out that essential product information that could have led to a sale, and reduce your company's (and client's) customer service expense. What else do your prospects and customers need to know?

Enthusiasm is Contagious

The other thing we can learn from Louis is that enthusiasm drives the helpful advice he provides to his prospects and customers. These extensive product descriptions wouldn't be nearly as effective if they weren't infused with the enthusiasm that comes from enjoying your work, as Louis clearly does.

While it would be disengenuous for a multimillion dollar industrial products or high-tech company to copy Iturra's home-grown approach to marketing presentation, copy for every product must include enthusiasm as its vital ingredient.

Writing copy with energy and enthusiasm creates better and more effective copy than recycling the same old marketing buzz-benefits everyone else uses in your business. If Louis can put as much enthusiasm as he does into describing the virtues of a band saw blade, then you can do it with the high-dollar technical products you're selling.

Building better products, being honest, showing what you know, and showing enthusiasm are the ways Louis Iturra has built his business and created a unique niche in his field. As long as he keeps doing this, he'll attract loyal customers and defend his business against larger companies and cheaper offshore competitors. This is what we marketing people call "building an invincible brand franchise." If you're fighting for market share in your field, you'd do a lot worse than taking a page from the way Louis plays the game.

Eric Gagnon (eric@businessmarketinginstitute.com), a director with the Business Marketing Institute, is author of The Marketing Manager's Handbook and The CRM Field Marketing Handbook.

Tools of the Trade: Modern Marketing for Construction Brands

Internet Marketing—Acronym Soup: Web 2.0, SEO, APPS, PPC, QR Codes

No question, Internet marketing is one of the most important tasks and responsibilities in construction marketing. But Internet marketing is much more than a website. Modern Internet marketing, often called Web 2.0, includes user-friendly website design, useful content and resources, social media integration and sharing, along with built-in search engine optimization (SEO) features that drive organic or natural search results. Mobile web is the hottest topic in marketing, followed closely by Mobile Apps or applications. And finally, Paid Search, often called pay-per-click or PPC is a tremendous lead generation tool for many construction marketing scenarios.

A great example of modern Internet marketing and Web 2.0 is the Construction Marketing Association. A resource deep and search-optimized website integrated with an award-winning blog, and all major social media networks: LinkedIn, YouTube, Facebook and Twitter. Importantly, multiple lead generation registration pages are available:

1. *Free email newsletter registration*
2. *Member registration/member login/member directory*
3. *Webcast event registration*
4. *Contact form*
5. *Whitepaper request and purchase*
6. *Award application and purchase*
7. *Certification registration and purchase*
8. *Career Center resume and/or job postings*
9. *RSS registration*

A visual example of Construction Marketing Association Web 2.0 marketing assets including website, blog, Twitter, Facebook, eNewsletter and whitepaper, appears below.

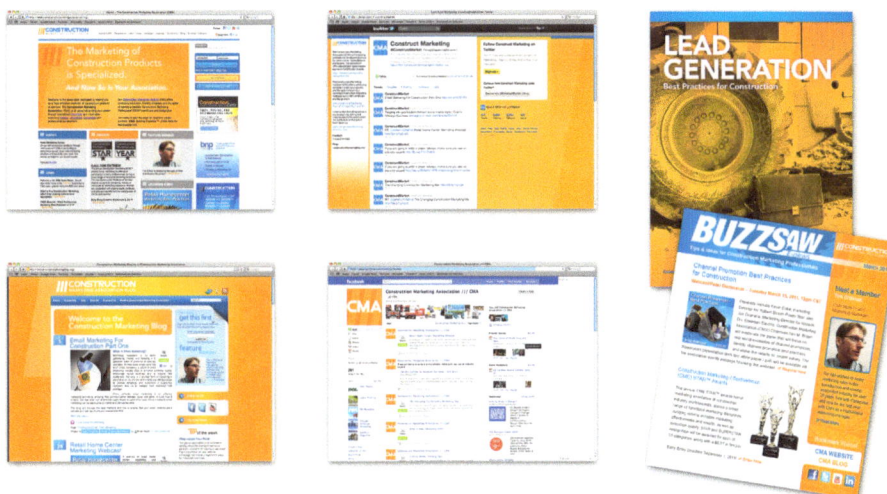

///CMA

SEARCH ENGINE OPTIMIZATION (SEO): TOP PRIORITY FOR CONSTRUCTION MARKETERS

As construction marketers implement next-generation websites that feature enhanced functions, many companies have not yet taken advantage of even the most basic **Search Engine Optimization (SEO)** techniques.

Developing your website, or retrofitting an existing website with, best practice SEO is critical to achieving improved **organic or natural search engine results**, thereby increasing website traffic and quite possibly sales and market share.

SEO is impacted by on-page coding, off page lnk-building, and social media presence. Some of the techniques and features that support search engine optimization include:

> *Meta tag coding*
> *Page Titles*
> *URL redirects, URL structure*
> *Site Maps and Text Links*
> *Link building, Reciprocal Links and Inter-Linking*
> *Keyword content or "landing" pages*
> *Blog and Social Media Integration*

Invisible to the user, **Meta tags** are HTML (or XHTML) coding for descriptions of a webpage's contents, thus enabling the search engine to correctly index the web page's contents. Meta tag coding is the most fundamental SEO technique and critical to most search results. Meta tag coding includes Meta descriptions, Header tags and Alt or image tags. In the past, Meta keywords were used, but are now less important.

Each webpage should have a keyword-rich **Meta description** (also relevant and specific to the page), approximately 150 characters in length including spaces. **Header tags** are brief headlines that should be coded at the top or header position of each page. **Alt tags** are the file names, image titles or descriptions for images contained on your website. These are useful when search engines index or "spider" your website since the engines automatically turn off images and read only text, including file names. Therefore, instead of image filenames such as "DCP0003.jpg," images should be re-named "KEYWORD.jpg," to increase search results.

Page titles or Title tags, although not technically meta, work with Meta Descriptions and are typically displayed in the Search Engine Results Pages (SERPs) as the title, along with the meta description. Title tags are the descriptive words at the top of the browser window that, more often than not, only list the company name or website address. Title tags should be simple, keyword-rich, and approximately 70 characters in length including spaces.

An often neglected SEO technique is setting-up **URL redirects**, or more specifically, a **301 permanent redirect** for your website. Search engines will index both the *www.domainname.com* and *domainname.com* versions of your website. This scenario creates what is known as *duplicate content,* thus **diluting** the search authority of both.

Also called a **canonical redirect**, the 301 permanent redirect is vital to proper search engine optimization and improved rankings. A simple way to test whether your website has a 301 redirect in place is to type *"yourdomain.com"* into your browser address bar then hit "Enter". If the URL does not automatically change to *"www.domainname.com"*, then the 301 redirect is NOT in place to resolve canonical issues; therefore, it is not optimized for the search engines. The redirect must be done at the hosting server level, and can often be completed via hosting tech support requests.

Another important SEO determinant is **URL or domain structure**—specifically, keyword-rich sub-domains. When linking to website sub-pages that are often served dynamically via databases, the URL that appears on the "http" line often includes obscure database code with multiple back slashes or symbols. To eliminate this search engine hurdle, ideal URL structures use the base domain name, along with simple keywords or keyword phrases in place of this coding.

Site Maps are yet another SEO best practice. Typically a secondary navigation text link is placed in the footer of the web page, and linking to a sub-page with a simple outline of website content and sub-links. This is often called a Site Index. In the same location, redundant text navigation links for all primary navigation should be placed. Site Maps and Text Links allow search engines to index all of your website contents and sub-links to determine search rankings. XML Site Maps should be submitted to key search engines including Google, Yahoo, and Bing.

Link-building, **Reciprocal Links** and **Inter-Linking** are key aspects to search engine optimization. Why? Because most search engines rank websites based on how many links there are to that site. The practice of dedicating a website sub-page or pages to industry links, and/or requesting reciprocal links supports link-building. Link sources include paid and free directories like Yahoo and DMOZ. Industry blogs, publications, associations, and trade shows are also great sources. Bookmarks to your website or pages are a source of links. Place Share and Bookmark widgets on your website, and bookmark your website sub-pages with popular Bookmark sites like Digg, Delicious and StumbleUpon. Finally, Inter-Linking is text hyperlinks to other pages on your website.

Before posting your company's enhanced website on the worldwide web, be sure your website content includes keywords that correspond to the meta tags for those pages, or even dedicated landing pages or sub-pages for your site's top keywords. As referenced previously, these pages should use keywords in URLs, title-tags, Alt tags and meta code to ensure the best search results.

Now more than ever, **Blogs and Social Media** are major determinants of Search Engine Results. Best practice search optimization requires that your website link to your blog and social profiles. Ideally the blog is a primary navigation link, and a sub-domain of the site (ex. www.sitename.com/blog). Two of the most important determinants of website search authority are indexed pages and links to your website. Blogs support both with each blog post indexed as a new page, along with blog roll reciprocal links. More on this topic will be covered in the blogging chapter.

Placing social icons with hyperlinks to key social media profiles including Facebook, Twitter, YouTube, LinkedIn and Google+, along with Share or Bookmark icons is also important to building search authority. Counter tools like AddThis share tool, the Tweetmeme Retweet tool, Facebook Like button and Google +1 button also support social sharing and ultimately, search authority.

Below is a sample (Construction Marketing Association) homepage with numbered references to SEO features.

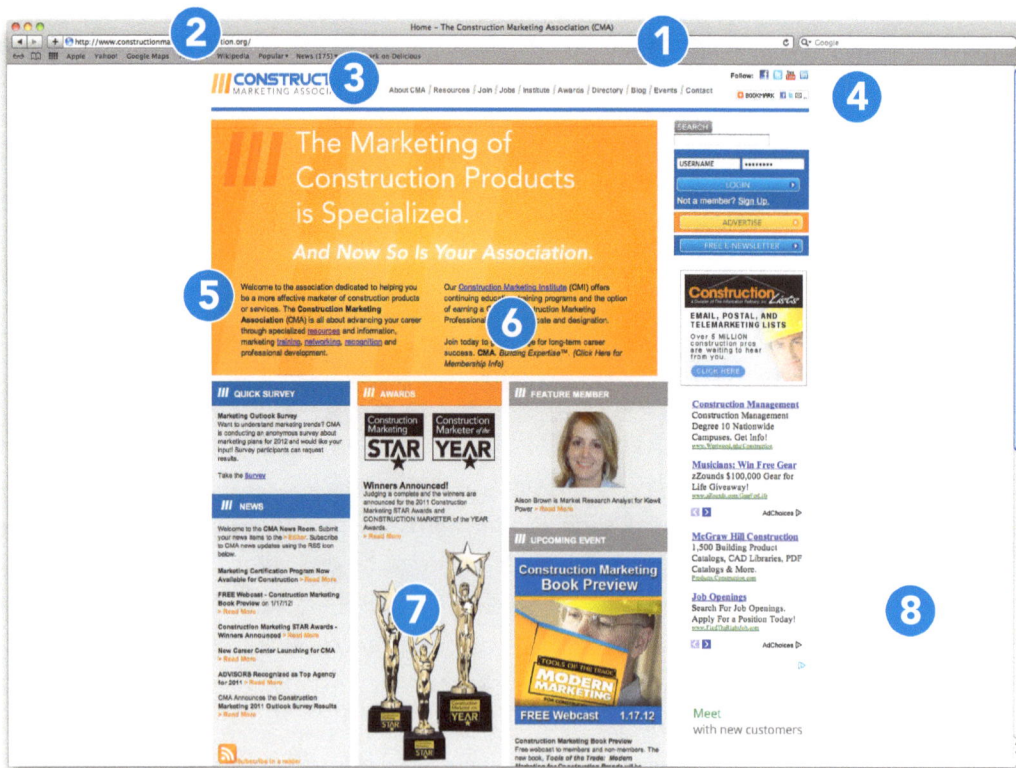

1. *Keyword-rich age title or Title tag*
2. *Keyword-rich URL or domain structure*
3. *Website navigation based on keyword analysis*
4. *Social sharing including hyperlinks to Facebook, Twitter, YouTube, LinkedIn, bookmarking and related*
5. *Keyword density of page content*
6. *Interlinking of text to other pages*
7. *Image Alt tags*
8. *Not shown, proper Meta-coding, site maps, URL redirects*

With a Search Engine Optimized website, organic or natural search results will flourish. There are several options for measuring search authority and search engine optimization (SEO). We prefer and recommend Google Analytics, but this does require installation of Google Analytics tracking code. Certainly test keywords with search engines to measure your search engine results page (SERP) placements. A free and robust tool is Hubspot's Marketing Grader.

BAD SEO PRACTICES

Blackhat SEO techniques are used in an effort to rank pages higher than they deserve to be ranked. Blackhatters use a variety of techniques to manipulate search engines, despite the risk of being banned, penalized in rankings, or ruining their reputation.

Some common blackhat techniques are keyword stuffing, hidden or invisible text, mirror websites, link farming, doorway pages, meta-tag stuffing, scraper sites, and hidden links.

Search engines take measures to prevent and penalize those utilizing blackhat SEO techniques. For example, Google Panda was an initiative by Google to penalize "thin content" with a lot of ads. Google Penguin is an algorithm update to Google Panda that targets link farming by evaluating incoming links. These algorithms are being continuously updated and are used to decrease search rankings of those websites using the techniques mentioned above.

SEO SUMMARY

With a Search Engine Optimized website, organic or natural search results will flourish. There are several options for measuring search authority and search engine optimization (SEO). As Google dominates search engine volume at nearly 70%, we prefer and recommend Google Analytics, but this does require installation of Google Analytics tracking code. Certainly test keywords with search engines to measure your search engine results page (SERP) placements. Google Adwords provides robust keyword analysis and testing. A free and robust tool is Hubspot's Marketing Grader (www.MarketingGrader.com). Finally, mobile versions of your website and blog support search authority, and Web 2.0, and is our next topic!

THE FUNDAMENTALS OF MOBILE WEBSITE CONVERSIONS

Driven by meteoric growth in smart phones and tablets, mobile web is the next big marketing thing! Current predictions indicate that one in two Americans (100 million americans – 3/6/12) now own a "smart phone" device. Mobile website conversions are the future for content delivery. Great websites are no longer sufficient for the task of business communications and interactions. Every company must establish a current and a future strategy for how to make mobile communication one of their primary resources. The opportunities associated with mobile-friendly website marketing cannot be ignored. But you must prevent technological overkill.

While your current website is most likely viewable on a mobile device, it is NOT mobile optimized. Attempting to click a link with your finger-tip on a 3.5 inch screen is quite a challenge. The ultimate goal is to structure your website to be user friendly on each and every mobile device. Ultimately, those users who visit your site via a mobile device need to be converted to leads, which requires convenient navigation and a logical site structure.

Essentially, mobile website conversion requires the development of stripped down versions of a larger website, with different versions for each mobile operating system. Android, iPhone and Blackberry control the market with 41%, 27% and 22% respectively through July, 2011 *(Source: comScore)*.

As an example, the mobile version of the Intel website is only nine (9) pages, compared to over 80,000 pages for the regular website. The most popular blog software, WordPress, offers built-in widgets for mobile website conversion.

One efficient option for mobile website conversion is through your content management system (CMS). Many popular CMS systems offer mobile Plug-In's. This usually strips out any complicated CSS and large image files. It "stacks" the site so it is viewed primarily vertically. To view a very rough example of this type in your URL at http://www.skweezer.com, and it will render a ultra-simplified mobile version of your website. Any Plug-In available from your CMS would allow for a much cleaner look. Google also offers a mobile site creator, per link below: http://www.google.com/sites/help/intl/en/mobile-landing-pages/mlpb.html

Another option for mobile website conversion is to build it from the ground-up. The same information that is relevant and important on your full website may not be relevant to a mobile viewer. Often times large amounts of copy and large image files are distracting and cumbersome. A mobile user will not read a mass amount of text, and they will not wait for a large file to load. Small image file sizes and minimalistic copy is important. Also be sure to make user navigation very simple. Be sure to set up a 'mirror' for your website and direct all mobile traffic to the URL http://mobile.yoursitehere.com. You will see several variations of this often times including m.yoursitehere.com.(i.e. www.knaack.com becomes mobile.knaack.com or m.knaack.com). This gives you a sub-domain to build mobile website under.

Due to the technical nature of a mobile website, it is important to have a skilled developer involved in the process. However, this is often why marketers choose the off the shelf solution even though it is not the best option. It is also a best practice to allow users to view your normal website if they so choose. The reasons they may want to do this include being connected via Wi-Fi or a hotspot, or load time is not a deterrent from viewing the full site. When choosing to design your own website remember to use large buttons, and if using a form ask for only the necessary information!

Mobile web technical development, while beyond the scope of this chapter, involves programming in HTML, PHP, CSS, along with specific requirements of each hardware operating system. Specifically Apple/Mac (iPhone, iPad), Android and Blackberry. Other mobile conversions technical considerations include the following:

> *LOGO: make it attractive but small, no more than 2-KBs in size*
> *NAVIGATION: include links to your main pages, places, and points of interest; reduce the viewer's need for typing*
> *CONTENT: make it clear, distinctive, and exact; keep it consistent with the content on your primary website; use snippets when possible*
> *GRAPHICS: use small images, sparingly; use images only where contextually relevant*
> *FOOTER: keep the footer simple and clean; avoid hyper-links*
> *KEEP THE CODE VALID: mobile browsers are not so forgiving as their PC counterparts*
> *FOCUS ON FLUID LAYOUTS: set widths by percentages rather than pixels*
> *TARGET SPECIFIC DEVICES: utilize unique style-sheets for each specific type of handheld device*
> *AVOID FANCY SCRIPTS: many mobile devices will choke on Flash or Javascript code; it may even lock up the viewer's phone*
> *USE AUTOMATIC MOBILE BROWSER DETECTION: success is in the redirection.*

Mobile device interfaces are small, typically limited in speed, and set to pre-defined dimensions. Craft you mobile website conversions to meet these restrictions, but provide the content that your business partners require and expect.

MOBILE APPLICATIONS OR APPS

Beside mobile website conversion, Mobile applications, Mobile apps, or Apps are Internet applications that use mobile devices including smart phones and tablets. Often mobile applications are tools like price calculators, configurators, even games.

Like mobile website conversions, mobile applications have to customize to each operating system (OS) including Google's Android, Apple's iOS, Blackberry, along with Apple iPad and other tablets.

After targeting the OS that your company wishes to reach, focus on your users' needs and what will make it easiest for them to reach you so you can assist them. Be efficient in your design and try to plan ahead of any potential problems such as network strength issues or low memory, and make sure that your designers and developers work in conjunction to achieve the most effective mobile application to effectively market your business through the use of this skyrocketing medium.

INTERNET DIRECTORIES

Building links, inbound links, or back-links to your website and/or blog are key to building search authority and improving rank in search engine results pages (SERPs). Advanced link building includes submitting your website, blog, articles and white papers, and news releases to online directories to achieve links. This blog shares top link building submission options for different types of content.

Website Directory Submission

In addition to submitting your XML sitemap to search engines, it is equally important to submit your website to various web directories to build links. Here we'll cover the top website directory submission sites we've used, including paid and unpaid.

Top 3 Web Directory Submission Sites (PAID):

1. *Yahoo Directory - The Yahoo directory is the best paid option for submitting your website.*
   Cost: $299 per year

2. *Business.com - Business.com is a great paid option, also a little pricy but worth looking at.*
   Cost: $299 per year

3. *Best of The Web - Best of the Web is a cheaper option for a paid directory and is quite popular.*
   Cost: $149.95 per year

Top 3 Web Directory Submission Sites (UNPAID):

1. *All The Websites - Allthewebsites.org has been around for some time and is one of the top free directories that hasn't switched to paid yet.*

2. *IllumiRate - Illumirate is a top free directory, but does take time for your listing to be verified.*

3. *ExactSeek - ExactSeek requires membership in order to add your URL to their directory.*

A Note on DMOZ:

In an effort to figure out whether DMOZ, the largest free directory on the internet, still allows users to submit their URL, we did some quick analysis of the DMOZ site. It is true that you need to literally dig through the categories until you find a place that best fits your website. We found that News/Weblogs is still taking submissions because we were able to see the "suggest URL" on the top right of the page. Keep in mind that DMOZ is extremely strict in which websites it accepts into its directory. In the past, when submitting client sites, we've noticed that it is really "hit or miss" when it comes to your site being approved. This is why we've taken it off of the top free web directory listings as it works for some, but not others. DMOZ does seem to influence search results a bit, so if you can get your website listed, we applaud you!

BLOG SUBMISSION AS A LINK BUILDING STRATEGY

When submitting your blogs, be sure to check out the site. While it isn't preferable to join sites that require you to add code to your website, in some instances this is okay – especially with blog submission sites like Technorati, where adding a "token" is only temporarily needed. Below we'll cover the top 3 blog submission sites we've used based on experience.

Top 3 Blog Submission Sites:

Technorati - Technorati is a very well known blog submission site. However, they have a tedious submission process. You must create a profile and then you are allowed to "claim" your blog. When doing this, Technorati will ask you to provide your feed link (rss feed burner), your facebook page link, your twitter link, and any blog profiles you know of that link to your blog currently. This shows how important it is to connect all of your social profiles, website, and blog! You will need to put a small code within a blog post, have Technorati check that it exists, and only upon approval can you then remove that token.

Blog Search - BlogSearch.com allows you to quickly submit your blog and confirm that you are the owner through an email verification process. Upon verification, they will review your blog and add it to the category you chose. The submission process takes under a minute!

Blog Catalog - Blog Catalog is another great blog submission site that requires you to validate your account through email before submitting your blog. Then, you can add your blog through your profile. A positive aspect of Blog Catalog is that there are a ton of categories to choose from to make sure you submit your blog to the most relevant listing. You will be required to verify your blog through adding Blog Catalog's link somewhere on your home page (you can do the footer if you do not want it overly visible).

There are hundreds of other blog submission sites. Keep searching for ones that work well for you.

ARTICLE SUBMISSION AS A LINK BUILDING STRATEGY

When submitting your articles to article submission sites to build links, it is extremely important to provide original content created by you or your company.

Top 3 Article Submission Sites:

Ezine – Ezine is a great site to submit your white papers and articles to. Membership is free and you create a profile as a person, not an organization. So, if you are the person who writes for your company, be sure to sign up as yourself. In your profile, you can connect your Twitter, Facebook, Google, YouTube, and LinkedIn accounts, which is great if you are trying to build a link relationship back to your website. Search engines can recognize that you are the original author of the content and give you authority in search results. It is important to follow all the steps Ezine outlines in generating article content. They will contact you if your first submission does not pass all of the guidelines and allow you to go back multiple times to fix it. Below is an example of the statistics page Ezine gives you to check on how many visits your articles have received:

Articlesbase – Articlesbase is the easiest and quickest article submission site to submit your articles and they get back to you about whether or not your articles have been approved quickly. Like all article submission sites, this one offers statistics on the number of times someone has viewed your article. Notably, they have a keywords performance, like Google Analytics, that shows you what people searched to arrive at your article.

Yahoo! Voices – Yahoo! Voices is the most strict article submission site. It is difficult to get your article or white paper submitted to this site as they seem to be a "three strikes you're out" type of site. So, make sure that your article follows all of their guidelines and is practically flawless in errors. They only give you two chances to resubmit your article and will then reject it if you do not pass the test. If you can get your article submitted to this site, it will certainly help you in search.

ADDITIONAL LINK SUBMISSION TIPS

As you submit to website, blog, article and white paper submission sites, and PR directories, be sure to avoid link farms and robot linking. It is detrimental to submit your sites to link farms in order to gain more back-links to your website. Google frowns upon this and the links, while high in quantity, will not be good quality links. Also avoid sites that claim they have robots to build your links for you – these are ways to hurt your website's authority in search results. Overall, if someone tells you that they can cut the amount of time you spend in link building quickly and cut down your marketing with "too-good-to-be-true" offers, they are lying to you.

A Note on Inbound Links, or Back-links, To Your Website

Inbound links, or back-links, are incoming links to your website. It's important to have other sites on the web point to your website, blog, social profiles, etc. Why? Because it adds to your search authority and allows search engines to see that others are giving you credit for being a good reference. Keep in mind, however, that there are inbound links that could hurt you: these could be links from "spammy" websites or sites that search engines deem "low authority." Likewise, if you've signed up for link farms, where you pay a site to generate hundreds of inbound links to your site, you risk lowering your search authority because search engines see that these low quality sites are linking to you. Curious to see which sites are linking to you? Try Open Site Explorer from SEOMoz.

You want to link to sites that are related to yours and will provide an additional resource for your audience. For example, as the Construction Marketing Association, we link to the AMA and BMA because we know that those are other associations you may be interested in. It most certainly helps if you can get major authoritative sites like this to link back to you to generate reciprocal links, mentioned in our blog on Link Building Basics, yet this does take some more work. Often you will have to contact the organization or business and ask if they are willing to link to your site because you think your site would provide an additional source of information for their customers/audience.

PAID SEARCH

Also called Pay-Per-Click or PPC, paid search is employed when organic or natural search is not achievable, or not possible. This is most often the result of a very competitive keyword category. Other reasons for Paid Search are high-ticket sales prices offset paid search costs. Or new competitive entrants use Paid Search to enter an established market.

Paid search options include Google Adwords, Yahoo! Search, Bing, paid Directory listings, link building and more. Following are the results of a recent (2011) poll identifying types of Paid Search used by construction marketers.

Types of Paid Search Used

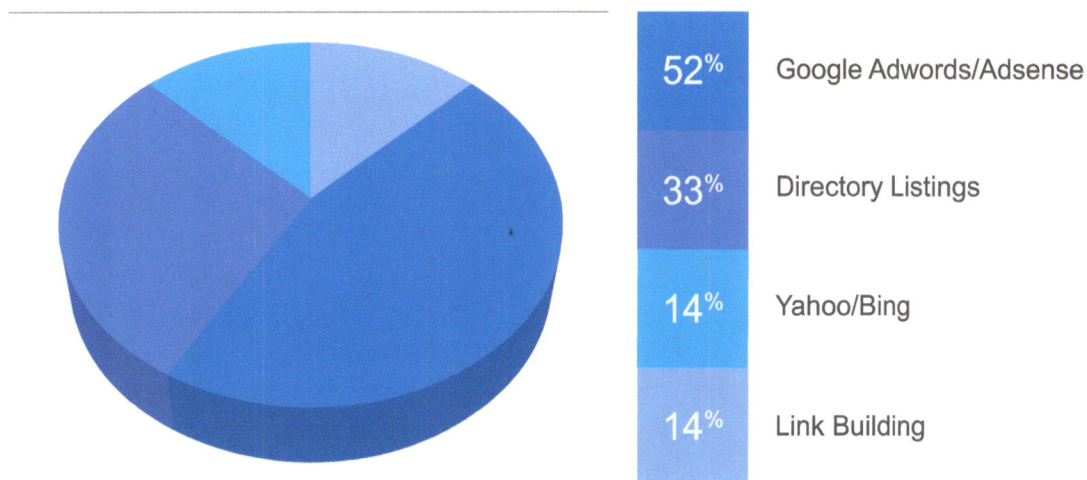

52%	Google Adwords/Adsense
33%	Directory Listings
14%	Yahoo/Bing
14%	Link Building

Below is an example of a search engine results page (SERPs), with explanations. Note that the top frame and right frame are Google Adword listings.

Anatomy of a Google Search Results Page

Below is a recommended ad group treatment.

EXAMPLE: STEEL BUILDINGS Tightly themed ad groups are important

Existing   Proposed

Metal Buildings

- Steel Buildings
- Metal Buildings
- Prefabricated Buildings
- Metal Garages
- Metal Barns
- Church Buildings
- Buildings Manufacturer
- Metal Building Company

Pre-fabricated

- Prefabricated Metal Building
- Pre Fab Metal Building

Garage

- Small Metal Garages
- Portable Garages
- Metal Garage
- Metal Garages

Kits

- Metal Building Kit
- Metal Buildings Kit
- Metal Storage
- Building Kits

Costs

- Metal Building Cost
- Cost of Metal Building
- Metal Building Quotes

Below is a screen shot of a Google Adwords Dashboard, along with call-out explanations.

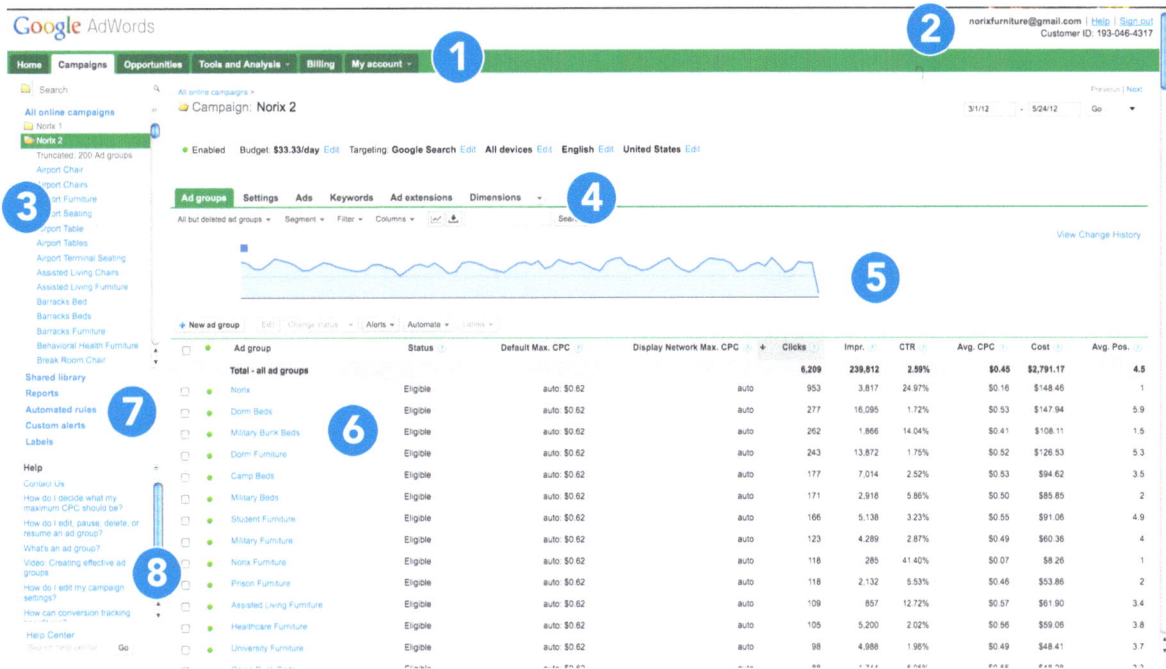

1. Main Adwords Navigation – This is where you will find the home screen, campaigns menu (pictured here), Tools and Analysis such as keyword research, Billing, and My account that has all information you need to manage your notifications and preferences.

2. Account name identifies which Adwords account you are logged in under, and displays customer ID# which you will need if you ever call Google for customer service.

3. Campaign Menu – Here you will see all campaigns that are being managed under this account

4. Secondary Campaign Navigation – Here you will see several 'tabs' that you can click on to manage your campaign settings; be sure to optimize each and every tab!

5. Here you can see a visual representation of how many clicks you have received from your campaign

6. This is a breakdown of all your campaigns currently running, with statistics on Budget, Status, Clicks, Impressions, Click-Through-Rate (CTR), Average Cost-Per-Click, Cost, and Average Position.

7. Other Campaign Information – Here you can see four additional navigation tabs that will allow you to look at shared library, build reports, create automated rules, and create custom alerts.

8. Help – This is where you can find out more to optimize your Google Adwords Campaign.

A Word About Negative Keywords?

The use of a negative keyword list is very useful in filtering out unwanted traffic, eliminating unqualified customers, and increasing your quality score with Google.

Negative keywords are a list of keyword or keyword phrases that help prevent your ad from being displayed to an unwanted audience for your PPC campaign. By doing so, you can keep your ad from showing up in unrelated searches that drive little to no quality traffic. This also helps you keep PPC costs down.

QR CODES FOR CONSTRUCTION MARKETING

QR codes are everywhere! The hype is backed up by statistics, such as 14 million American's scanned QR Codes in June, 2011 alone! (Source: comScore) Clearly most of what we encounter is consumer advertising and retail applications. So what about the construction industry? Are QR Codes an effective marketing vehicle? The answer is yes! And this chapter will demonstrate the what, where and how of QR Codes.

What are QR Codes?

Think of QR Codes (quick response codes) as a 2D version of a barcode. While barcodes provide simple information such as SKU or part number, quantities, dates, price, etc., QR Codes can perform object hyper-linking, meaning they can encode data in space that is two-dimensional. They can transmit text, find and open a website, or even download files. QR Codes offer several advantages over barcodes, one of which is that your prospective customer can read or scan them from a variety of angles, rather than having to be correctly aligned, as they would typically find necessary with using a barcode.

Each QR code generation service supports different QR code executions. Below is a comprehensive list of the information QR codes can support:

> *URL (scan to visit our website)*
> *Calendar event (scan to add our event to your calendar!)*
> *Contact information (scan to add _____ to your address book)*
> *Geo location (scan to check in at _____)*
> *Phone number (would automatically call given # when scanned)*
> *SMS (send a text message)*
> *File downloading (scan to download our product brochure)*

WHAT MARKETING APPLICATIONS CAN USE QR CODES?

Because these codes can be easily and quickly scanned by a smart phone application (app), they can be placed on all types of printed marketing mediums. QR Codes allow marketers to deliver static print communications to website-based registration pages, promotions, downloads and more. Print applications include:

> > *Magazine and newspaper ads*
> > *Newsletters*
> > *Business cards*
> > *Coupons*
> > *Direct mail, postcards, stuffers*
> > *Packaging*
> > *Signage and point-of-purchase graphics*

Below is an example of a trade print ad with a QR Code that hyperlinks to a website.

To Blog or Not to Blog: There is No Question

For many construction marketers, blogging has become a critical marketing tactic for several reasons. First, blogging reinforces thought leadership and subject matter expertise. You can publish very specialized content that is searchable for years to come.

Second, when implemented properly, blogging can have profound effects on search engine authority in many ways. Consider that each blog post builds indexed pages. Also blog titles, page titles, URL structures and image Alt tags all support SEO. The typical blog roll can build reciprocal links, and interlinking within a blog post can build back-links. Next, social sharing (Retweet, Facebook Like, bookmarking, etc) and linking to social profiles can build search authority. Finally, throw in Header Tags, keyword tags and Google Analytics and you have a powerhouse of search engine optimization (SEO) delivered to your website.

Third, your blog can be the center of your content marketing and social media program. When integrated with other social profiles, sharing tools and counter tools, blogs can effectively "automate" content deployment. How? With Retweet, Facebook Like and now Google+ counters, content is automatically posted in these respective profiles. Even LinkedIn profiles can be integrated for auto-updates.

Fourth, blogs can generate leads in a variety of ways. How? RSS registrations capture email addresses. Links to registration pages allow for email newsletter sign-ups. Placing offers within blog posts that hyperlink to registration pages can also generate leads. Additionally, blog comments often contain customer questions or requests. And finally, website analytics can identify traffic from blogs.

Despite all these extraordinary benefits, the daunting task of creating and managing a blog can be a deterrent. Our goal for the next section is to demonstrate that blogging can be manageable and extremely effective.

The term blog comes from the combination of the terms, web and log. A blog is defined as a website containing articles, referred to as 'blog posts' or 'blogs', that highlight subject matter expertise, industry news, or any relevant information to the audience you are targeting. These blogs often times include links and images adding value to the reader's experience. Managing a blog can provide your company with an opportunity to further extend your brand and the industry expertise you have to offer.

///CMA

BLOGGING PLATFORMS

There are several options for what platform or software to use for blogging. The two most popular options are Blogger, which is owned by Google, and WordPress. There are several other platforms, but these two dominate due to both user-friendliness and features. A plethora of Plug-Ins are available on WordPress, some of which can amplify your SEO efforts, making WordPress the leading platform in our eyes.

Keep in mind what you intend your blog to be. If intended to be a community where people come to interact and engage you might consider a platform such as Drupal, which is for building community sites. At the end of the day, WordPress offers an easy to use interface or content management system (CMS), coupled with excellent SEO-enhancing features, including Google Analytics. In addition, WordPress is extremely customizable. Not to mention, the basic version is free!

Still, costs can be incurred for design services, advanced development, hosting integration and ongoing content development. No matter what platform you choose, be ready for the next step of developing content and publishing regularly, the subject of our next section.

List of 5 Blogging Platforms

1. *WordPress*
2. *Blogger*
3. *Tumblr*
4. *Drupal*
5. *Joomla (Considered a Content Management System, but can be used to create a blog.)*

A WORDPRESS WALKTHROUGH

WordPress gives us the ability to customize a blog as much as we want. As long as a skilled developer is on hand, you can build an extremely user-friendly experience. The Construction Marketing Advisors specializes in blog design with integration of social media. A thorough process of building a destination to extend your brand is important. With WordPress you are given that rich user experience, along with a robust content management system (CMS) on the backend. This CMS is so amazing and easy to learn, we had to show you. Below you will see an example of a custom WordPress blog theme for the CMA's blog (ConstructionMarketingBlog.org), with numbered callouts for key elements.

1. *Custom Designed Blog*

2. *RSS feed subscription and search functionality*

3. *Blog post with Title, Author, Archive Categories, Tags and Date*

4. *Social media sharing and integration*

5. *Customizable widgets tailored to target audience*

6. *Images hosted and search engine optimized*

7. *Not shown, blogroll with reciprocal links*

///CMA

Following is a screen of CMA's WordPress content management system (CMS), with callouts for key elements below.

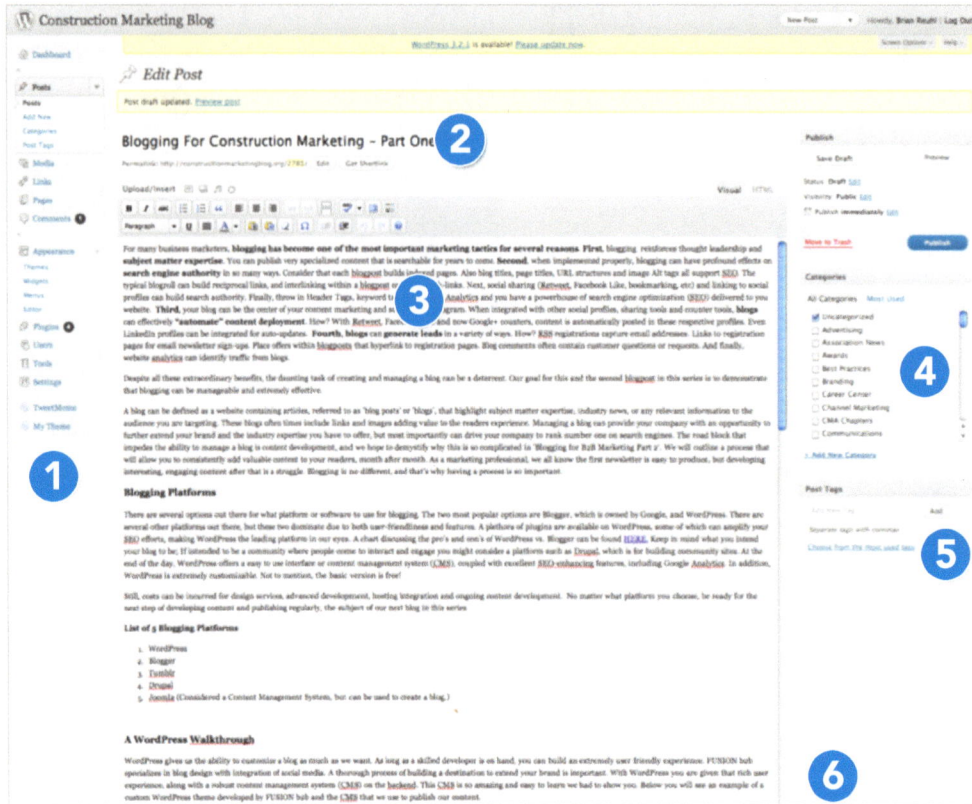

1. Main CMS Navigation allows you to manage all aspects of your WordPress Blog.

2. Search Engine Optimized Title and URL.

3. Content publishing area; ease of uploading text, images, and videos.

4. Archive Categories; Allows users to sort through content by topics they are interested in.

5. Tags; often referred to as keywords. Help users find interesting content, as well as help SEO.

6. Not Shown – Plug-Ins; often times they are used to help maximize SEO by amplifying each and every blog post.

IMPORTANT FEATURES EVERY BLOG SHOULD HAVE

> *Resource Links/Blog roll – a standard feature that benefits SEO and acts as a valuable resource to your readers to find industry content.*

> *RSS Feed – a Plug-In that allows your readers/visitors to sign up to be emailed when you publish a new blog. RSS = real simple syndication. We suggest using Feedburner, which is yet again owned by Google.*

> *Social Sharing – Add the social sharing features such as the Facebook Like button, the Twitter Retweet Button, the Google+ button, and the LinkedIn Share button. When your readers share your content it builds up your SEO and over time will drive your page rank higher on search engines.*

> *Image Optimization: images can be optimized for SEO in 3 ways; image file name, image title, image alt tag; use keywords.*

> *Tags and Categories – Both help users locate blog content; Tags are meta-tags that are indexed by search engines. Categories allow users to search blog archives by category name.*

> *Utilization of Bold Face and H1 Header tags – Both of these rich text-editing features help to build SEO. Be sure to use these when appropriate throughout blogposts to maximize SEO.*

> *Widgets on the sidebar – WordPress has a vast amount of 'widgets' available for use on the sidebar. Examples include Blogroll, Archive by month and Categories, Word cloud, recent Blogs, recent Tweets.*

> *Analytics – be sure to track and monitor your success with blogging. Before you even start blogging be sure to develop several key performance indicators (KPI's) that you will keep track of. This may consist of total visitors to your blog, click-through to landing pages, or form registrations. Google Analytics integrates with WordPress quite nicely.*

> *Plug-Ins – Currently WordPress has 17,126 Plug-In's available; for more info, link to: wordpress.org/extend/plugins/*

> *Call To Action – Each and every blog you write should have a purpose. Be sure to have a call to action to solicit a response from a reader. Often times these will be a link to a form the reader can fill out to receive ___ (insert offer here)___.*

> *Branding – Custom design should extend your visual identity and reflect company goals and vision.*

ONGOING BLOG MANAGEMENT

This next section will consider the ongoing management and implementation of the blog, focusing primarily on content. Other ongoing blog management considerations include building a blogroll and corresponding reciprocal links, updating other resource or content items like case studies, and supporting search engine optimization.

As mentioned, content is king! Content is the fuel that will keep your blogging initiative alive and relevant. What's more, when blogs are integrated with other social media including Facebook, Twitter and LinkedIn, these social profiles can disseminate your blog content.

The process of developing content is challenging, and requires a thorough process and schedule to ensure that your blog strategy stays intact. A Rule-of-Thumb is that the average blog does not begin to build authority until 50+ blogs are published. You do the math—one blog per week takes a year; two blogs per week takes six months. So be ready to consistently blog.

To guide content, define your target audience(s), then brainstorm and define a content strategy and plan. You will likely have primary and secondary target audiences, so specific content should be developed for each audience. Note that content should not just be about you or your company or prospects and customers will tune out quickly. Research and identify topics that are important to each target audience. Check with relevant publications (magazines), associations, bloggers and trade shows.

The content plan should have a ratio of content for each audience, company and product info, industry topics and other items like case studies, new videos (video blogs=vlogs). Curated content should be part of the content plan. That is, blogs or articles from other authors and bloggers, used with permission and credit (list the author and/or publisher name with hyperlinks).

The content plan should define a schedule, with blogs for the next week or month defined, and rougher ideas identified for later dates. Developing content over and over can become tedious so be sure to not carry the load alone! Research, identify and cultivate multiple sources of content. Some quick tips to make content management easier. Start with internal staff—solicit input and feedback from sales, customer service and technical experts from engineering. Reach out to other relevant bloggers. They are typically flattered to have there content curated with credit and links that build search authority. If an internal manager cannot dedicate time to ongoing blog content, outsource to a qualified agency or freelance writer.

25 BLOG CONTENT IDEAS

If the above tips and tricks do not demystify the process of blogging, it may be the week-in and week-out struggle with developing content ideas. To offer further assistance, we took the liberty of compiling 25 blog topic ideas so you can start blogging today!

25 Topics to Blog About for B2B Companies

1	Use your existing case studies or create a new one.
2	Profile staff member or industry professional.
3	Explain your corporate culture and mission.
4	Make a how-to post on a topic related to your company. Don't be afraid to share.
5	Post an FAQ or discuss a common customer support question.
6	Use your press releases (but please, don't copy-paste, refurbish them!)
7	Announce hosted events, trade shows, conferences, webinars or sponsoring events.
8	Talk about awards, recognitions or good reviews achieved by your company.
9	Blog about your company's history, how it started, the founders and their background.
10	Make a list of free resources in your industry.
11	Any holidays coming up? Put your industry spin on them.
12	Highlight a product or service. Don't sell; educate.
13	Share your presentations with others.
14	Make a statement about future trends. Any predictions for the future in your industry?
15	Add a personal touch – showcase your employees. What do they do, what is their day like?
16	Talk about problems in your industry and provide your solution. It's okay to rant and rave.
17	Provide tips for better productivity, processes, etc.
18	Share your company's stats (website traffic, sales, budgets, etc.) in a case study form.
19	Ask your readers a question. Get their input on decisions.
20	Showcase industry best practices, let them know you're on board.
21	Critique competitor's case study or white paper. Voice your opinion, but be fair.
22	Make a list of tools you use on daily basis.
23	Share what you've learned over the past month, or year.
24	Provide a guide for best resources, people, twitter followers, etc. in your industry.
25	Discuss recent or past industry related news and your take on them.

With a content plan, schedule, and ongoing content resources, there are several important elements to be aware of that should be used in each and every blog you publish, and things to do in support of the overall blog:

1. *Each blog title should include keyword search terms*
2. *Use keyword rich blogpost copy*
3. *Categorize each blog by keywords for archiving, and use keyword tagging for SEO*
4. *Images should use proper meta coding to support SEO*
5. *Keep blog length to 400-1000 words; break longer blogs into series*
6. *Use hyperlinks to resources, and links to offers to capture leads*
7. *Continually add relevant links to your blogroll, and request reciprocal links*
8. *Offer changing content and resources, ex: case study, project spotlight*
9. *Encourage social sharing and comments*

Social Media Best Practices

WHY CONSIDER SOCIAL MEDIA?

Social media is no longer just for personal use, the technology savvy, or hip consumer brands. Social media is fast becoming a major aspect of best practice construction marketing, and can no longer be ignored. This chapter will demonstrate why and how social media marketing (SMM) is integral to a modern marketing mix.

Why? *Social media is building a huge, continually growing body of marketing successes and case study examples that go beyond early adopters to all sizes and types of business brands.*

Why? *Top social media networks have robust analytics via user-friendly dashboards; often more measurable than traditional marketing.*

Why? *Social media significantly impacts search engine results, including improvements in search authority for brand websites when integrated properly.*

Why? *Top social media networks are adding many new business-friendly features, applications and tools that support business marketing initiatives and measurement.*

Why? *Social media is relatively low cost in comparison to advertising, trade shows and other traditional marketing vehicles; small budget marketers can compete with large budget competitors (a level playing field).*

Why? *Social media opens new channels, and can often reach niche targets that previously were too fragmented or cost prohibitive.*

Why? *Social media effectively supports other critical business functions including customer service, recruitment and publicity.*

SOCIAL MEDIA CHALLENGES

Like any marketing endeavor, companies and brands should carefully evaluate, plan, and manage social media or they will risk mediocrity, or even failure. While social media seems inexpensive with all social networks free to use time and agency resources aren't required to implement. Developing compelling content and effectively integrating social media with traditional marketing are major challenges.

This eBook on social media best practices for construction marketing will provide detailed tips and procedures for managing each major network: LinkedIn, Facebook, YouTube and Twitter.

We'll discuss how to conduct social media training, and then share our experiences in developing and managing content. Finally, we'll demonstrate how to measure social media marketing results to drive the bottom line.

Oh, with the pace of change in social media, be sure to check back soon for updates!

EVERYONE GETS LINKEDIN

LinkedIn has made significant strides to become the most effective professional social media site on the Internet. Growing by over a million users a week, LinkedIn showcases professionals from over 18 different industries and categories. Users are given a profile to build and expand, highlighting their professional accomplishments and allowing other LinkedIn users to connect, InMail, write recommendations and much more.

In terms of branding yourself as a professional in any industry, LinkedIn is a must. If a LinkedIn user has an active profile they will likely show up on search engine result pages. LinkedIn is a place to connect with past and present contacts/clients/customers, along with prospects and groups. There are several reasons to join the LinkedIn community and leverage this site to elevate both your company and career.

Why Join LinkedIn?

LinkedIn currently has over 100,000,000 users that are 'linked' to the companies they work for, and the people they work with. This is a great place to network, find leads, post jobs, and engage with companies and groups. This network of professionals is growing everyday and so are the capabilities of the network. Just recently LinkedIn allowed you to follow both profiles and companies, so you can get updates and news. LinkedIn also offers several robust tools to help your company build a presence on the site, such as a company page that links to your employees, products/services, blog and Twitter.

LinkedIn Profiles

Your profile is a landing page for your personal brand. You may ask why having a profile page is important to marketing your brand or company. Simple, your personal brand amplifies the companies brand on LinkedIn. Every single action that an employee makes on LinkedIn reflects upon the company's brand.

Having a great profile picture is where you need to start when building your profile. This is the first thing someone will notice. It reflects the level of professionalism that they can expect from you. Be sure to include a link to your company website and blog. Also, when you link your Twitter account to your LinkedIn profile, your Tweets will automatically feed into your LinkedIn status (and make you look active). Profiles should also be supported through the use of applications. These applications allow you to add Powerpoint presentations, PDF's, Videos, Events, Blog Feed and more. Next, build your connections starting with associates, clients, vendors and business contacts. You can upload your email address book to identify more connections. LinkedIn Groups are an excellent source of connections, which leads us to our next subject.

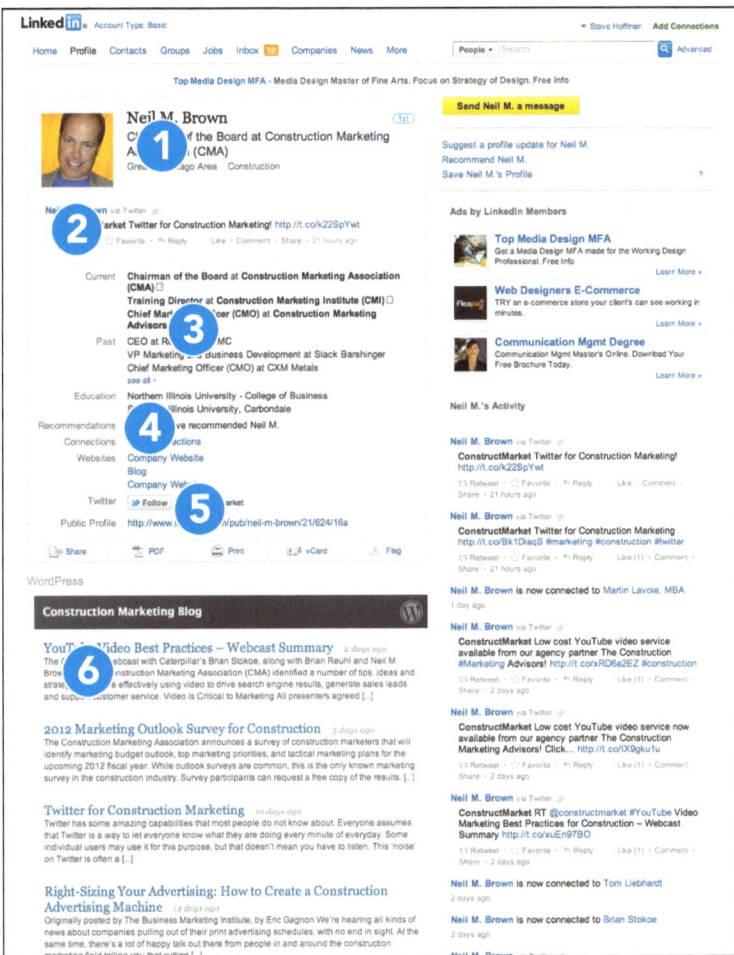

Here is a LinkedIn Profile page

1. Profile Information including Name, Position, Specialities, Location and Industry

2. Status Update – post articles, news, or company info. Also have the ability to integrate with Twitter.

3. Current and Past Positions, Education highlighted.

4. Recommendations and Connections

5. Links to websites and Twitter account

6. Applications: Here you can see the Construction Marketing Blog and the four most recent blog posts

Not Pictured
A. Contact Information
B. Groups and Associations
C. Events

///CMA

LinkedIn Groups

LinkedIn was created for business professionals to communicate within a trusted network. These discussions happen within LinkedIn groups and fuel most of the interaction across the whole site. LinkedIn Groups opens a world of possibilities and allows you to accomplish several business activities. Your personal profile allows you to join and display up to 50 groups that you belong to, which you can use as a way to demonstrate your areas of expertise.

Groups can either be open or closed. If you join an open group you immediately become a member. Open groups are important because they allow search engines (e.g. Google, Bing, Yahoo) to index the content displayed in those groups (content in closed groups does not get indexed). Closed groups are good for controlled content, membership oriented groups/associations, or even alumni networks that require you to have actually attended a specific school. These closed groups also allow you to capture emails if you are the group administrator (this will be discussed further under the category of owning a group). Overall, groups are an important strategy to attract industry professionals to a specific topic, and use as a marketing vehicle.

Join, Introduce, Participate

You can identify relevant LinkedIn Groups via keyword search. Joining larger groups is always a good idea, because it means your posts will have a larger reach. However, larger groups may mean that interactions may not be as valuable when it comes to building a business relationship. Whenever you join a new group be sure to introduce yourself with a discussion post. Let the group know why you have joined the group, what your professional interests are, and request a connection. Be careful not to be too self-promotional or sales-oriented. Provide useful or educational information and let the user decide whether to contact you. The number one rule behind any social media interaction is to give value, then ask for value in return. As an example, before you ask for people to sign up for and attend your webcast, be sure to post articles and comment on discussions happening within the group.

Build your Network through Groups

Some people are inherently social and have no issues with increasing the size of the LinkedIn network because they have so many contacts outside of LinkedIn. For those who don't have a large network of connections, LinkedIn allows us to network with anyone in the entire world at the click of a button. LinkedIn limits your ability to connect with someone by forcing you to tell them how you know them. Groups give you the bridge to connect with someone that you may not have a previous connection with. If you are within any group you belong to, you have the ability to look at the members list. Within that list you can see who you are already connected with, and those who you are not yet connected to. You can request a connection with anyone in that group by going to group member profiles, click on "invite to connect", then select Groups, and what group you would like to connect with them through (you may belong to multiple groups with one person). If you already have joined your maximum of 50 groups, you can leave a (e.g. smaller) group and join another and continue to grow your network with the steps above.

LinkedIn Group Administration

Understanding how to start and manage a group yields several opportunities for the person who is the group administrator. Content control and management falls onto their shoulders, and if someone is abusing the group guidelines or policies the administrator can remove their post, and even remove them from the group if the post was egregious. As group administrator you capture everyone's emails who joins the group (if it is a closed group; if it is open you do not receive their email information). If the group is branded, or covers industry or company relevant content it will show up in Google results (if the group is an open group). Lastly, owning a group showcases your industry expertise and elevates you to be seen as a subject matter expert within your network on LinkedIn.

LinkedIn InMail Strategy

Once you leverage LinkedIn Groups to increase the size of your network you can engage your connections with direct contact through InMails. InMails act as an email within LinkedIn, and send a message to the user's email notifying them of the message you just sent them. Often times, individuals on LinkedIn will have their personal email attached to their profile so they are more likely to read the message you sent them. You can send up to 50 InMails at once, and make it seem like you sent it directly to one person (be sure to check the box to not show recipient emails). Use a descriptive title for your message, as well as a "short and sweet" body paragraph that gets to the point. Let them know you understand their time is valuable and thank them for taking the time to read your message. InMails are great for several things, here is a list:

1. *Thank someone for connecting.*
2. *Group invites*
3. *Event invites*
4. *Company page invites*
5. *Research (poll, question, survey)*
6. *Promote a new whitepaper or case study*
7. *Business opportunities*
8. *Corporate web site invite*
9. *Social media invite (please like, follow, watch, etc.)*

Be careful about spam, or InMail that is too frequent or self-promotional. As always, provide value in your offers and communications.

LinkedIn Company Page

Most people define LinkedIn as a digital resume. This definition fails to underline the power of LinkedIn for highlighting your company. Having a fully functional company page on LinkedIn will act as a resource to anyone interested in working with you or your company. LinkedIn will assist you in creating your company page, by giving you a step-by-step walk through. Below is a list of six steps to complete and optimize your company page within LinkedIn.

Steps to Complete Company Page

1. *Have all employees listed under your company (on their personal profiles)*
2. *Fill out company description (use same company description used on other social mediums)*
3. *Add your company logo*
4. *Build a following*
5. *Ask for and receive recommendations for your company*
6. *Create a Products and Services page – This will allow you to highlight your companies products or services, and link to websites, videos, registration pages, brochure downloads and more.*
7. *Ask for recommendations for your products/services*

Here is CMA's LinkedIn Company Page

1. *Company Description*

2. *Services Offered Section*

3. *LinkedIn Ads*

4. *Number of Followers, Services, & Recommendations*

5. *Main LinkedIn Navigation*

LinkedIn Applications

LinkedIn has a number of powerful applications that allow you to maximize the effectiveness of your personal profile on LinkedIn. These applications include SlideShare, Google Presentations, Behance (portfolio display), Events, Amazon Reading List, and LinkedIn Today. All of these applications have strengths. There are more applications on LinkedIn than listed below, but these are the most business friendly, useful applications.

- **SlideShare** – *This robust application allows you to upload any size Powerpoint presentation you want to your LinkedIn profile. However, PDF's can also be uploaded to SlideShare (their orientation can be either portrait or landscape). This is a great application to show off presentations you've given, and a way to highlight your expertise through a presentation. You can also show off the company you work for by uploading a presentation that they've given in the past, a PDF of a brochure, or a capabilities sheet.*

- **Google Presentations** – *This application is just like slideshare, however it gives you the functionality to add video to your profile on LinkedIn.*

- **Events** – *Do you attend a lot of live events? If so, this is the application for you! Events gives you the functionality to add a running list of the events you are planning on attending, as well as the events you've already attended. Show off all that traveling you are doing to your peers and add a little bit more character to your personal profile by showing where you are spending your time.*

- **Amazon Reading List** – *If you do a lot of reading, I suggest adding this application to your profile. If you constantly have a book that is inspiring you to work harder and smarter, show it off to your professional colleagues! Often times knowledge is a springboard for business innovation, and it comes from dedicating time to those books on your shelf. Show off the books you are devoting time to, and how they are influencing your career and company.*

- **LinkedIn Today** – *Recently LinkedIn released their news platform called "LinkedIn Today" that aggregates content from around the internet. This is a great source to find industry articles, relevant industry information, and what the people within your professional network are interested in. The best articles that are shared the most, and have the most comments are elevated to the top of LinkedIn news, so you see only the most important articles first. The first time you go to the LinkedIn News portion of the site they will suggest industries that have news that is relevant to you. Be sure to follow these and tell LinkedIn what industries you are interested in. These news articles are aggregated primarily from twitter, so you will see a 140 character format for article descriptions. This is a great resource for anyone that is interested in real-time news.*

LinkedIn To Do List

Below is a list of 17 things you can do on LinkedIn today!

1. *Add your company website, blog and Twitter to your profile*
2. *Request connections with your existing networks (Email address books, your company, customers, suppliers, partners, alumnus and more!)*
3. *Join and display groups in your industry, interest and expertise, up to 50!*
4. *Introduce yourself to the groups, request connections in each group*
5. *Post questions, answer questions in groups and LinkedIn Answers area*
6. *Promote relevant content, events, offers to RELEVANT groups (Don't spam!)*
7. *Promote relevant content, events, offers to your connections via InMail (Don't spam!)*
8. *Add presentations (convert PDF and Powerpoint files to SlideShare)*
9. *Add events you are attending or promoting*
10. *Create a company page, or link your profile to the existing company page*
11. *Create discussions*
12. *Give recommendations (professional reference)*
13. *Add your reading list*
14. *Post industry news*
15. *Share documents*
16. *Post status updates*
17. *Advertise on LinkedIn*

A Network Like No Other

With so many business professionals participating on LinkedIn, this network is typically the easiest social media platform to understand. Still, most people are not leveraging the many features and applications LinkedIn offers. Be sure to complete your profile and link to your brand website, blog and Twitter. And take advantage of LinkedIn groups, InMail, company pages and applications.

For those involved in business development, LinkedIn provides rare insight into contacts at large, complex companies that would be impossible to identify otherwise.

As a rule-of-thumb, spend 15 minutes a day on LinkedIn to ensure that you build both your personal brand and company brand like no other network.

FACEBOOK TAKES OVER THE WORLD

Everyone is talking about how Facebook can help benefit your business, but rarely do they ever talk about the basics. The real trick to any successful Facebook marketing strategy is a strong foundation. That foundation is built through understanding Facebook, its features, and how it leverages social connections around the world.

Facebook has made signing up extremely easy for everyone, and it is evident with over 750,000,000 users. In order to create a business page you have to sign up for a personal Facebook account first. So it's important to spend time creating your personal Facebook Profile. As most people have a personal Facebook, this eBook will focus on the Facebook business page.

Over time, Facebook has become increasingly business-friendly by adding important features that benefit businesses. How? First they increased the ease of uploading photos and videos by adding a quick up-loader tool. This allows images to be loaded faster onto the site, as well as high-definition images and videos. Another major change Facebook developed is the redesigned business pages. The new business pages shifted the design layout so now images are across the top, and the navigation is on the left hand sidebar. Also the page administrators navigation is in the top right hand side, above the usual advertisements you see throughout the social networking site. Other major changes include Facebook Insights additions (Facebook's analytics platform), SEO benefits of having a Facebook page, the process of developing a custom tab and Facebook Advertising. The biggest innovation that Facebook ushered into the marketing revolution was the development of the Social Graph, which was introduced in 2010 at their annual F8 Conference.

Setting up Your Business Page

Facebook will guide you through setup, and take you through six steps of creating your business page.

1) Add an image – This is the most important, yet simple step in setting up your Facebook business page. This image should be your company's logo. If you do not have a logo this is a great time to create one! Be sure to make your logo large enough that it can easily be read on your page.

2) Import contacts – You can import your contacts in two ways. First, you may import by creating a contact file (easy to follow directions can be found on Facebook). The second way is by signing into your email account and Facebook will automatically import your contacts. This is an easy way to build fans for your business.

3) Provide some basic info – People want to know about your business! Tell them where you are located, your phone number, website, and general information about your business.

4) Post status updates – The reason a Facebook page is so important to your marketing strategy is the ability to stay in contact with your customers easily. They are able to see important information you are posting such as links, photos, videos, or events. You can let them know what the company is up to at any time, from anywhere.

5) Promote your page on your website – You are able to build the amount of people who "Like" your business by adding a Like button directly to your website or blog.

6) Set up your mobile phone – You are able to update your business page from anywhere with your mobile phone. Facebook will give you an email that is unique to only your page where you can email status updates!

Once you have your Facebook Business page optimized you can begin to build relationships with your customers. You can begin to create custom tabs that are industry specific. For example, downloadable product brochures, videos, or even a contact form! This unique feature will differentiate your Facebook page from others, and will encourage users to "Like" it. Adding offers, promotions, giveaways, and content to your Facebook page is a great way to bring customers in.

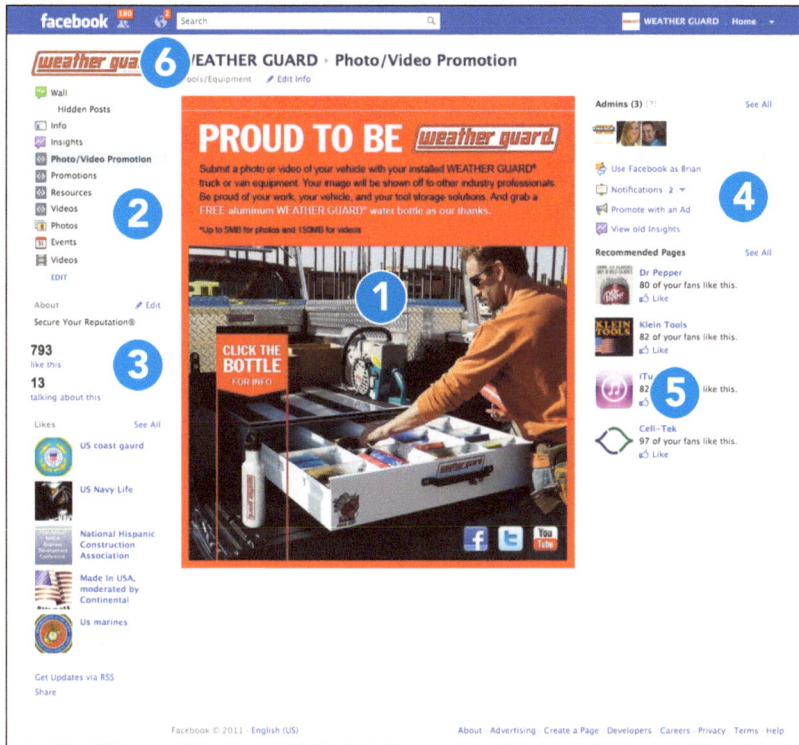

The Facebook business page shown demonstrates a custom tab for *WEATHER GUARD®* truck equipment. It shows a promotion that allows users to submit a photo or video and receive a free water bottle.

1. *Custom Facebook Landing Page*
2. *Facebook Page Navigation*
3. *Number of Likes*
4. *Administrator Options/ Navigation*
5. *Facebook Ads*
6. *Profile Image/ Company Logo*

The Weather Guard photo gallery is used to post photos from the promotion.

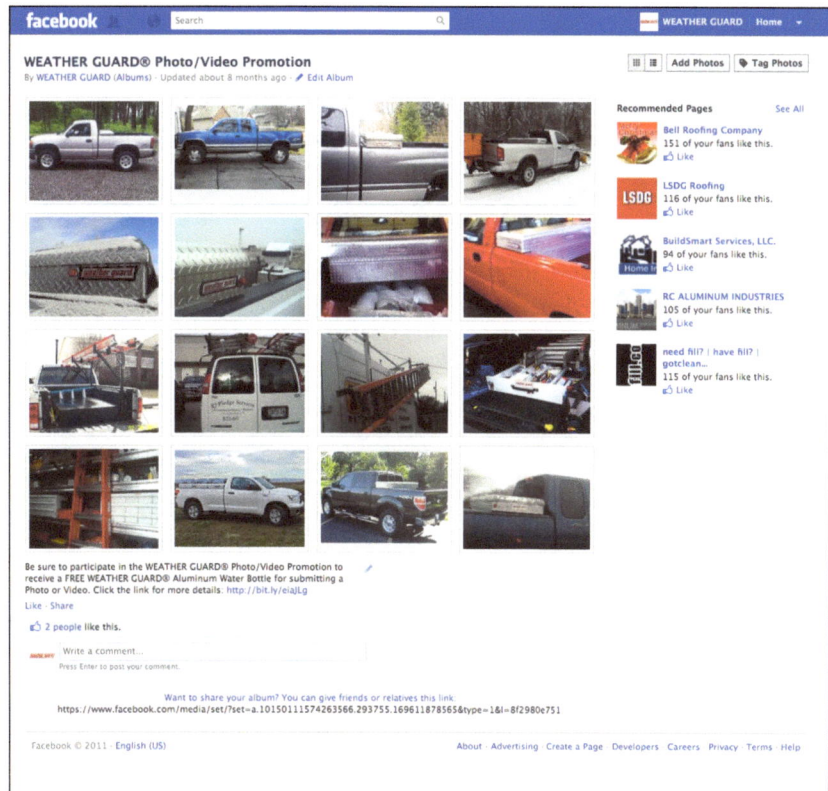

Easy Ways to Engage Customers with your Business Page

1. *Status Updates*
2. *Photos*
3. *Videos*
4. *Events*
5. *Articles*
6. *Locations (check-ins or store locations)*
7. *Promotions*
8. *Contests*
9. *Coupons*
10. *Links to brochure or presentation PDFs*
11. *Links to relevant resources*
12. *Industry tips and tricks*
13. *Custom tabs*
14. *Ask questions, answer questions, request feedback*
15. *Surveys and market research*
16. *Monitor your social media (check it daily!)*

Get the Word Out!

Once your Facebook business page is established with information and content, you need to get the word out! Here is a simple list of tactics to engage in:

1) Invite your Facebook friends: make sure to invite friends that you know will positively engage with your company. I would also be sure to invite your employees to your Facebook page.

2) Add your Facebook page to your Email Signature: every email you send is an opportunity to invite someone to your Facebook page. Let them know you are proud of the content you are putting on your page.

3) Email Blast: build a customized HTML email inviting everyone on your email list to engage with your social media pages. If you don't have an email list start building one! Also know your audience: If you work with end users, reps, and dealers think about sending several different emails that will intrigue that audience to engage with your Facebook Page.

4) Advertise on Facebook: Facebook uses extensive targeting methods to make sure your advertisements get to a specific group. Recently added ZIP codes to targeting methods available.

Integrating your Business Page with other Social Media

Once a business page has several 'Likes', it is a good idea to integrate it with other social media initiatives such as LinkedIn, Twitter, YouTube or a blog. This is done through applications on Facebook. YouTube videos can be directly posted to your business page wall, or under your 'video' tab on Facebook. Your Facebook posts can directly feed your Twitter account. LinkedIn can be linked to your Twitter account as well so it can then be posted to three different social media sites all at once! We always suggest that your blog be a major source of content for your Facebook. Whenever you have a new blog it should be brought over to your Facebook, and it should link to your blog. That one blog post will then populate your Facebook, Twitter, and LinkedIn accounts.

Custom Facebook Tabs

Facebook has made huge changes in the realm of creating a custom Facebook tab. In the past custom tabs were hosted by Facebook and utilized Facebook Markup Language (FBML) which was Facebook's version of Hypertext Markup Language (HTML). Since so many custom tabs were being created, Facebook hosting all of the content became burdensome so they decided to have any custom tabs hosted on exterior websites. This was implemented to speed up the user experience of Facebook, as well as give the custom tab developers more freedom to code and make their custom tabs much more robust! The process of creating a custom tab has switched from a beginner/intermediate skill level to now an Advanced/Expert skill level. The ability to develop, host, and edit HTML is key to being successful with any custom Facebook tab initiatives you may undertake.

Custom tabs can also be used as a welcome page on Facebook. When a user first visits your page they would be greeted with "Welcome to our Facebook Page! Click Like Above". Below is an example of Construction Marketing Association's custom landing page:

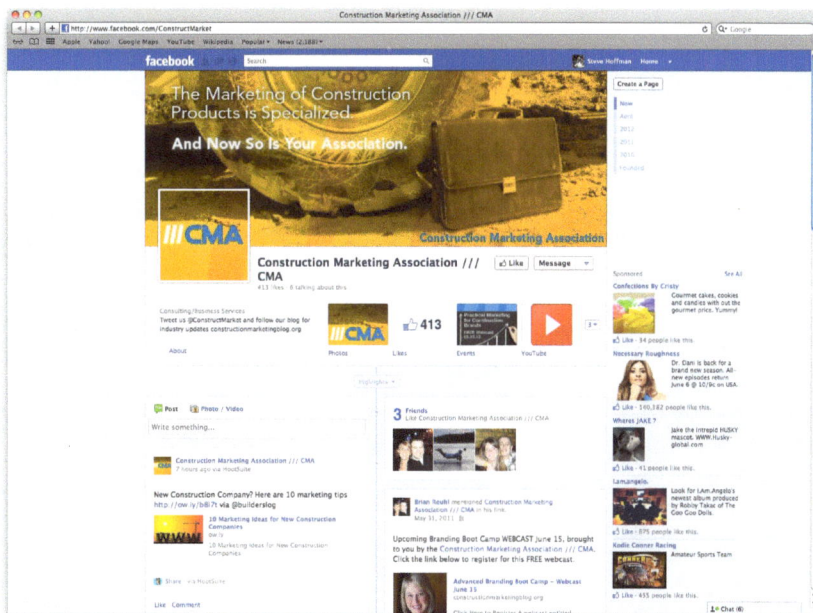

To make a custom tab for your default landing page, follow the directions below:

1. *Click edit page (you can find this directly under your profile picture)*
2. *Click manage permissions*
3. *Click down on the default landing tab box and select the custom "welcome" tab you have created.*
4. *Click save changes, and you will have a custom landing tab on Facebook!*

If you are unsure about how to create a Custom Facebook Tab contact Construciton Marketing Advisors to discuss how we can work together to create a custom Facebook Tab and optimize your Facebook page.

Basic Facebook Definitions

Following are some basic Facebook definitions.

Profile Page: The main destination for personal Facebook pages. Someone's profile page highlights his or her picture, user information, and interests. When you view other profile pages you first see their wall.

Facebook Wall: The wall is located within a profile page. It allows other Facebook users to post links, pictures, and events. This is one way to communicate with other users, by posting content on their wall.

News Feed: Located in someone's Home screen when they first log into their personal Facebook account. Updates of friends and pages come up on the news feed. When you post a status update, this is where a user will see it.

Group: A social page within Facebook that allows users with similar interests to connect on any given topic. You can create groups, or join an existing one.

Friend: A social connection between two Facebook users. A friend must be requested, and the recipient of that request must accept.

Fan Page: A page within Facebook that represents a topic or company that you have the ability to 'Like'. This is the primary location of businesses on Facebook.

Like: A term on Facebook to show that you are interested in a given Fan Page, topic, or content. Often you will see 'Like' buttons on blogs and news articles with a counter. By clicking, an abstract of the article will post on your Facebook wall, and demonstrate your interest and expertise to your friends and business network.

Personal vs. Professional Facebook

When you create your own personal Facebook profile you need to keep in mind who you want to connect with, and what your goals are. If you are looking to get your business into social media you should be very aware of the content you are sharing on this social media site. Initially everyone saw the personal benefits of having a Facebook profile, but overlooked the professional opportunities that exist. Facebook can serve as a way to network with business prospects, current customers, or fellow employees. Remember, that you never know who you will work for, or with, in the future and you should always act professional for this reason. You have control over what content is shared on your profile, so be sure to keep it clean, lean and professional. Think in terms of personal branding, and how you conduct yourself will ultimately reflect your professionalism and highlight your industry expertise. Remember to utilize your personal profile to amplify your companies marketing goals on Facebook.

Try It Out

The easiest way to learn about Facebook is by trying it out. Set-up your account and start connecting with your business contacts. There are several things you cannot learn unless you sign up. Soon enough you will be an expert Facebook marketer!

Facebook Business page for Crane Composites, a manufacturer of Building Products.

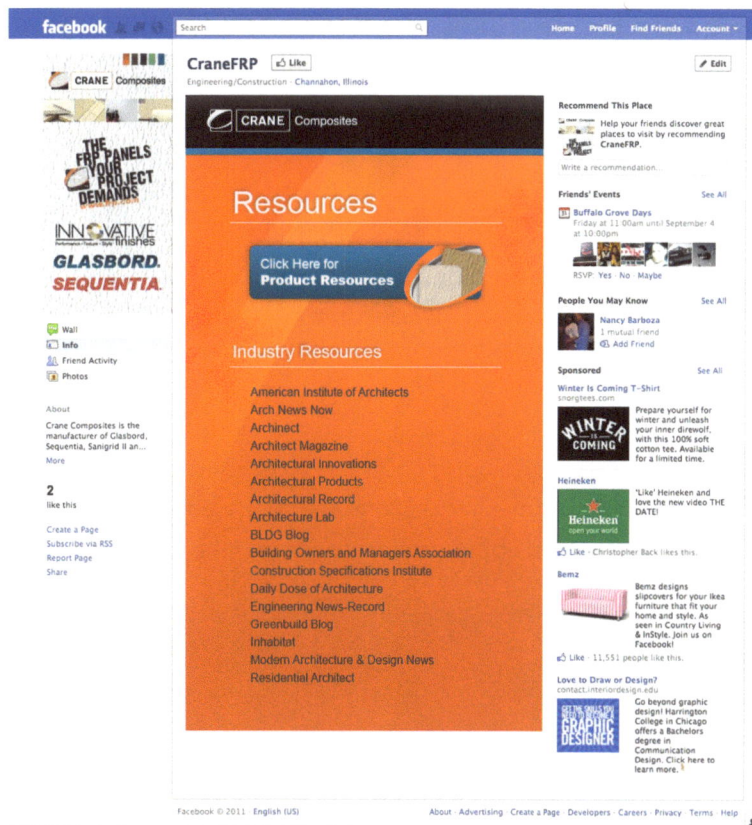

VIDEO ECLIPSES THE INTERNET

Some pundits project that video will soon dominate all content on the internet. While this seems unlikely, video is the fastest growing marketing vehicle, doubling in volume from just 2010 to 2012, and triple digit growth expected thru 2015! *(Source: Cisco)* Not surprisingly, YouTube dominates video usage with 43% of all views. *(Source: comScore).*

VIDEO GROWTH

Video Growth Chart By Year

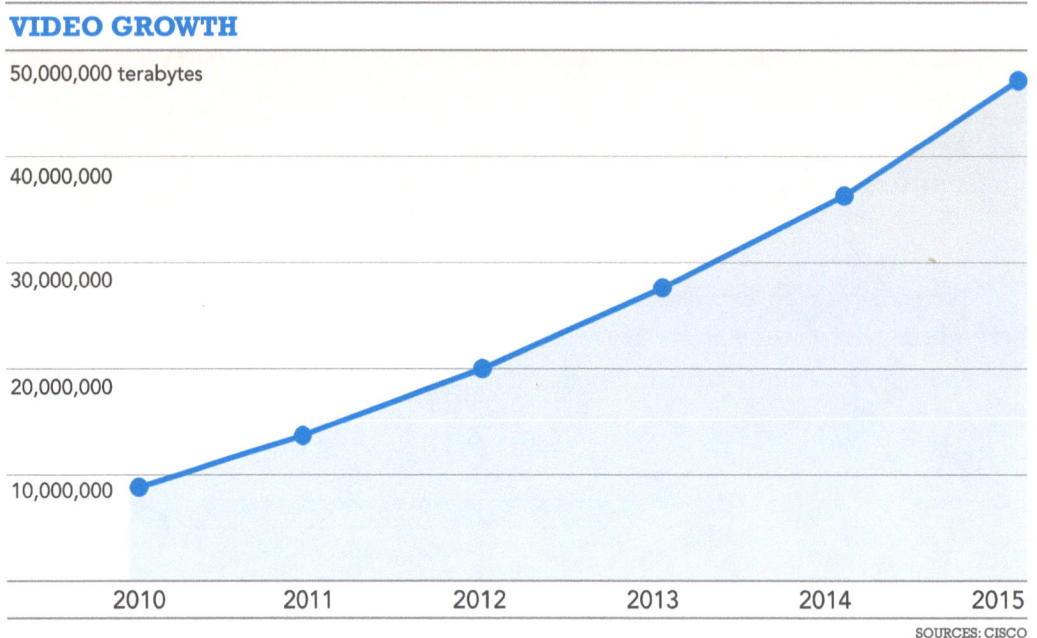

SOURCES: CISCO

Why consider video? According to Forrester Research, "any given video in the index stands about a 50 times better chance of appearing on the first page of results than any given text page in the index." Need more convincing? Google purchased YouTube. In sum, video is now critical to search engine results.

Consumers are increasingly flooded by blog content, news articles and reviews. Humans simply can't consume that much text. Consumer preference will therefore shift toward video as the primary way to learn about products and services. (Source: - MarketingProfs)

Video is becoming even more strategic now that mobile marketing is integral to every marketing campaign. With the emergence of smart-phones and mobile device growth, a large portion of the population can view a video from anywhere, and it will be more convenient than attempting to read text off a 3.7 inch screen.

Mobile Growth Chart

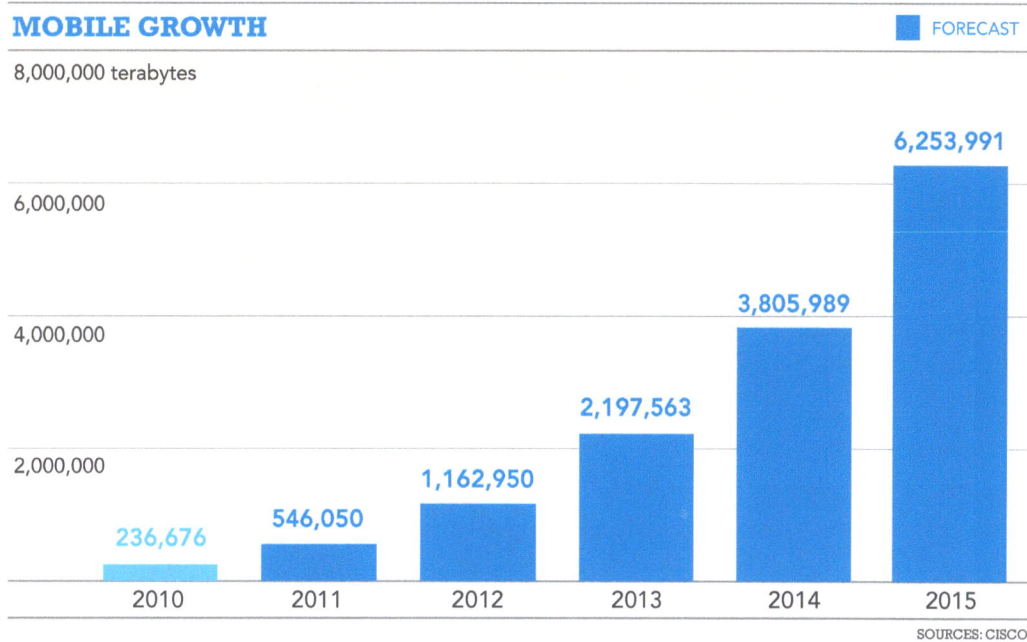

MOBILE GROWTH ■ FORECAST

8,000,000 terabytes

Year	Terabytes
2010	236,676
2011	546,050
2012	1,162,950
2013	2,197,563
2014	3,805,989
2015	6,253,991

SOURCES: CISCO

Do Your Homework

Just like any new marketing initiative, start with research. Look at your competitors' YouTube channels. Identify YouTube channels for publications and associations in your category. Then search for video and YouTube best practices including award winners outside of your category.

Next, develop a plan for your video marketing initiative. First, consider who your target audience is. For example, if your target is CEOs versus maintenance engineers, different levels of execution are clearly required. Your targets will also help determine the types and subject matter of videos. Later in this chapter, we provide a list of different types of videos that can range from slick capabilities productions, to simple interviews with employees using your iPhone. Finally, your video plan should include a schedule of video topics and detailed actions including scripting, videotaping and editing.

YouTube Basics

Since YouTube controls the video market, it only makes sense to explain the details of how to implement your YouTube channel. Following are the steps:

1. Go to www.YouTube.com
2. In the top left of the website you will see "Create Account", click here.
3. Fill in Information accordingly and choose your brand name as the "Username" in the required fields (note 20 character username limit)
4. Go to your channel and upload custom backgrounds by clicking on "Themes and Colors" and then click "show advanced options." Note that your custom background must be less than 256kb.
5. Now upload your video(s). Note that videos must be no longer than 15 minutes and 2GB in size. Note that the most recent video upload will be in the top position, but you can use the YouTube admin tool to move any video in the channel to the top position.
6. Next optimize each uploaded video for search by choosing a title with keywords, along with a keyword-rich description of the video content.

Keywords are fundamental to your video success and are any significant words or phrases that are used to describe the contents of the video. YouTube will suggest keywords to you, but they are often inaccurate. Spend 5 minutes brainstorming keywords to add. This will dramatically increase your search result ranking.

Here is the YouTube channel for KNAACK® Construction Storage Equipment.

1. *Video*
2. *Channel Name*
3. *Video Description*
4. *Profile Information*
5. *All Videos Published*
6. *Search All of YouTube*
7. *Search Just Channel*

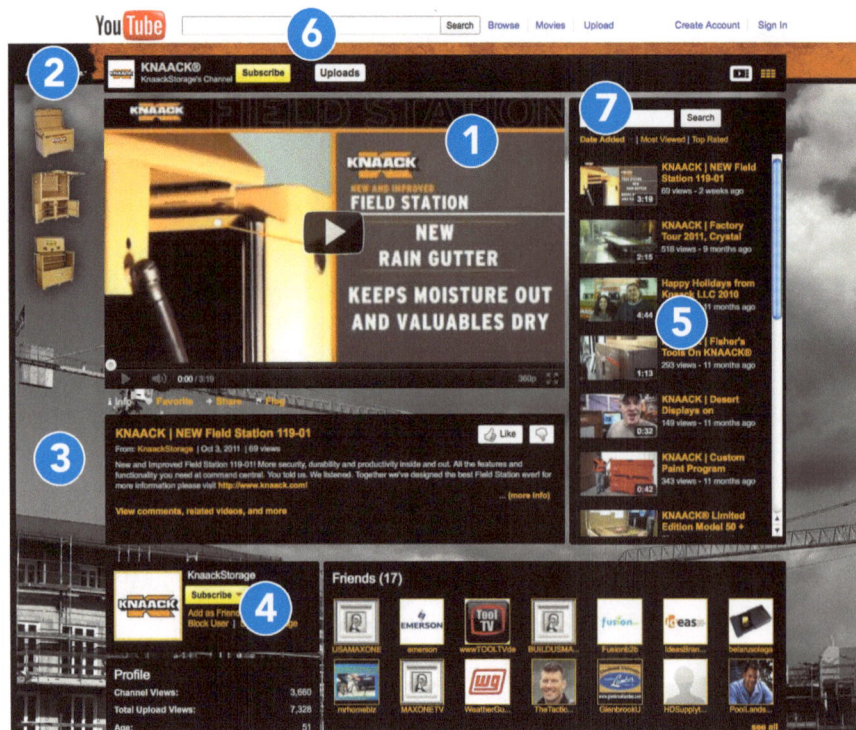

Tools of the Trade: Modern Marketing for Construction Brands

Video Content Ideas

1. The Elevator Pitch – A 30-60 second video that highlights your company or brand's unique selling proposition (USP). Think about how much time you spend in an elevator before getting off on your floor. That is how much time you get to set your company apart from others!

2. Slick Capabilities Piece – A polished overview of your company or brand with animation, sound and professional voiceover. We recommend 1-3 minutes.

3. Customer Testimonials – Ask your best customers or clients to sit down and speak about your products/services. Have a couple of questions ready and give them time to think about their responses before shooting.

4. Executive Briefs – Record "C" level executives speaking about a new product/service, new program initiative, or simply the state of the business. The executive can introduce the company or brand, or say thank you to customers. Keep it short and focused. 1-2 minutes in length.

5. Webcasts – Many webcasts or virtual seminars are training in nature, so sharing these with customers is relevant. Since many are longer in time, you will have to break up the video into 15 minute increments. As such, we recommend titling video series as Keyword 1 of 2, 2 of 3, etc.

6. Case Studies – Document successes with summaries of customer problems and solutions. If video is not available, still photo images can be used with support copy, and perhaps a customer testimonial!

7. Redeploy Powerpoint Presentations – This is so easy, simply record a voiceover timed to Powerpoint slide transitions. How many old Powerpoints do you have?

8. Employee Interviews – Interview key sales, technical, customer service and other staff about their role in serving the customer, new program, etc. Make sure the selected interviewees are upbeat and articulate!

9. Use Your News – Have a new product, program or project? Interview those involved for the insider perspective. The clip can also be used in a video press release.

10. In the file cabinet – Dig into all of your old files, and videos that you've forever held onto, but never knew what you were going to do with them. Did you run a commercial on TV ten years ago; well use it! Take all of this old content, and post it onto your branded YouTube channel and let people view it. You may not expect these tactics to work, but they often "bring people back" to when all TV commercials were like that. In fact, people may even get a laugh out of it when they think about how video used to look that way.

11. Reduce, Reuse, Recycle – We are referring to video of course… Be sure to take ALL video that you create across any and all departments, and use it to add content to your video content planning and strategy. Most video, with simple editing becomes some of the best content your Video strategy needs.

12. Executive Summaries of Collateral Business Materials – If I asked you to turn your brochures into a video you may say it's impossible. I encourage you to create short executive summary videos of what that brochure encompasses and then encourage viewers to download the catalog off your website, and offer them a link to reach the content. You just increased your website traffic AND got someone to download your brochure. This applies for all collateral materials such as sell sheets, product brochures, white papers, blogs, and anything you can think of. Summarize the content in 30 seconds and include the link to the content!

13. Travel Much? - When you are on the road attending conferences, trade shows, and all day events record some video! This video can be reused across several different channels, and with simple editing can be a hit for your video strategy. If you run into customers at these events, or you are on location with a customer ask them for a 30 second interview.

> **Here are some quick questions to always have in your back pocket:**
> a. *Introduce yourself and tell us about your company*
> b. *What are the biggest challenges you face in your business*
> c. *How did my company help you achieve better results*
> d. *Allow them to give a shameless plug at the end of the video; they are doing you a favor, so give them some value in participating.*

14. Formal Round Table – Invite industry peers and experts to be recorded about the industry outlook, current trends or emerging technology that are prevalent to your industry.

15. Q&A session – This is exactly what it sounds like. You are the interviewer, and you ask an expert questions about your industry.

16. Email your Video – Most Email Service Providers (ESP's) will allow you to embed video in emails, or link to video download. This is just another way to spread your videos.

17. VLOGS – Yes, you learned a new word! Combining a blog post with a video is called a VLOG. Again, keep it short and sweet and people will share your video. At the end of a VLOG be sure to ask for viewers to Retweet, Facebook Like, or Social Bookmark your video, and share it with their friends and colleagues.

18. User Generated Content – Ask your clients to create videos that give an outsider's perspective lon your company. B2C isn't the only category allowed to have users generated creative content.

19. Video Press Releases – Are you sick and tired of writing press releases? Spice it up and show those editors their time is valuable. "I know you are busy and so are we, that's why we created this one minute video to highlight the importance of our press release." Be sure to transcribe the video underneath so they still have a written piece to refer to.

20. Embed Video on Your website – This adds an interactive element to any website. It may be an introduction video to the company, or as simple as thanks for visiting our website be sure to visit our _____ page to find out about our great products/services. This also gives you download credit on YouTube.

21. Video Transcription – If you blog or post your video to your website be sure to write out all of the content within the video. This allows search engines to index the content of the video so you are optimizing your search results. I like to refer to this as "double dipping" because you get twice the effectiveness out of one video!

23. Product/Service Videos – This is a MUST have piece of video content. Showing off your products and services in video allow viewers to see real applications of products, or add a visual identity to a service that your company offers.

24. Advertisements – Did you recently put an ad in an industry publication? Create a video describing the execution and layout of the advertisement and why you felt like that publication was the right solution. If you created a commercial be sure that is added to your video content strategy. Just because you take a traditional approach with your marketing efforts, doesn't mean it wouldn't make a great video.

Video & Social Integration & Promotion

Once your YouTube channel is established, how do you promote it?

First, have a YouTube logo and hyperlink on your website and blog pages. Next include the YouTube logo and hyperlink in all employee email signatures. Certainly all forms of Internet or electronic communications should include the YouTube logo and hyperlink, even PDF documents can have active hyperlinks.

With these promotion basics accomplished, now you can distribute individual videos via other social networks. Embedding the video in other social networks dramatically increases the amount of views and elevates your video in search engines. Be sure to post videos on Facebook, websites and blogs. Tweet about the video with links. Include the video in a press release. When it comes to distributing your video, dare to dream of all the possibilities, and remember to ask for engagement from your customers. "What do you think of this video?" is a great place to start.

A Place for Twitter

Twitter has some amazing capabilities that most people do not know about. Everyone assumes that Twitter is a way to let everyone know what they are doing every minute of everyday. Some individual users may use it for this purpose, but that doesn't mean you have to listen. This 'noise' on Twitter is often a deterrent to most people even giving the micro-blogging platform a chance. Micro-blogging is the technical name for the service that Twitter offers. Using 140 Characters or less (spaces and punctuation count) you have to write the message you want others to see. This leaves the door wide open for tech-savvy businesses to become subject matter experts.

Initial Set-up

Once you sign-up for Twitter be sure to follow the steps they outline for you, and fill out your bio and information completely. Also let people know why you are on Twitter by telling them you are interested in the construction industry. This allows people to find you by your interests, and will help you find other users interested in construction marketing. If you are curious about whom is most influential within your industry or a given topic check out WeFollow.Com, where they list Twitter profiles and rank them in specific categories. Make your profile more inviting by adding custom color schemes, or even a custom background image, and a hyperlink to your website.

Construction Marketing Association's Twitter Page

1. *Custom Twitter Background*
2. *Twitter Timeline with latest Tweets*
3. *Tweet Here*
4. *Trends-What is "Hot" right now*
5. *Follow Suggestions*
6. *Main Analytics on Twitter*
7. *Main Navigation*

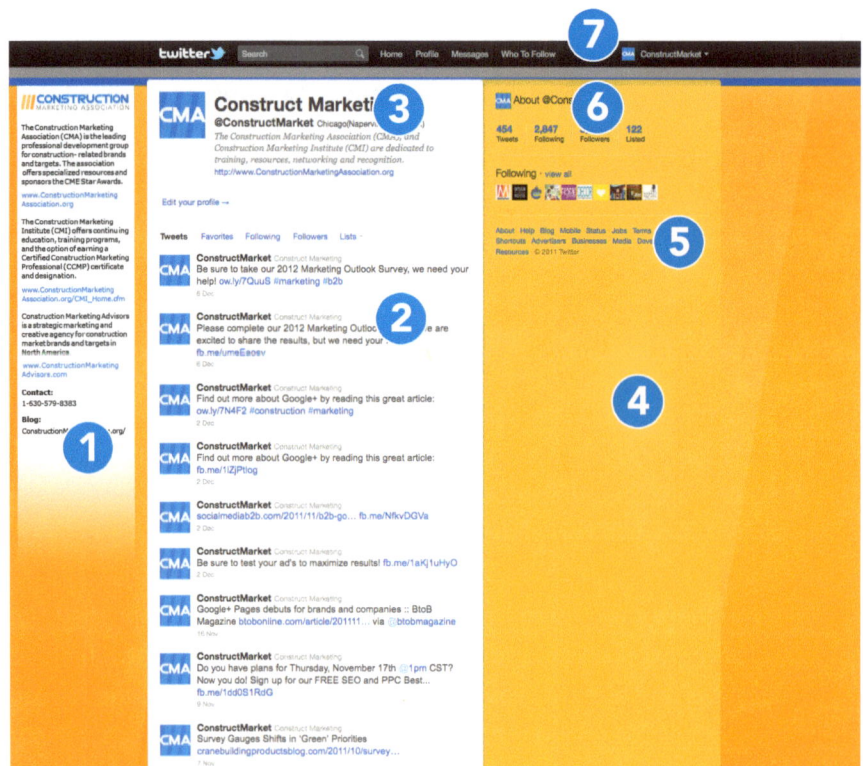

Tools of the Trade: Modern Marketing for Construction Brands

What can Twitter be used for?

A News Source – Our world is moving deeper and deeper into the digital age and our source of news needs to be up to the minute, and sometimes even up to the second. You can utilize Twitter's power to be your source for news. Every top news channel in the world is tweeting what's going on locally and across the world. Look up your favorite news source and stay informed.

Knowledge Source (Best Practices) – People on twitter are some of the most knowledgeable at what they do. When you follow someone on twitter you can tap into that knowledge bank and learn from the best. Who doesn't want to hear from thought leaders?

Industry Specific – No matter what industry or sector you come from, someone is on Twitter talking about it. If you want to hear what is popular and catching people's attention in your industry you have to get on Twitter. Listening to others is the best way to get a handle on what's hot and what's not, and to stay on the cusp of the up-and-coming. Learn from the best in your industry so you can become the best!

Listen and Share (Engage) – Ever heard the saying "You were given two ears and one mouth, so you should listen twice as much as you speak?" Well that is a great way to approach Twitter. Before you jump in and start tweeting, be sure you understand how to use Twitter in the most effective manner by listening to how others do it. Listen, and then speak. If you are confident that people are going to listen to what you have to say, don't hesitate. Someone out there is going to listen, but be sure to thank them for becoming a follower!

Cross-Pollination – Social Media is all about sharing, and Twitter is no different. Gaining influence on Twitter comes over time. Once you have people's attention and your following is growing, be sure to invite them to your other social media outlets. 'Like me on Facebook' and 'Connect with me on LinkedIn' are all great strategies to engage in on Twitter.

Link Sharing – Once you get on Twitter you will begin to see a plethora of links. Nearly every Tweet has a link on it, because you can't get the whole story in under 140 characters. If what you say is interesting enough people will click the link. Now this may be your first interaction with short-links, but have no fear. Short links allow you to take up less of the 140 characters that Twitter gives you. Links are integral to your strategy of sharing content on Twitter. Be sure to let people know where the link will send them, and they will be more likely to click.

Marketing – Twitter can add another touch point to your marketing mix. This allows for you to become an industry leader and send traffic to your website, or your blog. Twitter is also a great platform for offers and promotions. If you are curious on how to track how successful your Twitter efforts are please continue reading until the chapter titled Measuring Social Media on page 34.

Food for Thought – Ever have an interesting thought pop into your head and you felt like you should share it? If you've ever had a construction marketing revelation and wanted to let people know about it, Twitter is the perfect outlet. Remember that it is all about thinking outside of the box. People are more likely to engage with the unconventional because it will catch their attention. This strategy also adds an altruistic feel to your Twitter account, and people may see value in following you.

Word of Mouth – If you've ever wanted to attempt a viral marketing campaign, Twitter can help. The infamous Tweet button can now be found on almost every site you may get your news from. If you share great content on Twitter, others will spread the word for you. Just focus on putting out interesting, engaging thought provoking tweets and your loyal following will do the rest of the work.

Trending Tweets - When you first sign into Twitter, you will see Trends on the right hand side of the screen. This is where you can see what everyone is talking about. You may not be interested in what is happening around the world (60% of twitter users are outside of the U.S. which means often times things are in a foreign language) but you can change your trends to reflect your geographic location and what you may be interested in.

Advertising – Seeing that people tend to spend time engaging on Twitter, they have recently added advertising options. Promoted Twitter Accounts, promoted tweets, and promoted trends are the three basic options Twitter now has. Pricing is based off of each engagement a Twitter user has with the specific option. Retweeting, link clicking/sharing, and following are all examples of engagement. A robust metrics dashboard is given to advertisers. We can all hope that this dashboard will soon be released to everyone using twitter for business, as measurement becomes increasingly important.

Applications / Utilities – Seeing that Twitter does not have a robust dashboard offered to its users, people have created ways of keeping track of your account. Programs such as TweetDeck and Hootsuite offer Twitter users an easier way to track conversations that are happening on Twitter, and measure results. These applications are free for basic use.

Hash Tags – You may often times see a world preceded by a "#" sign, which is defined as a hashtag on Twitter. This means that people who search for that given topic will be alerted to what you have written. For example I would write:

New! Blogpost Titled Twitter basics for Construction Marketing #construction #marketing".

This tweet above now alerts people interested in marketing and construction." Hash tags are very important to reaching more people, and leveraging the word of mouth aspects of Twitter.

You need to be aware of the different ways Twitter can be used and find what works for you, and your business. No one-way of using this micro-blogging platform is right. Before doubting the power of Twitter, sign-up, and start to network and connect with people in your industry. Soon you will have a powerhouse of followers who listen to what you and your company are saying.

GOOGLE+ JOINS THE GAME

Since there are still mixed reviews across the web, we decided to dig through all the jabber about this high-profile social network. We found some helpful resources to look into that will hopefully clear up the social clutter. To start with, it does not hurt to claim your Google+ business page. Why? At the very least, so no one else grabs it out from under you first.

How do I create a Google Plus Business Page?

Set-up is free and easy, similar to Facebook's business pages. You will need to be sure to have a Google+ account (which you can build from a Gmail address) before creating your business page. Hubspot offers a killer e-book on how to create and utilize Google Plus Business Pages.

Show me the Numbers!

Compete generated a 2011 analysis on how popular the site became since launch. Highlights include:
- In 7 months (through December 2011), Google Plus generated:
  - *20 million unique visitors to it's main landing page (half of Twitter's unique visitors).*
  - *50 million visits*
  - *200 million page views*

NetworkWorld has also discovered some interesting stats on the social site:
- Two-thirds of Google+ users are men, in contrast to Facebook having a higher user base of women.
- CEO Larry Page claimed Google+ had 90 million users as of January 19, 2012 (compare this to Facebook having around 800 million)

Simply Measured also posted a study on Google Plus brand page adoption and engagement trends based on the Top 100 Interbrand Brands' Google+ pages.

Key study takeaways include:
1. Companies post and engage primarily during work hours, Monday through Friday. You won't see the numbers spike as high during the weekend. 86% of engagement occurs during work hours (5am to 5pm) and 89% of engagement happens Monday through Friday.
2. Most posts are visual. In fact 65% of engagement comes from photo and video content.

Importance of Photos on Your Google Plus Business Page

After reviewing the above, it brought us to an important discovery from Simply Measured's results and why photo posts are important. Google Plus was actually built for image sharing. Think about this: Google owns Picasa. Picasa has an image editor on Google+. Whenever you create a post with a link, it automatically generates a picture button where you can click through the images found on that page and choose one to put alongside your post.

Here's another thought: Wonder why the newer social network Pinterest is doing so well? It's purely pictures that stimulate visual interest and then generate re-pins (re-sharing). In summary, it may be useful for your Google Plus Business Page posts to have pictures alongside the content.

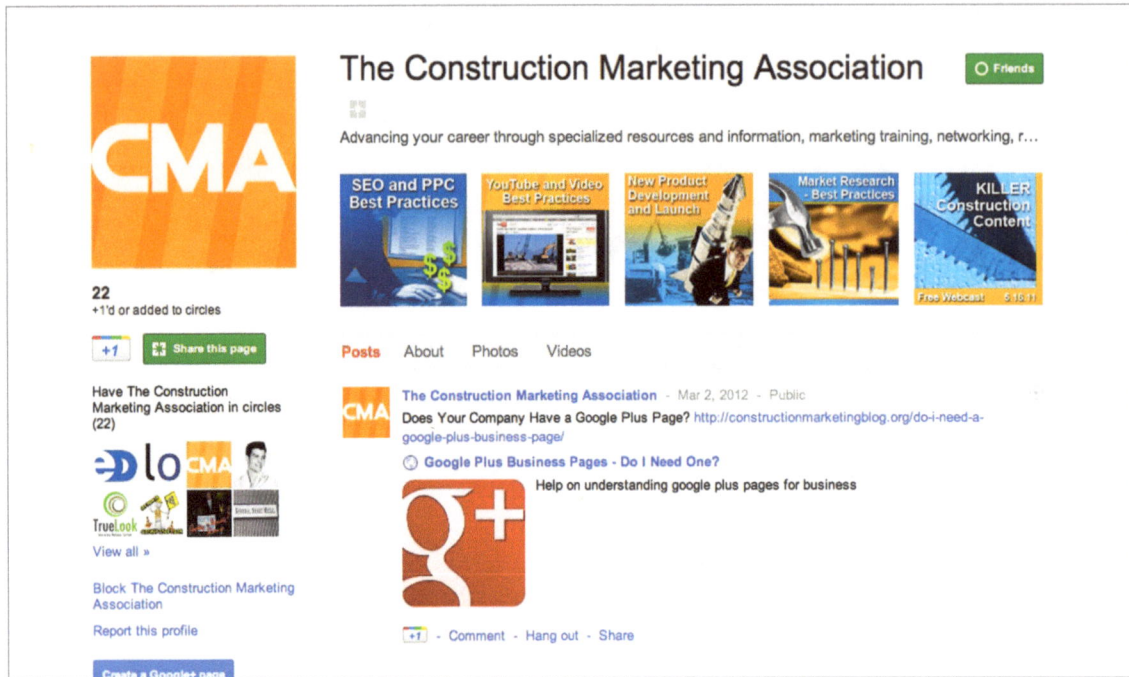

What's the deal with that +1 button?

Simply put, the more +1s a page gets, the more resourceful or popular those who viewed and +1'd the page perceived it. This is super helpful when browsing the web: you can get to the top pages quicker rather than digging around for them. More so, result pages that feature +1 content from your circles will appear sooner, mainly because Google thinks if you are connected with an individual, you may share the same interests.

There are reasons to believe that the +1 button is good for search engine authority. It encourages higher Click-Through Rates (CTR); if people see more +1s, they are more likely to click that link, not to mention the fact that it is a SEO tool created by THE top search engine (Google). Mashable recently posted a great blog on how the +1 button affects search engine optimization (SEO).

Keep in mind – you cannot +1 other pages unless you are logged into a Google+ account. Also, just because your site has several +1s, this does not mean it gets ranked higher in search results.

Are you concerned about how your Google Plus Page is performing? Check out this cool Google Plus Analytics tool that Simply Measured created that shows your Google Plus Business Page's analytics.

Social Media Training – 5 Steps

The importance of social media in construction marketing continues to grow, with more and more examples of companies and brands realizing financial results. The promise of social media is improved search engine results, increased website traffic, real interaction with customers and prospects, and ultimately measurable revenue generation. In addition, a huge opportunity exists to unleash employees, and involve staff as brand ambassadors to amplify your social media initiatives.

As we have all experienced, social media takes a great deal of time. So gaining the support of a "small army" of brand ambassadors is intuitively appealing, but not without issues or problems that can be minimized with guidelines and training. To that end, following are 5 Tips for Social Media Training in your organization.

1. *Create a company social media policy guide*
2. *Seek, recruit and develop thought leaders as editors*
3. *Develop a social media plan*
4. *Conduct staff training*
5. *Ongoing communications and reporting*

A SOCIAL MEDIA POLICY?

Depending on the scope of your organization, a simple to extensive social media policy will provide guidelines to staff AND partners to ensure corporate and/or brand objectives. A policy will also ensure messages and tone are consistent. In addition, dealing with negative situations and unprofessional conduct can be defined, including disciplinary actions. The policy can serve as a training vehicle with detail on corporate and brand social media assets and procedures. Below is a sample guide for Intel.

Below is a link to policies for hundreds of corporations, along with Intel's policy.

http://socialmediagovernance.com/policies.php
http://www.intel.com/sites/sitewide/en_US/social-media.htm

RECRUIT SOCIAL MEDIA EDITORS

The new media revolution has transformed marketers and other employees into authors and publishers. While marketing, communications and PR staff have always participated in content development, ideally a broader social media program will recruit and leverage thought leaders and subject matter experts across the enterprise. Content is king in social media and thought leadership can come from engineers, executives, and yes even sales people. Ideally, marketing assumes the role as managing editor, guiding content strategy, editorial calendars and assignments. Which leads us to the next tip, planning.

DEVELOP A SOCIAL MEDIA PLAN

Like all marketing plans, goals and objectives should be defined. We suggest both overall objectives and specific goals for each of the top social media platforms including blogs, LinkedIn, Facebook, YouTube and Twitter. Some of the obvious objectives are Fans and Followers, however, keep in mind that quality is more important than quantity.

A basic part of planning is benchmarking or evaluating other companies and brands social media. Certainly evaluate competitors, but also analyze those brands recognized for best practices. Obviously you want to deploy social media better than competitors, and understand what some great new ways to leverage the different platforms for marketing results.

Developing and managing content is one of the biggest undertakings with social media, so assigning a social media project leader or managing editor is critical. This person should bring together key thought leaders and subject matter experts for brainstorming, planning and scheduling. This person should publish a detailed content schedule, and coordinate content for all platforms. Ideally, the plan will coordinate social media integration. Content development and management is the topic of our next chapter!

CONDUCT SOCIAL MEDIA TRAINING

So you have recruited the dream team of subject matter experts (SMEs) who likely have little (or zero) editing or social media experience. Both content and social media platform training will be required. Not to mention, you still want to enlist the small army of brand ambassadors that are your employees to comment, Retweet, Like and bookmark corporate blogs, posts and Tweets.

First, conduct platform-specific training including Blogs, LinkedIn, Facebook, YouTube and Twitter. Be sure to engage in detailed training for your editor team and basic training for employees. Following are some specific training considerations for each social platform.

Blogs

1. Train Subject Matter Experts (SME's) and employees how to Retweet posts
2. Train SMEs and employees how to Facebook Like blog posts
3. Train SMEs and employees how to bookmark blog posts including Digg, Delicious, etc.
4. Train SMEs and employees how to comment on blog posts

LinkedIn

1. Train employees how to link corporate website, blog and Twitter to their individual profiles
2. Train employees how to list company, brand, industry and partner events via the EVENT application on their profiles
3. Train employees how to upload company SlideShare presentations converted from brochure PDFs or Powerpoint presentations to their individual profiles
4. Train employees how to link their profiles to the company page
5. Train employees how to add LinkedIn connections, along with tips for business development
6. Train employees how to join up to 50 LinkedIn groups, and provide guidelines for group discussion posts
7. Train employees how to use InMails to communicate thought leadership, offers and programs to their respective connections

Facebook

1. Train SMEs and employees how to set-up their Facebook personal page
2. Train SMEs and employees how to Like the Facebook business page
3. Train SMEs and employees how to comment on Facebook business page posts
4. Train SMEs and employees how to post updates and share content on the Facebook business page
5. Train employees how to find relevant customers and prospects and engage with them on Facebook

YouTube

1. *Train SMEs and employees how to set-up their individual YouTube accounts*
2. *Train employees how to view company YouTube videos*
3. *Train employees how to comment on company videos*
4. *Train employees how to share and embed company videos*

Twitter

1. *Train SMEs and employees how to set-up their Twitter profiles*
2. *Train SMEs and employees how to Follow relevant Twitter profiles*
3. *Train SMEs and employees how Tweet and Retweet content including URL shorteners and hashtags (#)*
4. *Train SMEs and employees how to use external programs and applications including HootSuite, TweetDeck, WeFollow, etc.*

ONGOING COMMUNICATIONS AND REPORTING

Communicating social media activities, measures and successes is key to building interest and participation among employees and key contributors, while building management support. Providing frequent reporting and sharing successes will create enthusiasm. Depending on the scale of your enterprise, weekly or monthly reporting may be sufficient. Such reporting can be combined with ongoing training programs. Recognizing individual's contributions is another key aspect to these group meetings.

Measuring results of your social media program includes the metrics of individual platforms, which we cover later in this book for each platform. In addition, website traffic and analytics should be included. Finally, social media monitoring tools like Radian6 that measure conversations across the Internet should be used.

Now, go train someone!

Advertising—The King of Traditional Marketing

Pre-Internet (1995), advertising was king…the only game in town. Advertising was indisputably the leading marketing tactic. Client-side Advertising Managers hired Advertising Agencies. And Webster's Dictionary defined marketing as the advertising of products and services (1973).

A lot has changed. An April 25, 2011 issue of Advertising Age proclaimed that Ad Agency has become a dirty word. For big retail and consumer brands, advertising spending continues to grow. For business-to-business marketers, annual surveys continue to point to declines in advertising budgets.

Still, advertising is one of the biggest budget items and most expensive elements in the marketing mix, whether print, broadcast television or radio, or online. Media placement costs are significant, and ad production costs can be prohibitive to all but the biggest brands in any given category.

For brands that can afford advertising, it offers the advantages of reaching large and targeted audiences. Advertising can be deployed relatively quickly, with controlled timing and a controlled message. Great advertising can break through the clutter and get noticed, building brands and driving sales. Ads with direct response offers can generate measurable leads. Following are select advertising sample from Construction Marketing Advisors.

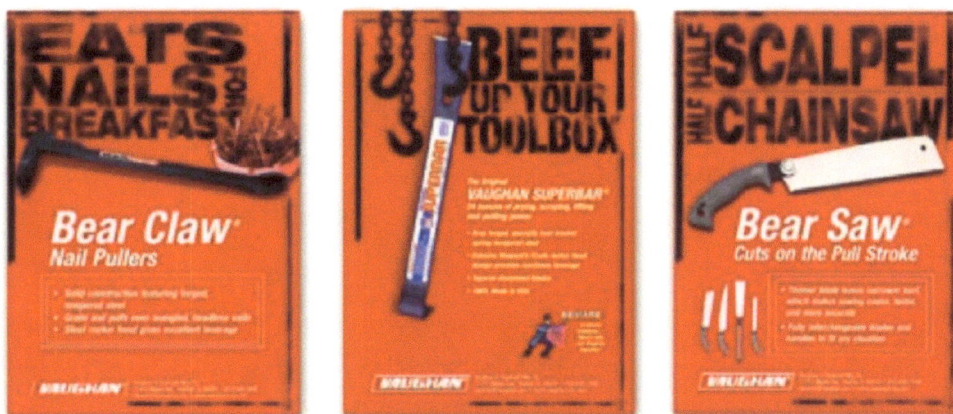

For companies in the construction category, advertising is likely dependent on which segment of the industry you participate in. Product and service brands targeting construction prospects and customers likely employ some level of trade print and online advertising.

Best practices print advertising calls for a strong headline and/or visual to get the reader's attention, light copy to invite the reader, not dissuade. Ideally, it also includes an offer or call-to-action that leads to a measurable lead. The offer can be to call a toll-free number to request a quote, or a website address to register for a free sample. Or as mentioned earlier, a QR code that links the prospect to a website. Below are examples of award-winning ads for FC Lighting from Construction Marketing Advisors. The layouts have all the essentials: strong headline and visual combination, minimal copy, and a call to action.

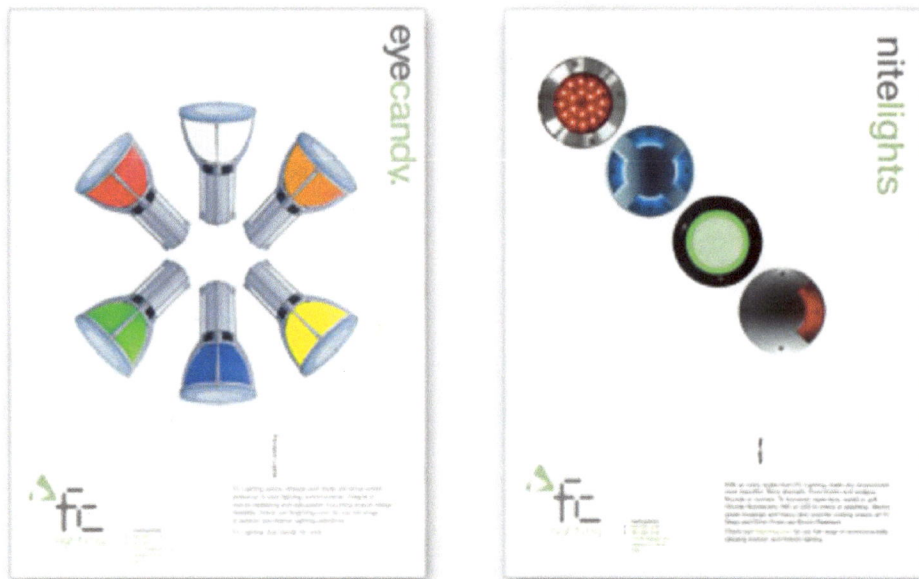

Architectural, engineering and construction firms likely do very little advertising, save limited trade publication advertising. Construction brands that sell to consumers through retail home improvement stores may participate in limited broadcast advertising. Sometimes these brands will participate with in-store flyers or circulars. Below are examples of flyer/circular advertising for Home Dept and Lowe's for building materials manufacturer USG.

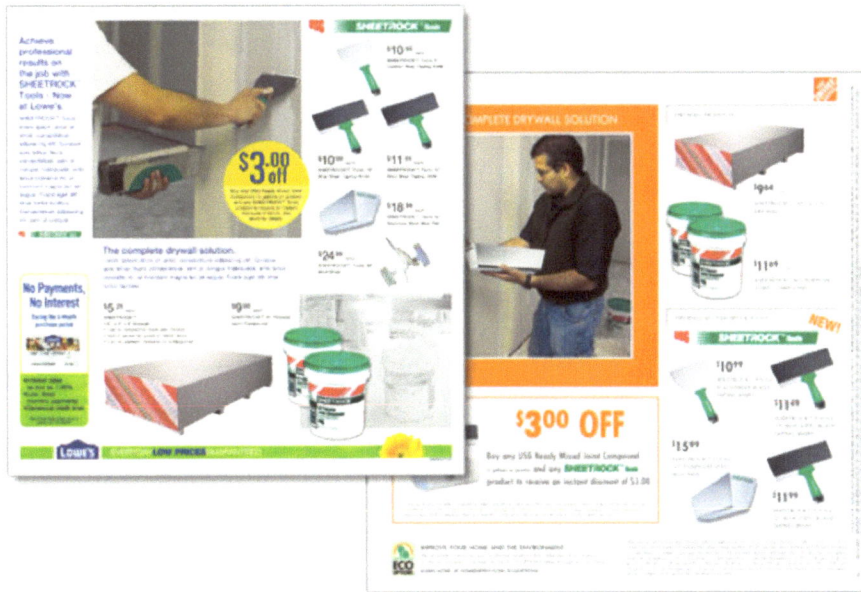

BANNER ADS

With the growing importance of the Internet, electronic display ads, typically called banner ads or banners, are gaining a larger share of advertising budgets. The obvious advantage of banner ads is the ability to hyperlink directly to a website or registration page to generate a lead. Another advantage of banner ads is that they can animate to catch attention and communicate different messages and offers.

Banner ad sizes can vary by each Internet publisher, however the Interactive Advertising Bureau (IAB) has developed display ad unit guidelines*, defined by pixel width and height. Electronic ads are typically developed in HTML or Flash, with file sizes kept to a minimum to ensure fast loading. Below are several examples of banner ads for construction brands from Construction Marketing Advisors. (*Source: www.iab.net/iab_products_and_industry_services/508676/508767/displayguidelines)

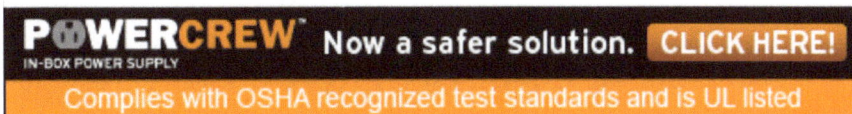

PRACTICAL TIPS FOR ADVERTISING TESTING

Advertising is one of the most expensive elements in the marketing mix, whether print, broadcast or online. And because of the fickle and subjective nature of advertising, seemingly great ideas can flop, while unexpected approaches surprise even the most experienced marketers. With substantial financial investment at stake, it makes sense to gain insight into customer reaction.

There are a variety of options for advertising testing. The extent of testing depends on the expected advertising budget-both ad production and placement. Clearly a $1.3 million Super Bowl spot requires more elaborate testing than a $20,000 print ad.

So what are the advertising testing options? And when should you use one testing type vs. another? Most experts agree on two broad types of advertising testing: concept testing and copy testing.

Concept testing is sometimes called pre-testing, and is generally exploratory using headlines, rough layouts or storyboards. Concept testing typically uses qualitative research techniques including focus groups or in-depth interviews to gain insight into effective ad concepts, identify problems or issues, or to generate new ad concepts.

In contrast, copy testing evaluates different executions of an advertising campaign using finished (or close to finished) ad executions. Copy testing typically employs quantitative research techniques including surveys to measure recall or recognition. Larger sample sizes can provide a level of statistical validity that may be important with larger investments.

What's more, you may use both types of testing for an important or expensive advertising campaign, using concept testing for the early stages of campaign development, and copy testing to select the final ad option.

Finally, advanced copy testing using quantitative techniques can also involve physiological measures including eye-movement analysis, galvanic skin-response methods and brain-wave analysis. Although these are often too complex or expensive for most requirements.

And what would a section about advertising testing be without an example of an actual ad test. Earlier this year, Construction Marketing Advisors conducted an ad test for client BOSCH Power Tools. Per above ad testing types, this was definitely a copy test using finished print ads with a striking visual (ala Cyborg) and varying headline, copy and the treatment of the direct response offer.

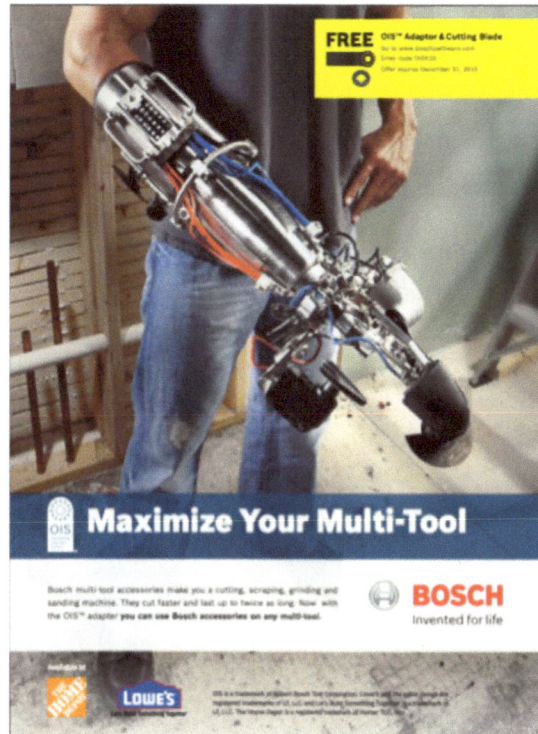

We set-up a survey using the free web-based SurveyMonkey tool and posed four (4) questions:

1) *Which headline do you prefer most? Which headline would you stop and read?*

2) *Which copy version do you prefer most?*

3) *Which Free Offer treatment and layout position do you prefer most?*

4) *Please rate overall preference of each ad on a scale of 1-5 (1=hate, 5=love)*

The ad test was emailed to a random list of remodelers, the target audience from the circulation of Hanley-Wood's Remodeling magazine. We received hundreds of survey responses making the copy test statistically significant, and most importantly, a clear direction with a large percentage of respondents selecting the "Maximize Your Multi-Tool" headline and copy. The preference for "offer treatment" was even more pronounced with nearly 68% preferring the offer in yellow, top right position (an unconventional offer position, and unexpected outcome).

SMALL ADS DELIVER BIG RESULTS!

There is no question that advertising's role in the construction marketing mix is evolving to driving prospects to a registration page or microsite with offers that capture information for future marketing.

One inexpensive but extremely effective ad placement option are classified ads in trade publications that often cost hundreds, not thousands. Classifieds are typically located in the back of a magazine–sometimes several pages, with no editorial. Small ad sizes using 1 or 2-colors require strong headline hooks, and simple direct response vehicles like website addresses or 800 telephone numbers. See classified ad examples below from Construction Marketing Advisors.

Publicity: PR in the Age of Social Media

Publicity is defined by Merriam-Webster dictionary as the dissemination of information to attract public interest. Per the Publicity Insider blog, publicity is the simple act of making a suggestion to a journalist that leads to the inclusion of a company or product in a story. Newspapers, magazines, TV programs and radio shows have large amounts of space to fill and depend upon publicists to help provide story ideas, interview subjects, background information and other material. *(Source: Publicityinsider.com/pifaq.asp)*

We define publicity as the free placement of content, quotes or brand references in public or professional media. The term publicity is often used synonymously with public relations or PR, and sometimes media relations.

PR encompasses a number of activities or initiatives such as news releases or press announcements, article writing and/or placements, media relations, press events, press conferences and press tours. PR can also include investor relations and crisis communications.

The popularity and use of free publicity is historically counter-cyclical. Simply stated, PR increases when the economy tanks. In the midst of this seemingly extended downturn, PR is certainly gaining priority in the construction marketing mix. At the same time, PR is changing significantly. So how can you refine your PR to realize greater results?

This chapter will examine how PR has changed, and how your PR program can change to leverage new PR opportunities. Next, we'll focus on the specifics of PR distribution options.

SO, HOW HAS PR CHANGED?

PR has changed more in the last few years than the last 30 years combined. How? The changing roles of journalists and marketing practitioners, and the rapidly increasing use of social media in PR.

No doubt, the recession has taken a toll on journalists with layoffs, and those remaining have greater workloads, tightening budgets, and added responsibilities of writing for multiple mediums. According to the 2010 PRWeek/PR Newswire Media Survey, 59% of traditional (print) journalists are the author of a blog, and are also expected to contribute to online news, Twitter and other channels.

With greater workload, the research tools used by journalists might identify opportunities for marketing practitioners. Not surprisingly, Google and other search engines rank highest for research tools, 95% in 2010 per the PRWeek survey, followed by company websites (93%), Wikipedia (47%), newswires (36%), social networks (33%), and blogs (32%).

SOCIAL MEDIA EMERGENCE

While the hype of social media pervades marketing practitioners, the use of social media for publicity is growing rapidly, and becoming a major part of both journalists and practitioners PR activities. According to the survey, in 2010 79% of journalists had a Facebook profile, 46% had a LinkedIn profile, and 58% had a Twitter profile. Only 11% had no profiles. Twitter realized the most dramatic increase from just 22% in 2009.

In addition, 43% of PR practitioners use social networks to pitch media, with 76% using Twitter and 49% using Facebook. One of the key reasons practitioners use social media – Search engine results! Often posts to social media channels rank higher than even company websites for key search terms. And as noted above, journalists use search engines 95% of the time for research.

A discussion of PR and social media would be incomplete without acknowledging the growing importance of blogs. Per above, 59% of traditional (print) journalists wrote blogs. In addition, 45% of journalists had quoted a blog in an article, and journalists used both general blogs (24%) and company blogs (23%) for research. On the practitioner side, 66% are targeting bloggers more than before. "The corporate, brand or subject matter blog can be the hub of an integrated PR program, using social media channels for distributing blogposts and other news," suggests Heather Hawes, Program Manager for the Construction Marketing Association.

THE NEWEST RULES OF PR

So what are the implications of the changing PR landscape to practitioners or client-side marketers? Clearly PR strategies and tactics should embrace these changes, and leverage the opportunities. "Now more than ever, practitioners should be deploying blogs, Twitter, Facebook and YouTube profiles, Wikipedia pages, and Bookmark/Share links on website pages. The blog and all profiles should be linked to the website, which should have RSS feeds. News announcements should be formatted to include links to these assets and other relevant information sources," shares Heather Hawes. "The integration of PR and social media delivers powerful results that make both tactics more critical to the marketing mix. What's more, publicity is a key source of content for social media, and more than ever, content is king."

The Construction Marketing Association (CMA) is a good example of effective PR and integrated social media. Heather Hawes, Program Manager for the association and Construction Marketing Advisors agency sums it up. "Just a couple of years ago, we would email a news announcement to trade editors. We still distribute to trade editors, but we also post news on our websites and blogs with RSS feeds, use Twitter, Facebook, and social bookmarking tools to distribute the news and submit to free news distribution services. If the news item is big or strategic enough, we will submit to paid distribution services. Finally, we can measure placements with alerts and searches. Its faster, deeper and more measurable."

NEWS DISTRIBUTION TIPS

As you might expect, there is no "silver bullet" or single solution that addresses all PR distribution needs. Most marketing practitioners use a combination of approaches for getting news and PR releases in front of editors and influencers.

The Construction Marketing Association, and PR programs for clients of Construction Marketing Advisors use several options for news distribution. Heather Hawes, Program Manager shares her process. *"First we post news on our websites and blogs. This allows for Retweeting and bookmarking. Next we distribute to our own editor (email) databases. The news announcements are also formatted to include links to these respective Internet domains. Depending on how "big" the news item is, we will then distribute using both free and paid services. We still realize the majority of placements through our own, custom editor lists."*

"Distribution services increase news reach and placements, particularly across the internet, and with blogs that would be hard to identify," adds Hawes. No question, there are more PR distribution service options than ever.

The following table lists some of the top news distribution services, ranging from free to substantial fees for more value-added services. The table includes CMA's ranking based on quality, cost, distribution and Google PageRank.

Top News Distribution Services

#	Name	Fees	A/G	PageRank
1	dir.yahoo.com	$80	250k RSS, 30k journalists	PR7
2	sbd.bcentral/.com	$395-$675	Nat'l/Regional Selects/200 Industry Selects	PR7
3	www.business.com	$415-$715	85,000 registered journalists	PR7
4	www.botw.org	$285-$485	300k RSS, 8k news & broadcasts	PR7
5	www.site-sift.com	$0-$49	60,000 editors/journalists/bloggers	PR6
6	www.joeant.com	$0-$199	Vertical Industry Selects	PR6
7	www.ableseek.com	$240-$350	300k outlets/Monitoring	PR6
8	www.skaffe.com	$380	250k RSS, 30k journalists/bloggers	PR6
9	www.123world..com	$0-$30	Country and Industry Selects	PR5
10	www.goguides.org	$0-$29	Websites, RSS Feeds, Blogs	PR5

So which service should you use? Per above, depending on the importance of the news, you may opt for free distribution for minor releases, to the highest level of services for news that requires the broadest distribution, or specific features like financial disclosure compliance which BusinessWire and PR Newswire both support.

Our staff often uses a combination of free and paid, thus ensuring that multiple news sources will pick up the news. CMA ranks PRWeb highest by virtue of the combination of reasonable fees, broad distribution and high Google PageRank. Upon review, Businesswire and PR Newswire are the top-end services, and very similar.

Although Businesswire pricing is more reasonable for smaller clients. We have experienced excellent search results using 24-7pressrelease.com and Free-press-release.com. After this exercise, we are inclined to further evaluate PR.com. Following are some additional services we found but did not analyze.

Top News Distribution Services

#	Name	PageRank	#	A/G	PageRank
1	Newswire Today	PR6	7	PR Leap	PR5
2	Press Release Network	PR6	8	PR Zoom	PR5
3	Thomas Net News	PR6	9	Pressbox.co.uk	PR5
4	PR Log	PR6	10	Free Press Release Center	PR4
5	PR-Inside	PR6	11	EcommWire	PR4
6	ClickPress	PR5	12	PR Free	PR4

TRADE SHOWS AND EVENTS

Trade shows and events are staples of construction marketing, and often one of the top budget line items. On the brand side, manufacturers exhibit at industry events and might participate in networking events.

When marketing architectural, engineering or construction (A/E/C) services, exhibiting at trade shows is less common, but participating or sponsoring industry networking events is a major aspect of a typical marketing program, and is covered in the A/E/C marketing chapter.

Finally, virtual events including webcasts are gaining popularity due to cost efficiencies and lead generation. Following are some best practice marketing considerations for both trade shows and virtual events.

Trade Show and Event Marketing Best Practices

Most brand manufacturers manage an extensive trade show program exhibiting at multiple shows for key markets. No question, trade shows are one of marketing's biggest budget line items including exhibit construction, storage, transportation, erection and space rental, not to mention staffing and travel expenses.

While trade show investment is high, often results measurement is weak or lacking. Why? Because more often than not, exhibitors rely on card readers for the sole measure of leads and results, trade show booths lack customer interaction, and little or no pre-show or at-show promotion or communication takes place.

Still, trade shows can attract thousands of customers and prospects, along with editors, channel partners, prospective employees and other important contacts. For certain categories like construction equipment, trade shows are critically important to allow for product demonstrations, client meetings and entertainment. In addition, trade shows are typically produced with conferences, educational workshops, and association meetings that offer additional opportunities for promotion and networking.

Many marketers in construction markets have reduced trade show marketing budgets, most often by eliminating certain shows. For the remaining shows on the schedule, be sure to properly promote your exhibit via pre-show and at-show communications. Often trade show producers will provide email lists of registrants, some free of charge. Certainly, email and contact customers and prospects prior to the show, with your exhibit location, invites to hospitality events and related. Prior to the show, schedule customer, prospect and editor meetings.

Next, be sure to enhance customer interaction with attractive exhibit design, graphics and video. Create a "buzz" before and during the show with promotions, contests, celebrity appearances, hospitality and entertainment events.

Finally, measure trade show results via multiple mechanisms: card readers, contest registrations, editorial placements, sales personnel notes and more.

Following are the trade show exhibit design winners for the annual Construction Marketing Association STAR Awards™ including Polyglass USA, and McGraw-Hill Construction.

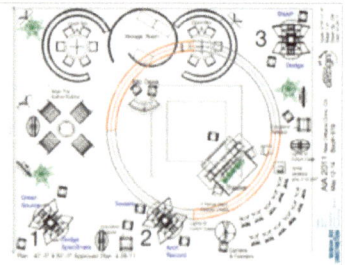

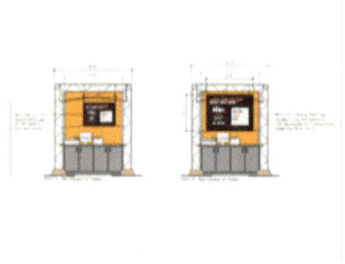

Tools of the Trade: Modern Marketing for Construction Brands

VIRTUAL EVENTS

As mentioned, virtual events are gaining popularity due to cost efficiencies, lead generation and more. In fact, monthly webcasts by the Construction Marketing Association are the top lead generation source of all marketing tactics for CMA.

Whether webcasts, webinars, web conferences or virtual trade shows, managing virtual events requires both careful planning and ongoing execution. Clearly, webcasts can be an excellent resource for training and thought leadership. But content, recruitment, promotion and management can be challenging.

Start with a plan that defines content and frequency. What topics are of interest to your customers and prospects? Be sure to not just be a sales pitch or commercial for your company or you will lose interest and participation fast. If possible, recruit opinion leaders for given topics, or multiple subject matter experts (SMEs) as panelists. If necessary, offer an honorarium.

Regarding frequency, an annual event may not be frequent enough, possibly losing interest and continuity, while a weekly or even monthly event may be too frequent to manage. Consider segmenting your content and audiences, so you communicate less frequently, and provide more targeted content. Frequency rules-of-thumb? No more than every 3-6 weeks, no less than every 180 days.

Be sure to allow adequate time for communication and promotion of each event. Email is a natural tool for communicating, with hyperlinks to event information and registration. But news releases, social media posts and more should be leveraged to build awareness and registrations. Below is a flowchart of communications and support for the Construction Marketing Association webcast training program.

Call for panelists
• LinkedIn
• Google

PR
• CMA Website
• Email Editors

Optional survey
• CMA Website
• LinkedIn

Newswire Distribution
• PR web
• Free PR

Social Media
• Blog
• Facebook
• Twitter

E-Newsletter

Post-Webcast
• Thank you e-mail
• Blog summary
• Archive/download

Execute Webcast

Social Media
2 day reminder

Social Media
1 week reminder

LinkedIn
• Group posts
• InMail

///CMA

Besides email, PR and social media, promote the event on your website, including a dedicated event page. If the event is really important, use Pay-Per-Click (PPC) advertising and/or banner ads. Even use telemarketing to remind key customers and prospects.

Other tips for successful virtual events include list building, offers, surveys, questions and follow-up. If possible, build your list through new sources and media partners. Offer registrants a copy of the presentation or whitepaper for attending. Use polling or surveys to inject the experience and perspective of registrants. Dedicate time for questions and answers. Always follow-up with registrants (that did and did not attend) with a thank you, and offer for more information, including on-demand versions of the event.

Finally, select a web conferencing vendor based on the scale and technical requirements of each event. A list of top web conferencing vendors (2011) from the Web Conferencing Council appears below. (Source: http://webconferencingcouncil.com/)

Top Web Conferencing Vendors

* VIA3
* GoToMeeting
* WebEx
* LiveMeeting
* Acrobat Connect Pro
* iLinc
* Connect
* Sametime
* WiredRed
* Yugma

Direct Marketing

Direct marketing is a broad term that encompasses several marketing disciplines including direct mail, email, database marketing, and to a lesser extent, telemarketing and direct response television advertising. Historically, direct marketing has been closely tied to direct mail, a medium that continues to lose marketing budget allocations to more cost efficient and measurable digital media. Acknowledging this trend, the Direct Marketing Association (DMA) has repositioned itself to be interactive and direct marketing, not direct mail.

Following are some best practices for direct mail, email marketing and database marketing.

DIRECT MAIL IS ALIVE AND KICKING

Like advertising, prior to digital media, direct mail was one of the top marketing tactics. Direct mail continues to be an important medium for reaching new customers, as well as providing time-sensitive information to captive customers lists. Why? Because direct mail can get delivered to decision makers that might not open email, direct mail can be personalized, and now direct mail can easily integrate with digital media.

Despite such nicknames as "junk mail" and "snail mail", when targeting the C-Suite or other hard to reach decision-makers, direct mail can break-through the clutter and get "special delivery" to individual contacts. Clever direct mail can be designed as dimensional pieces (e.g. large boxes), custom die-cuts shapes and sizes, or oversize postcards, all to get noticed.

With variable printing, customized messages can help engage the prospect. Below is an example of a die-cut mail piece with variable printing of a company name and first name/last name for WEATHER GUARD® truck equipment.

Per our earlier chapter, with QR Code technology, printed direct mail can now be scanned and linked to website content, offers and registrations. So integration of print and digital campaigns is possible.

Like email, direct mail is only as effective as the quality of the list. Especially in the construction industry with massive layoffs, list hygiene must be carefully evaluated for accuracy. Often mail lists (and email lists) are from trade magazine subscriber lists. Make sure that a high percentage of the list has been qualified in the last year. Typically, publishers and/or list brokers will state, 90% qualified within 120 days. If the list has not been qualified for longer than one year, the quantity of return-to-senders will be quite high, but is often refundable from the list broker.

When possible, develop and maintain your own list using customer contact information from sales, customer service, requests for quote, training registrations and related. Merge lists from trade shows and website registrations into a central database. Add distributors, sales reps and editors to your mail list. And promptly remove return-to-senders.

The negatives of direct mail include the high cost of printing, and of course, ever-rising postage costs. For this reason, postcards offer a good option for inexpensive printing and reduced postage rates for postcard sizes up to 6" x 11".

Email Marketing: The First Social Media

Rumors of my demise have been greatly exaggerated! Email is not dead. On the contrary, email marketing is growing. According to a January 2011 survey by BtoB magazine, 63% of respondents were likely to increase spending on email in 2011 (second only to websites) with 29% keeping spend constant. Also, The Email Marketing Institute recently released Q1 2011 email results stating, "North America Email Trends and Benchmarks Results showed a 39.2% increase in average volume per client from 2010 to 2011."

Following is some background on email marketing, along with email tips and tricks. Next, we will share email testing tips, measuring email campaigns, and a Glossary of Terms.

WHAT IS EMAIL MARKETING?

Long before blogs, Twitter and Facebook, marketers used email to communicate with customers and prospects in a similar way to direct mail; deploying a message to a list, with an offer, to generate a response.

The elements of email marketing include the list, the email layout and copy, the subject line and the offer(s). Most emails are distributed by email software or an email service provider (ESP). For a modest fee, the ESP provides an interface to design or upload the email (copy, images, html files), upload or manage lists, and provide metrics or dashboards on campaign results. The ESP also has built-in features for opt-outs and removal of duplicates (de-dupe).

WHY CONSIDER EMAIL MARKETING?

The major reason to consider email marketing is because it works, and in comparison to direct mail, email is a bargain. While list costs (when required) may be similar or slightly higher than mail, email does not have printing or postage costs. And when using email software or an ESP, the metrics or campaign measures are robust including open-rates, click-through-rates (CTRs), bounces and opt-outs. The immediacy of email is untouchable by any other marketing medium. And the combination of metrics and immediacy allow you to test subject lines, even offers (more on testing later). Certainly email integrates nicely with websites and e-commerce. And email campaigns can easily be customized, personalized and otherwise targeted to the individual or market segment. Finally, email lends itself to ongoing communications with customers and prospects who opt-in to newsletters and related communications.

But email marketing is not perfect. In email's infancy (around 1998-2000), open rates and click-through-rates were stratospheric until spam-blocking firewalls rained on the parade. Then anti-spamming legislation almost killed email. Now with spam-ware adopted by all email hosts, email open rates are much lower, averaging 10-20% for a business-to-business category (including construction).

Despite these issues, with the marketing mix rapidly evolving to Internet, SEO and social media, email is an important conduit to these electronic assets. And the promise of communicating quickly and inexpensively to captive customers and opt-in lists generated from all these Internet assets is too good to pass up.

So the holy grail of email marketing is how to be more effective; how to maximize campaign effectiveness. To that end, the balance of this section will share email marketing tips and tricks!

EMAIL TIPS AND TRICKS

1) The List: the foundation of any email (or direct mail) campaign or program is the list. Obviously, home-grown customer lists have the highest potential for opening, followed by opt-in email lists from a variety of your own sources. The problem with email lists in business-to-business is employee turnover. A good portion of email (or mail) lists become inaccurate over time, thus requiring ongoing efforts to purge hard-bounces, or non-deliverables (reported by most ESPs).

Purchased lists are available from publishers, associations, list brokers and online databases. List costs typically range from $100-$400 per thousand records. Often the list seller will not provide the list, but will distribute your email to their list to maintain control. Following is a list of sources for your email list.

Sources of Email Lists
Publisher lists
List brokers
Association lists
Online databases
Website registrations
Website contact forms, questions
Customer phone inquiries including RFQs
Sales contacts
Email has forward to friend feature
Trade show scans
Warranty registrations
LinkedIn connections
RSS registrations
Research people and companies using directories like Jigsaw

List hygiene, or continually cleaning your list, is critical to email success. When using an ESP, un-subscribers or opt-outs will be automatically purged from the list. If not using an ESP, you must perform this task manually. Hard bounces are invalid email addresses and should be removed from the list. Soft bounces should be tested as these can be out-of-the-office auto-responders or server issues on the client-side.

2) Email Design: there are 3 elements to be considered with each email design—subject line, layout, and offer(s) or call-to-action.

One of the most basic email success factors is to avoid spam subject lines. Spam filters are employed by most email providers today. Each closely looks at the subject line and message body to determine the likeliness of spam. Here is a list of what spam filters hone in on that you should avoid:

Free / Act Now / All New
50% Off Call Now Subscribe Now
Earn Money Discount Double Your Income
You're A Winner! Million Dollar Opportunity
Why Pay More
Special Promotion Information You Requested
Amazing Cash Bonus
Promise You Credit
Loans As Seen On Buy Direct
Get Paid Order Now Please Read
Don't Delete Time Limited While Supplies Last
Stop No Cost No Fees
Satisfaction Guaranteed Serious Cash Search Engine Listings
Join Millions Save Up To All Natural
You've Been Selected Excessive $ or !

We recommend testing subject lines, to be covered in the next section.

Regarding email layout, simple and brief is a good start. A combination of copy and visuals or images is another key. Treat the email layout like a print ad with a strong headline, light support copy, and clear offer (big buttons are good!). Email newsletters can have multiple content areas, but ideally, stay away from long-copy and use abstracts with READ MORE hyperlinks to full text. The added advantage of links is the opportunity to measure the click-through.

Always have complete contact information including phone, website, email, and links to your social profiles. Ensure that the unsubscribe link is easy to find.

Following is a sample of an email design from Construction Marketing Advisors targeting architects, which included a product highlight, as well as a project spotlight:

3) Email Software and Email Service Providers: We recommend using email software or an email service provider for all email distribution. Why? If you mail from your own email system, you can be blacklisted by the receiver. Second, ESPs will optimize against spam filtering. As mentioned, ESPs provide user-friendly tools for list management and even design. And ESPs offer great dashboards for measuring your email campaign. Finally, ESP fees are very reasonable.

List of Top Email Service Providers (ESPs)

iContact

Benchmark Email

Constant Contact

Mailigen

Pinpointe

Campaigner

GraphicMail

Vertical Response

MailChimp

4) Other Tricks of the Trade

One of the most important considerations for email success is timing, or when you distribute the email. For business-to-business markets, we recommend Tuesday through Thursday, after 9:30 am, or 1:30 pm. Why? Because Monday morning will have a back-up of email, and coupled with staff meetings, email will more likely be deleted. Also, emails overnight will be more likely deleted due to the quantity of other emails everyday. Fridays in the summer, forget about it. If you are doing nationally distributed emails, be sure to take into account different time zones. If marketing to consumers, weekends are actually preferred timing.

Another consideration for email success is frequency. If you bombard your list with emails, recipients will unsubscribe. If you email twice a year, there will be no continuity. Somewhere in between is a happy medium. Each scenario is unique. Do your customers and prospects use or buy your product (or service) frequently? Is your product complex, or require a lot of information, generate questions? A rule-of-thumb would be no more than weekly, and no less than quarterly. This is why a monthly eNewsletter is a popular frequency, delivering continuity without annoying your target audience.

Finally, to ensure deliverability, add a message to your emails along the lines of, "Please add our email address to your email contacts/address book to ensure that you receive our emails." Again, ESP software may have this feature.

EMAIL TESTING

One of the advantages of email is the ease of testing and optimizing campaigns. Before sending an email out to your full email list, test each campaign, keeping all (email) elements constant but change one variable. This approach is often referred to as A/B Testing. Since this type of testing is an industry standard, email service providers (ESPs) allow you to do this easily. It is vital to run tests when you are trying to decide on subject lines, layouts, or an offer.

To conduct the test, simply email one or more versions to a small list. Depending on the list size, typically 50-100 email addresses is sufficient. Next, measure and compare open rates for different subject lines, or click-through rates (CTRs) for different layouts or offers. Lower open rates or CTRs should be dropped in favor of higher open rates and CTRs. If all versions test low, go back to the drawing board or consult an expert.

Following is a list of email elements you can test before sending out an email:

>	*Subject Line*
>	*Offer/promotion/Call-to-action*
>	*Layout of the email*
>	*Design (colors, images etc.)*
>	*Level of personalization (Mr. _____ vs. First name)*
>	*Content (balance of written copy and visuals)*
>	*Headline/Title*
>	*Mobile Version*

MEASURING EMAIL CAMPAIGNS

As marketing budgets have become more restrictive, tracking, measuring and reporting have become increasingly important. Any ESP you choose will have a robust measurement dashboard that will allow for easy analysis and reporting. Below is an example of what an ESP dashboard looks like:

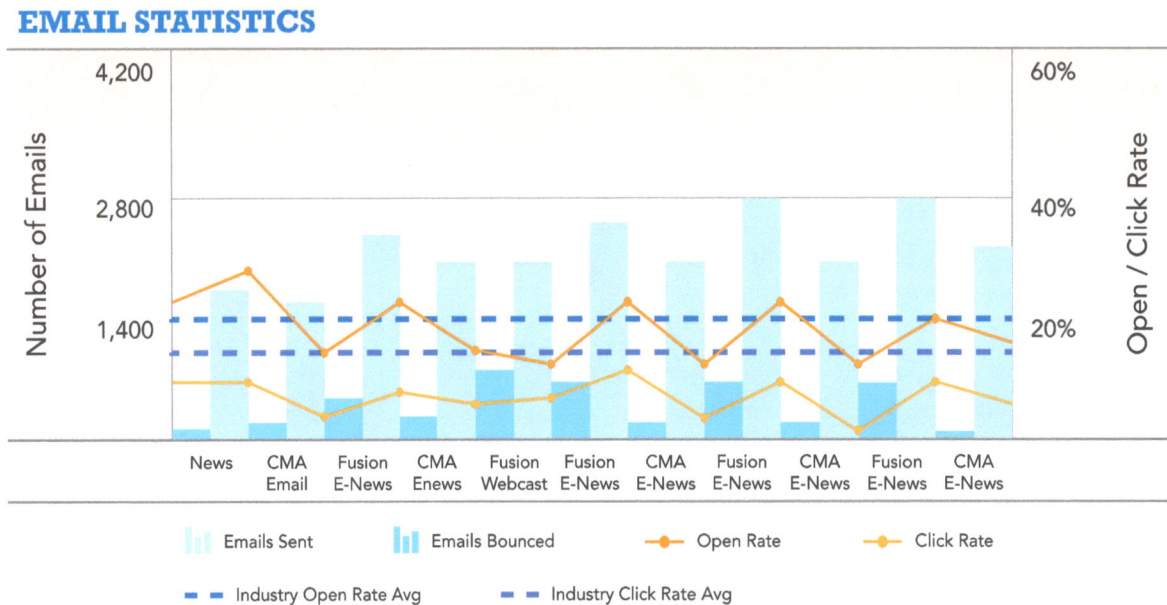

EMAIL STATISTICS

A typical ESP dashboard will report and track the following:

    a) Emails Sent

    b) Hard and soft bounces (see glossary)

    c) Open rate

    d) Click-through-rate (CTR)

    e) All of the Above

When measuring an email campaign success you need to track the progress of your goals. The typical open rate for business-to-business (B2B) markets is between 10-20%. If your focus is CTR then be sure to measure and track that statistic. The typical B2B CTR is 10%. Measuring and tracking your email ensures the success of future email campaigns.

Remember to always test, optimize, execute, track and report your email campaigns for maximum results!

GLOSSARY OF EMAIL TERMS

If you are new to email marketing there may be some basic terms you do not know yet. We have compiled a list of what we see as the most important email marketing terms. Note: This is not a comprehensive list.

Blacklisting – Lists of domains and IP addresses that have been reported or accused of sending spam. You can check blacklists at www.openrbl.org and www.dnsstuff.com.

Bounces – Emails that have been sent back to sender because the recipient email address was invalid or presently not working. Hard bounces are bad email addresses and should be removed. Soft bounces are most often out-of-the-office notifications, or temporary server issues.

Click-Through-Rate (CTR) – Hyperlinks within the email that are tracked by the # of times it is clicked on by email recipients, especially offers. Most ESPs report CTR.

Click-through tracking – Measuring the number of clicks that occur on each link in an email message.

Customer Relationship Management (CRM) – The ability to keep track of every interaction with every prospect and customer and keeps tracks of trends and tabulates results of such notes on an aggregate scale. Essentially, an intelligent interface that allows keeping notes of every action, sale, phone call, email, fax, etc.

CSV – A file format in which each new field is separated by a comma. This file format is used by ESP's to build email lists, where each email is separated by a comma. Outlook and other email services allow you to export your entire address book in this format.

Database – A storing of records. Databases are made up of tables. Tables are made up of columns and rows. Data is stored in a field (aka cell). Popular types of web databases include SQL and MySQL.

De-Duping – The act of removing duplicates from a list.

ESP – ESP stands for Email Service Provider. An ESP is a specific type of Application Service Provider (see ASP). iContact is an example of an ESP.

HTML templates – The most common programming language for emails. The acronym HTML stands for Hypertext Markup Language.

Mail merge personalization – The ability to, on the fly for each email, insert data from the database into specific fields in an email. For example, one may place Dear _____ in an email. When each email is sent out, a call to the database is made to retrieve the actual first name of that subscriber. It then 'pastes' this data into the email. Dear John, Dear Judy etc. will result.

Message scheduling – The ability to set a time in the future for a message to start to be delivered to recipients.

Open Tracking – The ability to keep track of the number of opens ("reads") a message gets.

Opt-in – A term that refers to any subscriber that has specifically requested an email newsletter. If they have signed up through your website, they are opt-in.

Opt-out – See 'Unsubscribe link' below.

Spam – Unwanted email that was sent without the permission of the recipient. Also known as unsolicited commercial email.

Unsubscribe link – The link at the bottom of each email which allows visitors to unsubscribe or modify/update their information.

Whitelisting – Opposite of blacklisting. Many ISPs have lists of sites with which they have built good relationships with and trust. If your sending fits their standards, it may be possible to add yourself to a whitelist. If you are on a whitelist, your mail has a much better chance of being delivered.

WYSIWYG Editor – Stands for "what you see is what you get." Allows users to create their own HTML newsletters right on the sending page, without knowing HTML.

SIX DATABASE MARKETING STRATEGIES

Despite high interest in database marketing (DBM), many marketers still have not implemented DBM. One of the reasons for this is a lack of practical information. Depending on your objectives, you should consider one or more DBM strategies including: 1) Segmentation, 2) New Customer Acquisition, 3) Customer Penetration, 4) Customer Retention, 5) Marketing Intelligence and, 6) Measuring Results.

1—Segmentation

Segmenting customers and prospects into various classifications is the first step in DBM. The most basic level of segmentation involves classifying, coding or sorting customers and prospects by type, size or potential.

Business marketers can utilize Standard Industrial Classifications (SIC codes) established by the federal government to categorize most business types. Other typical classifications include sales revenue, employees, product purchases, purchase interest etc.

A higher level of segmentation involves profiling, scoring, or modeling of customers and prospects. Profiling identifies frequencies (percentages) of different categories, for example, financial services comprise 17% of XYZ Corporation's customer base. In addition, the 80/20 rule can be illustrated utilizing percentages, for example, 80% of XYZ profits are derived from the top 20% of customers.

Scoring, as the name implies, ranks segments or individual customers by some predetermined criteria, often sales or gross margin contribution. Dividing the ranked list into three groups is common to identify heavy, moderate, and light users. Mail order marketers utilize RFM, that is recency, frequency and monetary or transaction value, as criteria for judging customer worth.

Modeling employs statistical techniques like multiple regression to identify factors that correlate to high sales potential or likelihood of promotional response. Prospective customers can then be "fitted" to these models to determine which prospects should be priorities.

2—New Customer Acquisition

Identifying and communicating with high potential prospects is a goal of most marketers. The segmentation tools described allow you to focus on prospects that are "heavy users" or that fit predetermined criteria. DBM can be utilized to identify new customer "gains", and to track trends in new customer activity. Finally DBM can be used to target and manage prospect communications, marketing, and sales programs.

3—Customer Penetration

What is your "account penetration" level by customer? DBM can help identify penetration by comparing transaction data to total customer purchases. In addition, modeling "ideal" product mix by customer type will identify cross-sell and up-sell opportunities. Again, the segmentation step can identify opportunities.

4—Customer Retention

Strategies in this area have grown in importance since the high cost of new customer acquisition has been well documented. DBM can support the identification of lost customers to be reclaimed, dormant customers to be reactivated, as well as the Lifetime Value (LTV) of customers. DBM often is the foundation for implementing loyalty building strategies including continuity or points programs, recognition, and other value-added marketing or sales programs.

5—Marketing Intelligence

Sometimes a by-product of DBM is the ability to utilize the database as a marketing intelligence device. Segmentation supports intelligence gathering. Often a customer record will include unlimited text entries. Remote database access and "real-time" updating reinforce marketing intelligence applications.

6—Measuring Results

Tracking of marketing, sales, advertising and communications program results is possible by "capturing" customer/prospect responses, transactions, etc., in the database. Updating customer records allows the database to remain "fresh." In addition, coding and sorting allows for the testing of alternative programs or offers, with responses carefully measured to support ongoing improvements.

WHY DATABASE MARKETING?

Database marketing promises to deliver more effective marketing and communications, first by improving customer understanding through segmentation, and then by using this information to communicate with customers in a targeted, even personalized way. At least six DBM strategies should be considered including segmentation, customer acquisition, penetration, retention, market intelligence and measuring results.

New Product Development and Launch

What is new product development and launch? New product development (NPD) is one of the main activities that contribute to growth, and NPD is inclusive of new services.

NPD is complex, requires a lot of resources, and has a high failure rate (reported from 46% to 90+%). Effective NPD is growing in importance due to shorter product lifecycles, high costs, increased competition and more demanding customers.

Several independent research studies (and the recent CMA survey) identify a majority (70-85%) of U.S. companies use the Stage-Gate system for new product development systems; other companies use Value Engineering, QFD, TQM, internal systems or a hybrid of internal and other systems.

NPD typically begins with idea generation, customer input, research and testing, and/or competitive analysis (patent review, reverse engineering). NPD can range from simple product improvements, cost reductions and line extensions, to new product platforms, to breakthrough innovations that define new categories.

New product launch includes all activities that bring new products into the market, or commercialization. Following are results of a national survey conducted in 2011 by the Construction Marketing Association.

Survey Questions

1. Are you involved in new product development?
2. Are you involved in new product launch?
3. How many new products do you launch per year?
4. Do you use a new product development system or process?
5. If yes, what type of system?

Involved in New Product Development?

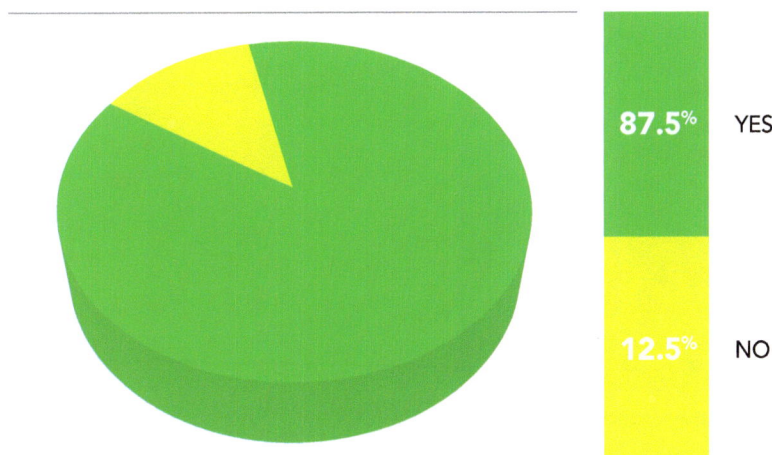

87.5% YES

12.5% NO

Involved in New Product Launch?

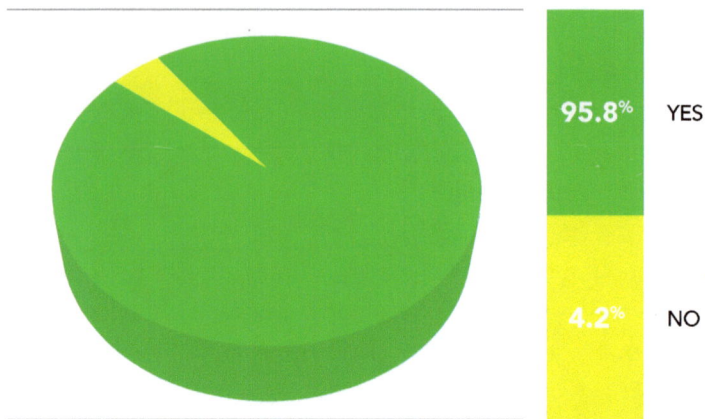

95.8%	YES
4.2%	NO

Products Launched Per Year?

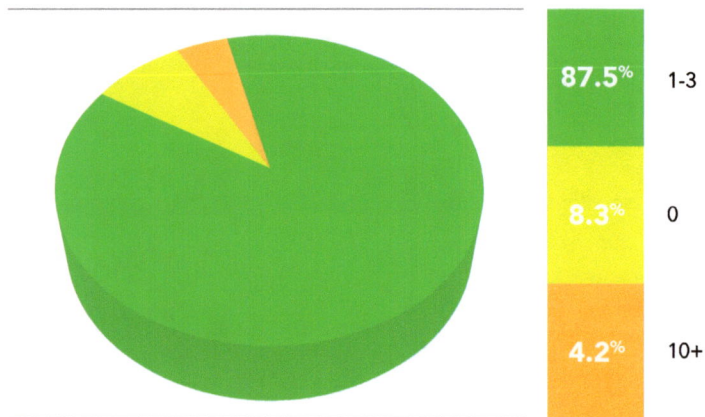

87.5%	1-3
8.3%	0
4.2%	10+

Type of System/Process?

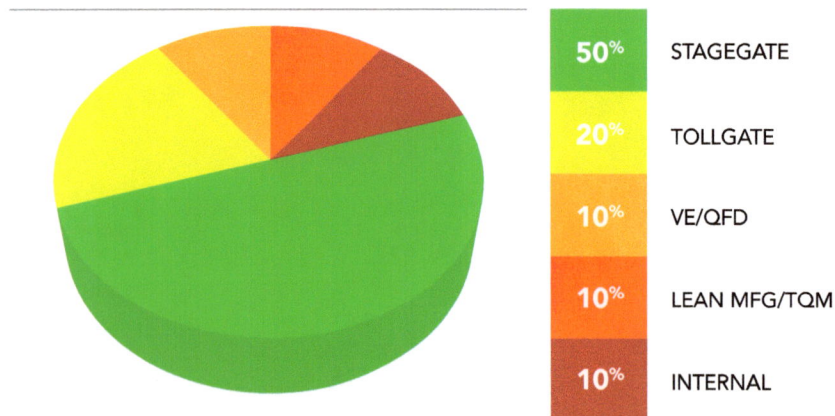

50%	STAGEGATE
20%	TOLLGATE
10%	VE/QFD
10%	LEAN MFG/TQM
10%	INTERNAL

Stage-Gate New Product Development (NPD) System *(Source: Product Development Institute)*

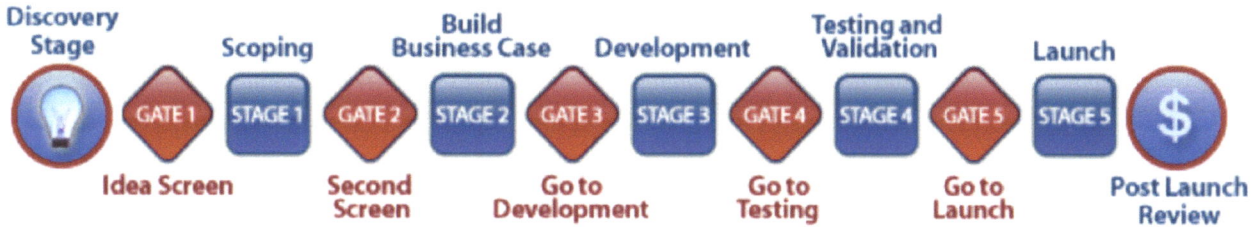

Stage-Gate System, Detail View

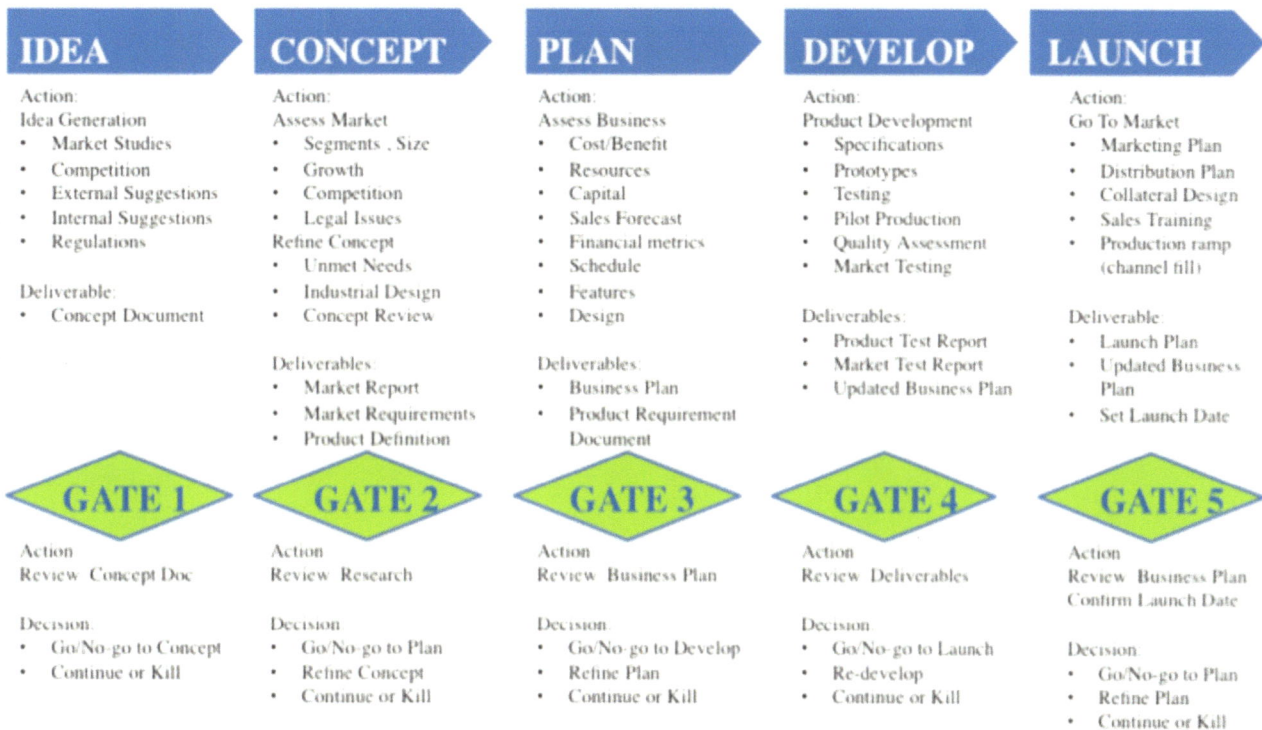

IDEA

Action:
Idea Generation
- Market Studies
- Competition
- External Suggestions
- Internal Suggestions
- Regulations

Deliverable:
- Concept Document

CONCEPT

Action:
Assess Market
- Segments , Size
- Growth
- Competition
- Legal Issues
Refine Concept
- Unmet Needs
- Industrial Design
- Concept Review

Deliverables:
- Market Report
- Market Requirements
- Product Definition

PLAN

Action:
Assess Business
- Cost/Benefit
- Resources
- Capital
- Sales Forecast
- Financial metrics
- Schedule
- Features
- Design

Deliverables:
- Business Plan
- Product Requirement Document

DEVELOP

Action:
Product Development
- Specifications
- Prototypes
- Testing
- Pilot Production
- Quality Assessment
- Market Testing

Deliverables:
- Product Test Report
- Market Test Report
- Updated Business Plan

LAUNCH

Action:
Go To Market
- Marketing Plan
- Distribution Plan
- Collateral Design
- Sales Training
- Production ramp (channel fill)

Deliverable:
- Launch Plan
- Updated Business Plan
- Set Launch Date

GATE 1

Action
Review Concept Doc

Decision:
- Go/No-go to Concept
- Continue or Kill

GATE 2

Action
Review Research

Decision:
- Go/No-go to Plan
- Refine Concept
- Continue or Kill

GATE 3

Action
Review Business Plan

Decision:
- Go/No-go to Develop
- Refine Plan
- Continue or Kill

GATE 4

Action
Review Deliverables

Decision:
- Go/No-go to Launch
- Re-develop
- Continue or Kill

GATE 5

Action
Review Business Plan
Confirm Launch Date

Decision:
- Go/No-go to Plan
- Refine Plan
- Continue or Kill

TYPICAL NEW PRODUCT DEVELOPMENT TEAM

One of the unique aspects of new product development (NPD) is the number and types of managers that are part of a typical project. Perhaps no other function in an organization brings together so many different departments and disciplines to a common project. Certainly marketing drives the project, but operations, engineering, purchasing, finance and top management and many other are all involved. Following is a visual representation of a typical NPD team.

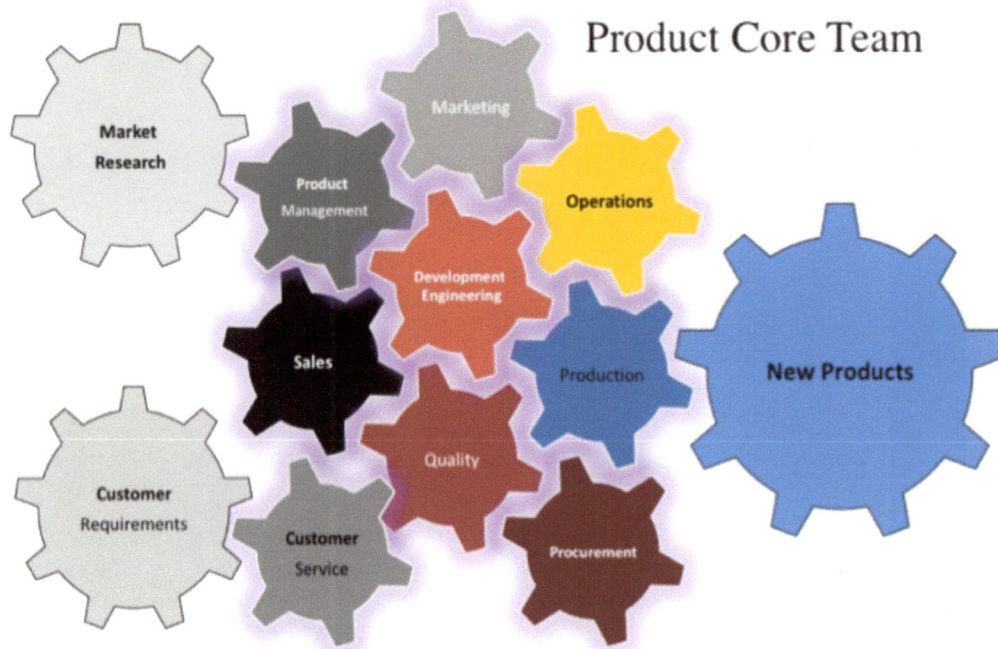

Product Core Team

A NEW PRODUCT LAUNCH CHECKLIST

Improving the effectiveness of new product development and launch is of critical importance to most companies as development costs can be stratospheric, coupled with extremely high failure rates. Certainly the new product development process is complex and multi-functional, including not just marketing—but also typically involving many departments such as engineering, operations, purchasing, executive management and others. The scope of this checklist does NOT address the many product development processes. Rather, the focus of this New Product Launch Planning Checklist is the marketing activities required to improve product launch effectiveness. No question that different markets or product types will require vastly different new product launch approaches and have different budget resources. So a New Product Launch Planning Checklist should allow for a range of market and budget scenarios. This planning checklist is based on a typical business-to-business (B2B) market scenario.

I. RESEARCH AND TESTING

A. Secondary Research (already published)
    i. Internet search
    ii. Syndicated research studies
    iii. Data from category publications, associations, websites, databases

B. Primary Research
    i. Customer interviews (also sales personnel, channel partners)
    ii. Customer/Channel surveys
    iii. Focus Groups
    iv. Test Markets, Beta Tests

C. Competitive Analysis
    i. Patent research
    ii. Reverse engineering
    iii. Branding/positioning analysis
    iv. SWOT analysis
    v. Pricing analysis
    vi. Market research to determine share, volume, channels

D. Testing
    i. Concept testing (interviews, focus groups)
    ii. Product evaluation (interviews, focus groups)
    iii. Copy testing (interviews, surveys or focus groups)

II. PRODUCT PLANNING

A. Market Definition
    i. Market segments
    ii. Customer identification (demographics, titles, units)
    iii. Channels

B. Product Definition
    i. Feature set, functionality, accessories
    ii. Prototypes
    iii. Competitive positioning (comparison, differentiation)

C. Sales Objectives (Revenue, Volume, Margin)
    i. Pricing (trade, discount schedules)
    ii. Cost analysis
    iii. Market share, other measures

III. MARKETING STRATEGIES/TACTICS

A. Branding
    i. Re-branding, Sub-branding
    ii. Naming
    iii. Identity (logo, graphic theme)
    iv. Trademark search, trademark registration, identity standards

B. Internet
    i. Website development, re-development, microsites, landing pages
    ii. Search engine optimization (SEO), search engine marketing (SEM)
    iii. Social media (profiles, followers, blog and forum posts)
    iv. Email campaigns (landing pages, registration forms)
    v. Webcasts, webinars, web conferences

C. Advertising

i. Media (research, planning, placement, traffic)

ii. Print (trade publications)

iii. Online (banners, directories, Google AdWords)

iv. Broadcast (TV, radio)

D. Publicity

i. News releases

ii. Press list

iii. Press kit

iv. Press events

v. Article (writing and placement)

vi. Media relations

vii. Distribution (internet, wire service)

E. Sales Promotion

i. Programs

ii. Training (sales, customer service, customers)

iii. Contests, coupons, sweepstakes

F. Collateral and Content

i. Brochures, product sheets, flyers

ii. Catalogs, manuals, instructions, installation manuals

iii. Educational pieces (white papers, guides, how-tos)

iv. Electronic versions for web, re-purpose above for web

G. Trade Shows and Events (national, international, regional shows, dealer open houses)

i. Exhibit design

ii. Booth graphics

iii. Pre-show promotion

iv. Inquiry management

H. Channel Marketing

i. Dealer or distributor programs

ii. Promotions

iii. Merchandising support, POP, packaging

iv. Training programs

v. Launch kits

vi. Retail line reviews

vii. MDF and Co-Op programs

I. Direct Marketing

i. Direct mail

ii. Database marketing

iii. List procurement, email, webcasts

j. Photography and Video (supports all tactics above)

Pricing for Profit

Successful pricing keeps your business alive and your customers satisfied, and you have several strategies and issues to consider.

Cost-plus pricing bases the selling price on the cost of producing the product plus a markup of your choice. The full cost of producing the product includes materials, labor, packaging, transportation, warehousing, distribution, marketing and any other costs that take your product to the sales floor, explains the University of Tennessee.

The formula for cost-plus pricing is total cost of the product multiplied by 1 plus your desired markup percentage. If you want to make a 50 percent profit on a $10 item, multiply 10 by 1.5 to determine a selling price of $15. The mark-up percent represents the percentage of the product's total cost that is profit.

The gross margin percent, on the other hand, represents the percentage of the selling price that is profit. In the case of your $10 item selling for $15, the profit margin would be $5. Your gross margin percent is the $5 profit margin divided by the selling price of $15, which leaves you with 33 percent.

Pricing can be done using the contribution margin, which is the profit a product makes once its variable costs are considered, according to the Small Business Advancement National Center. Variable costs are those that can fluctuate during a given time or season, such as marketing or transportation.

Calculate the profit margin of a product by subtracting the variable cost of a product from the selling price. The remaining amount must cover the fixed cost of the product and other expenses to keep your business running. If the contribution margin is too low, you can reduce the variable cost of the item or increase its selling price.

Volume pricing encourages a greater number of sales by offering discounts based on the amount of the product that is being purchased. The more people buy, the greater the discount. The more products you move, the greater your profits.

///CMA

PRICING ISSUES

Competitive pricing is a must in a market where undifferentiated products and services exist. Unless your particular product or service demands a higher price for a specific reason, the cheaper price is likely to prevail. Research the market and price your products within a reasonable range.

Managing price increases has its own set of strategies if you want to keep customers satisfied, according to Harvard Business School. You can try reducing the size or variable costs of a product to maintain a lower price. You can also be slow to increase your selling prices if the cost of materials increases and your competitors have already raised their prices accordingly.

Price fixing in any form is illegal, warns the U.S. Department of Justice. Price fixing can be a conspiracy by competing businesses to charge the same price for a given product. It can also take the form of holding prices firm, using a standard formula for calculating prices, having a minimum price schedule or fee and not disclosing or advertising prices. Price fixing includes any number of practices that eliminates or reduces pricing competition.

Unit III: Specialized Construction Channels and Segments

Within the broad construction category, there are both channel marketing alternatives and market segments that have very different marketing requirements and initiatives. So then, TOOLS OF THE TRADE, a book on Construction Marketing Best Practices must consider some of the different types of marketing. We identify two major channel options, the Distributor or Dealer channel, and the Retail channel, along with the A/E/C market segment, or marketing architectural, engineering or construction services. Each is radically different than the next including both marketing mix and marketing skills.

Those using TOOLS OF THE TRADE as the handbook/study guide for the Certified Construction Marketing Professional (CCMP) examination and program are instructed to select one category that most closely fits their marketing scenario.

///CMA

Marketing to Distributors and Related Channels

Most construction product brands that sell to professional construction firms typically sell to distributors. Beside the distributor designation, channel participants might be designated as dealers, wholesalers, jobbers, installers, manufacturers' representatives or brokers.

Distributor channel marketing tactics encompass a variety of activities including partner research, recruitment, retention, training, advisory groups or distributor councils, administration (including reporting) and fulfillment, call center or customer service, CRM and marketing automation, and legal requirements.

Channel promotion encompasses a variety of initiatives including Co-op marketing or market development funds (MDF); contest and sweepstakes; Spiff/Rebate and Trade-in programs; communication, training, certification and support programs; new product or program launch; special packaging or merchandising; event marketing (dealer demos, jobsite visits, entertainment, etc), sale premiums or ad specialties.

SURVEY SAYS

To further understand channel promotion, in 2011 the Construction Marketing Association undertook a national survey, with the following questions:

1. *Does your company/brand use Channel Promotions?*
2. *What type of Channel Promotions do you use for marketing?*
3. *Which Channel Promotions are the most effective?*
4. *Which Channel Promotions are the least effective?*

///CMA

Do you use channel promotions?

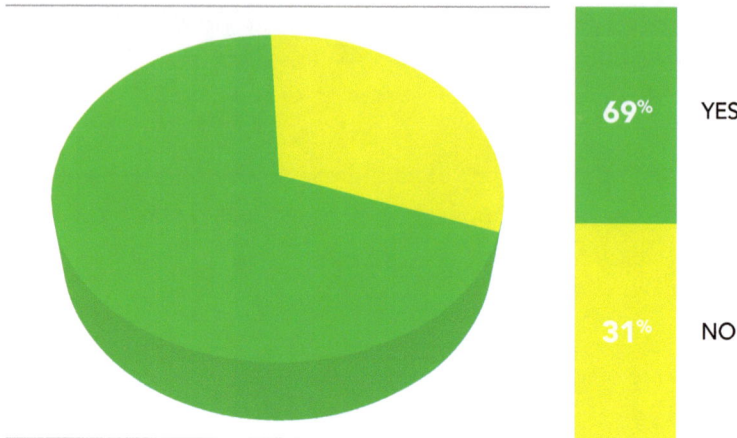

69% YES

31% NO

Types of Channel Promotions Used

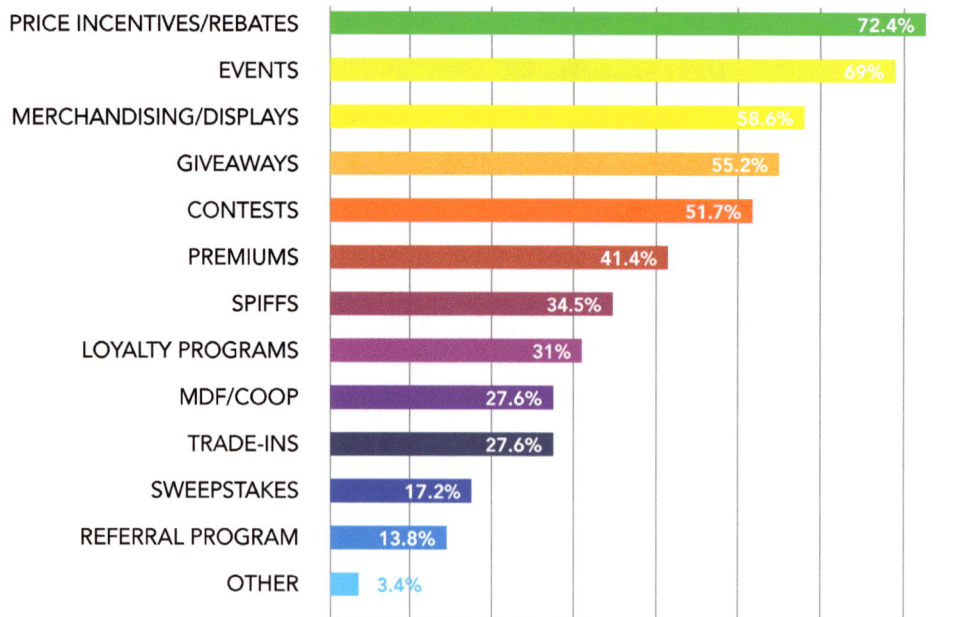

Type	Percentage
PRICE INCENTIVES/REBATES	72.4%
EVENTS	69%
MERCHANDISING/DISPLAYS	58.6%
GIVEAWAYS	55.2%
CONTESTS	51.7%
PREMIUMS	41.4%
SPIFFS	34.5%
LOYALTY PROGRAMS	31%
MDF/COOP	27.6%
TRADE-INS	27.6%
SWEEPSTAKES	17.2%
REFERRAL PROGRAM	13.8%
OTHER	3.4%

Tools of the Trade: Modern Marketing for Construction Brands

Most Effective Promotions

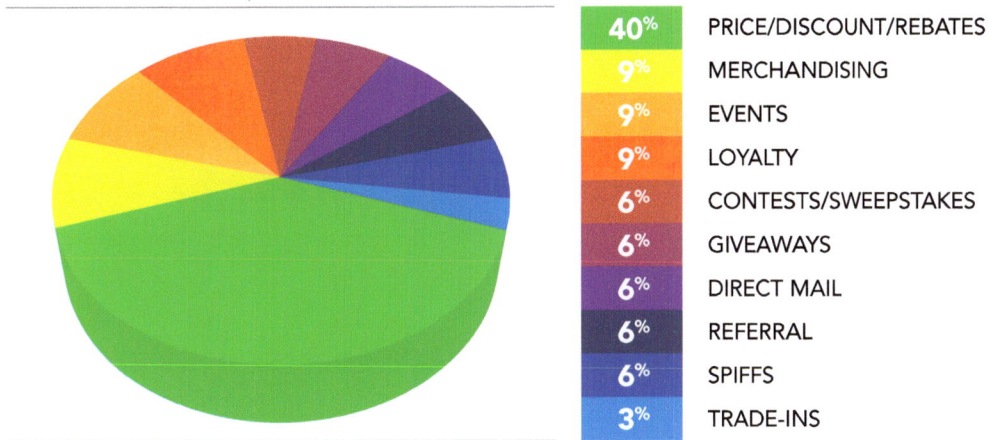

%	Promotion
40%	PRICE/DISCOUNT/REBATES
9%	MERCHANDISING
9%	EVENTS
9%	LOYALTY
6%	CONTESTS/SWEEPSTAKES
6%	GIVEAWAYS
6%	DIRECT MAIL
6%	REFERRAL
6%	SPIFFS
3%	TRADE-INS

Least Effective Promotions

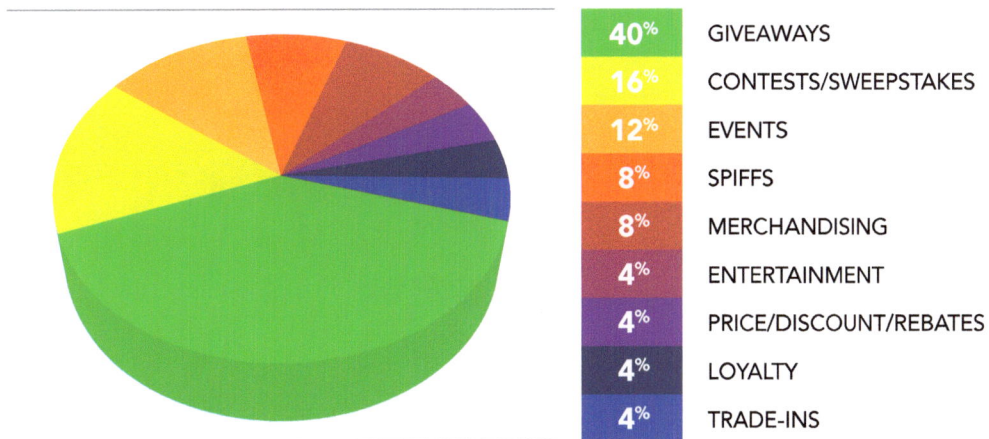

%	Promotion
40%	GIVEAWAYS
16%	CONTESTS/SWEEPSTAKES
12%	EVENTS
8%	SPIFFS
8%	MERCHANDISING
4%	ENTERTAINMENT
4%	PRICE/DISCOUNT/REBATES
4%	LOYALTY
4%	TRADE-INS

CHANNEL SALES POLICIES AND SUPPORT PROGRAMS

Manufacturers (and some services) will enter into Distributor Sales Agreements with channel partners that define pricing, incentives and services. These agreements will be based on a Sales Policy that defines price schedules, price incentives, volume pricing, price rebates and expected services.

Most manufacturers offer distributors and related channel partners price discounts. For example, a manufacturer will publish a suggested retail price, and allow a qualified distributor to purchase the product at a discount based on distributor margin. Typical discounts or margins are 15-50% (ex: large ticket items receive the lower discount). In exchange, the distributor will stock defined quantities of product, and depending on the specific market scenario, may undertake other services like display or end user promotion.

In addition to price discounts, the manufacturer may offer price rebates based on volume, along with cooperative (Co-Op) marketing or market development funds (MDF). These types of programs incentivize the channel partner, or reimburse marketing qualified expenses including advertising.

Distributor support programs may include catalogs and brochures, merchandising displays, promotions, contests and events, and new product information kits. Following is an example of a distributor sales program for Knaack Storage Equipment, called PROVANTAGE. The program includes a printed brochure, merchandising support brochure and website portal.

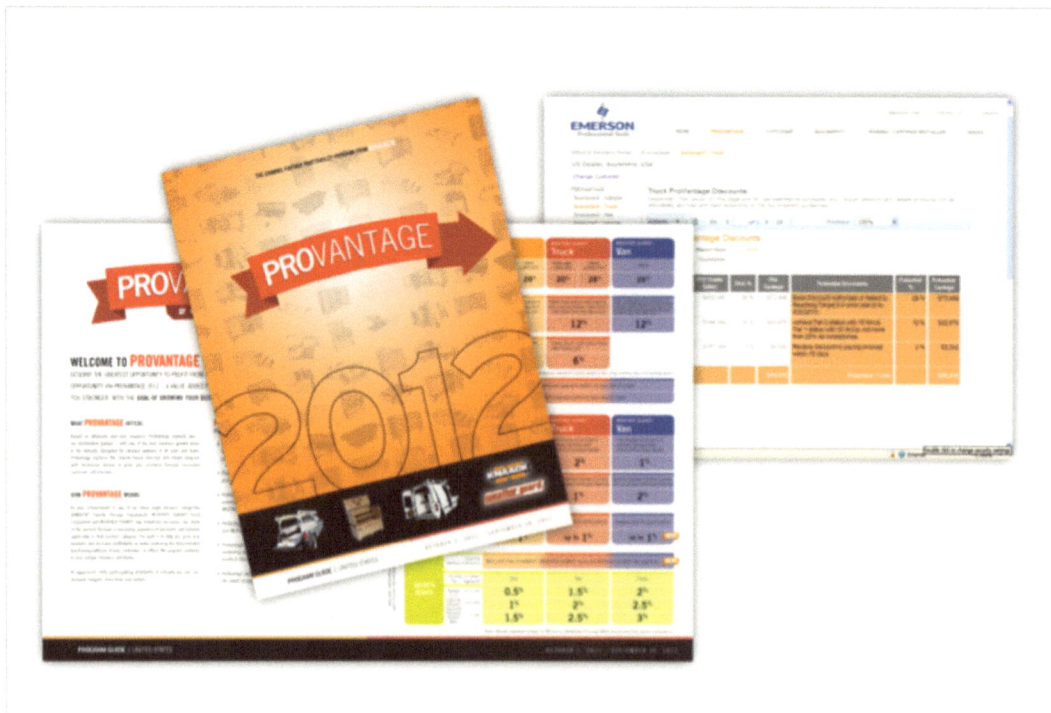

Following is an example of a new product introduction kit for Weather Guard distributors and dealers including brochures (English and Spanish), reinforced envelope with label, DVD video, and die-cut premium, from Construction Marketing Advisors.

Following is an example of a distributor sales promotion for Knaack and Weather Guard from Construction Marketing Advisors.

Following is an example of a distributor merchandising support program for Ideal Industries including showroom banner, counter mat, take-one free sample display, flyer and selection chart, created by Construction Marketing Advisors.

Marketing to Home Improvement Retailers

Home improvement retailers represent a very specialized channel for many types of construction products including building materials and supplies, fixtures, construction tools and equipment and more. In addition, some retailers have substantial professional contractor sales, including rental departments. This chapter will provide an overview of the retail home improvement category, share the results of a survey on retail marketing practices and describe retail merchandising and packaging with many examples. Next, the topics of retail line reviews and retail proprietary brands will be covered.

RETAIL SNAPSHOT

Retail home center and home improvement stores have a combined revenue of $132.54 billion; with overall home improvement channel sales totaling $205.9 billion in 2011. (Source: Home Channel News).

The retail home improvement category consists of several segments including big box home centers like The Home Depot and Lowe's, hardware cooperatives including Ace Hardware and True Value, Lumber and Building Material dealers (LBM's), mass merchants like Walmart and Sears Holdings, and specialty retailers that sell products such as paint, flooring, and farm goods.

The following chart identifies the largest home improvement retailers in North America by number of stores and earnings in 2011 (Source: Home Channel News).

Top Home Improvement Retailers

#	Retailer	Sales ($Mil.) 2011	# Stores 2011
1	Home Depot	$70,395	2248
2	Lowe's	$50,200	1749
3	Walmart*	$19,400	3868
4	Sears Holdings*	$12,200	3510
5	Menards	$8,800	263
6	Shermin-Williams	$4,780	3450
7	Tractor Supply	$4,230	1085
8	ProBuild Holdings	$3,300	439
9	Harbor Freight Tools	$1,650	380
10	84 Lumber	$1,430	258

*Mass Merchants, like Walmart and Sears Holdings, were not included in past rankings. However, they are included today because the influence of these stores on home improvement is so large. Mass merchants generated $33.12 billion in revenue, or about 16% of overall home improvement channel sales in 2011.

A recent survey (2011) on retail marketing practices by the Construction Marketing Association provides insight into this important channel. Following are the survey questions:

1. *What retail channels do you sell to?*
2. *What approximate percentage of sales are retail (vs. non-retail)?*
3. *What types of retail initiatives do you undertake?*
4. *What types of products do you sell to retail?*

Retail Channels Sold To

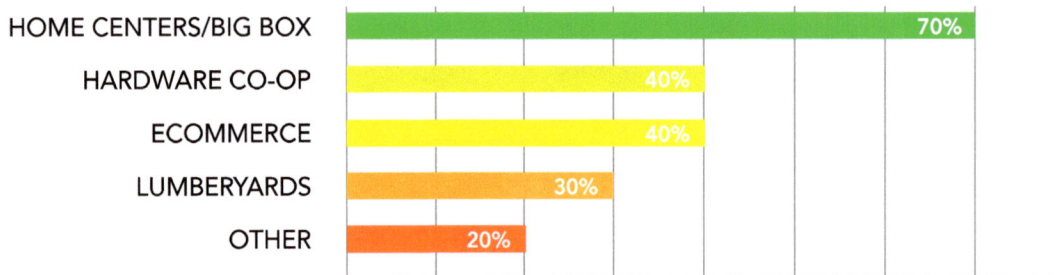

Channel	Percentage
HOME CENTERS/BIG BOX	70%
HARDWARE CO-OP	40%
ECOMMERCE	40%
LUMBERYARDS	30%
OTHER	20%

Percentage of Retail Sales

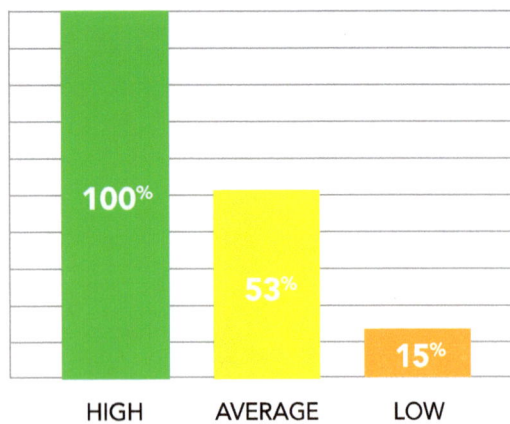

	HIGH	AVERAGE	LOW
	100%	53%	15%

Types of Retail Initiatives

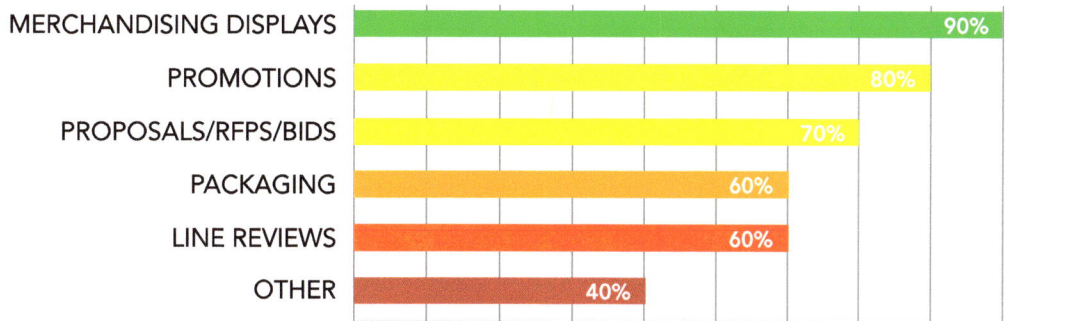

MERCHANDISING DISPLAYS									90%	
PROMOTIONS								80%		
PROPOSALS/RFPS/BIDS							70%			
PACKAGING						60%				
LINE REVIEWS						60%				
OTHER				40%						

Type of Products Sold

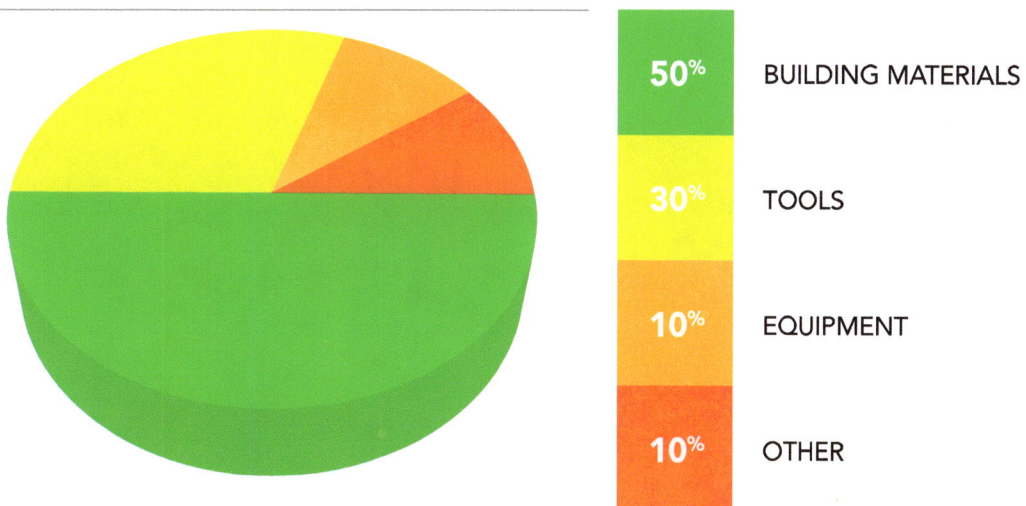

50% BUILDING MATERIALS

30% TOOLS

10% EQUIPMENT

10% OTHER

///CMA

HOME IMPROVEMENT RETAIL MERCHANDISING AND PACKAGING

Merchandising is the visual presentation of products in the store including all types of displays, signage and in-store promotions.

Planograms are used to specify merchandise sets by department and stock keeping unit (SKU), and corresponding point-of-purchase (POP) signage.

Typical merchandise sets include in-line (bays for home centers), end caps and solution centers. Promotional displays include in-aisle stack outs, quarter pallets (QPs), bin merchandisers, clip-strips and various dispensers.

Typical POP signage includes channel headers and posters, laminated how-to instructions, shelf-talkers, banners, ceiling danglers, or floor decals. Each retailer has departments and guidelines. Sometimes a retailer will appoint a category captain to oversee category management. Following is an example of category management for The Home Depot "Tool Corral".

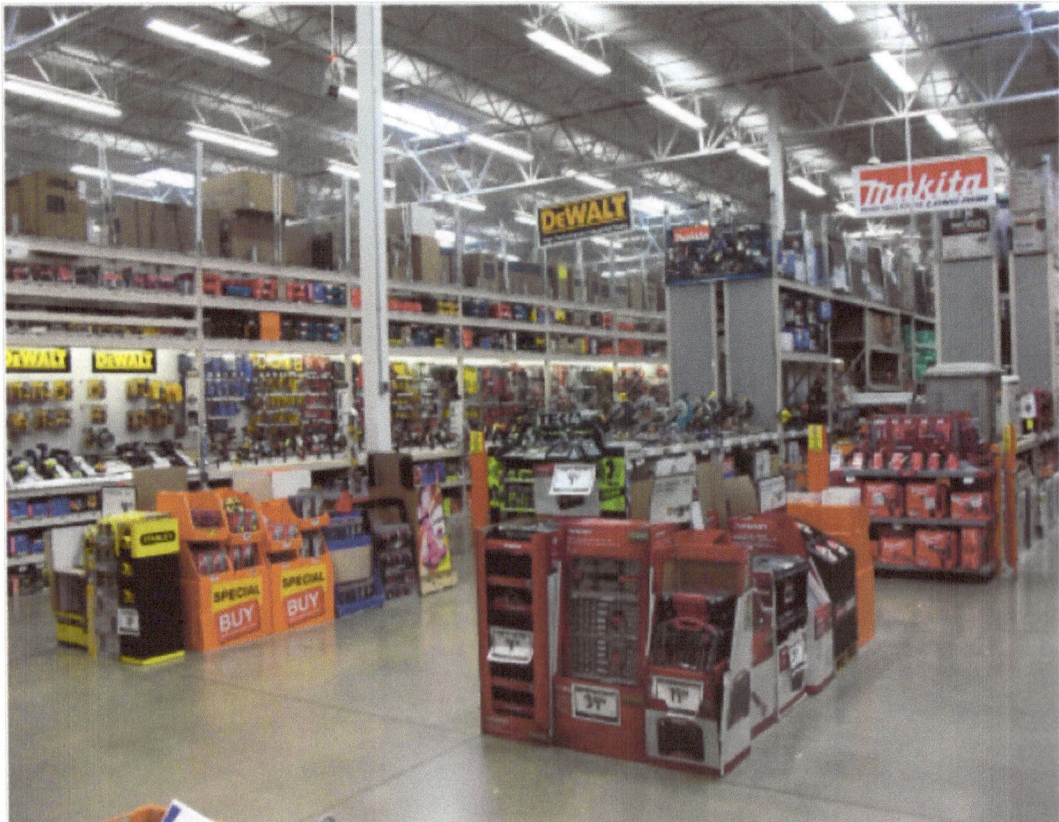

Tools of the Trade: Modern Marketing for Construction Brands

Following is an example of category management for Lowe's tool department, or "Tool World".

Following is an example of a category management planogram for power tool accessories from Vermont American.

Following is an example of a merchandising planogram brochure for hardware chain Do it Best from National Div. Stanley, created by Construction Marketing Advisors.

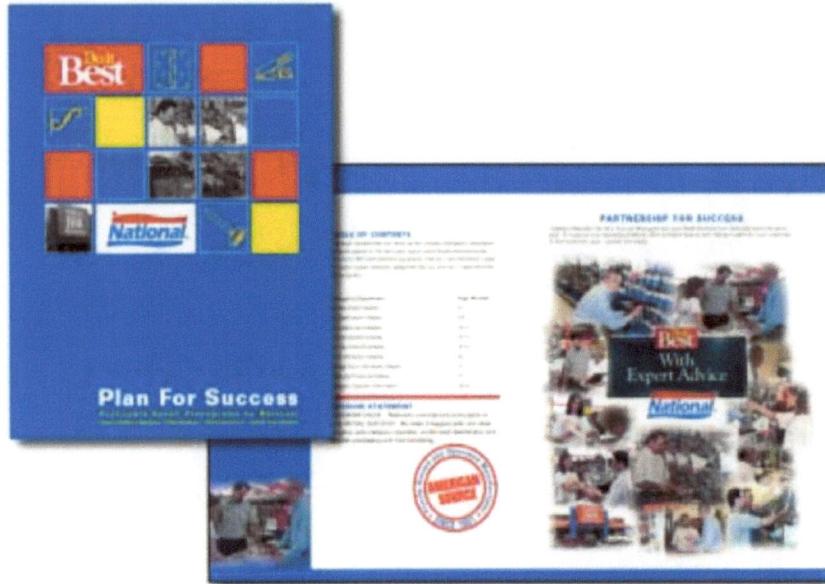

Following is an example of a category management planogram for RIDGID jobsite and truck storage equipment by Construction Marketing Advisors.

Tools of the Trade: Modern Marketing for Construction Brands

Following is an example of a Home Depot end cap with quarter palette display, and "conversion cart" portable display.

Following is an example of a Home Depot clip-strip display, and a gravity-fed display.

HOME IMPROVEMENT RETAIL PACKAGING

Each retailer will have packaging requirements related to bi-lingual or tri-lingual, bar codes, and for some products, security strips (Sensormatic). Following are several examples of home improvement packaging including blister card packaging for Ideal Industries, Bosch and Vermont American.

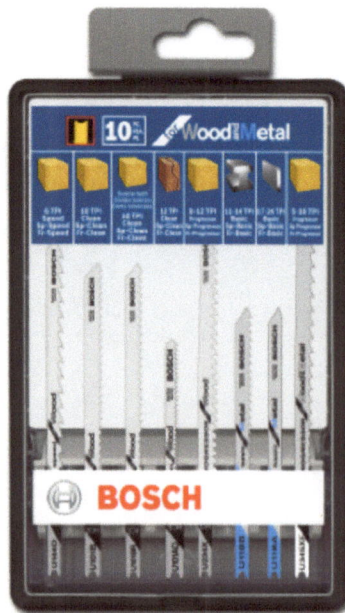

RETAIL LINE REVIEWS

Retailers continually evaluate their vendors and merchandising mix with point-of-sale (POS) data, margin analysis and supplier performance (fill-rate 95%+, inventory turns, sales per square foot).

Depending on the product category and/or department, line reviews are typically 1-year contracts, but could be up to 3-5 years. For certain product categories or departments, the retailer will hold online price auctions.

The key product/category supplier is often appointed category captain and may be responsible for promotion and merchandising support. This incumbent supplier must continually defend their business.

Depending on the product category, a retailer will often seek one or more national or pro brands, and a price brand, which often is a proprietary (house or private label) brand. Some line review trends to consider:

> *Retailers focused on SKU rationalization and vendor consolidation*
> *Retailers are requesting more frequent line reviews, and demanding more support*
> *Note that home center retailers seek pro contractor business; likewise seek pro contractor brands*

A challenger brand (not in the retailer) can win placements with special promotions

> *Approach differs based on narrow or broad line supplier*
> *Identify the department or category merchant and pitch*
> *Provide market intelligence (share, equity, brand support)*
> *Hardware co-op is different; pitch individual stores, as well as corporate buyers*

Incumbent suppliers and challenger brands can defend or gain placement with home center retailers through proactive merchandising and/or promotional support. Following are examples. Below is an example of advertising flyers or circulars for both Lowe's and The Home Dept from USG, by Construction Marketing Advisors.

///CMA

Following is an example of a bi-lingual free-standing insert (FSI) announcing a promotion, (buy a truck box get a free vacuum cleaner), in support of a merchandising display placement for Ridgid Truck storage.

PROPRIETARY RETAIL BRANDS

Power retailers in the home center channel are becoming increasingly active in developing brands, and dictating manufacturers' branding initiatives, from packaging and merchandising, to even product assortment. They are demanding custom or retailer-specific packaging and/or merchandising from manufacturers. At the same time, power retailers are launching retailer "proprietary" brands, or appointing and sometimes sponsoring new category brands. In some categories, consumer and contractor brands are appointed.

Home Depot Category Management

The Home Depot has instituted a long-term strategy to focus entire product categories on one or more national brands, along with a corresponding "price" brand, that is often a retailer proprietary brand. With a full-time buying office in China, Home Depot has openly stated an objective to source 15% of its products from China.

As an example, in outdoor lighting, Home Depot offers Malibu lighting, with a large dedicated display and seasonally, in-aisle pallet stacks. Directly adjacent to Malibu is the Home Depot brand, Hampton Bay, with a similar packaging design.

In the hand tool category, Husky and WorkForce are Home Depot sponsored and proprietary brands respectively. In power tools, Black & Decker is the appointed consumer brand, while DeWalt and Ryobi are contractor brands. Recently, Home Depot sponsored Rigid Tools as a "contractor brand", even though Rigid was known for plumbing tools. With Home Depot sponsorship, Rigid entered the general power tool market with drills, saws and other lines. Tool merchandising is closely coordinated in the "Tool Corral" with signage, displays and promotions.

Lowe's Knows Merchandising

Across the street (literally in many markets), Lowe's is demanding (during line reviews) that manufacturers provide packaging that can only be used with Lowe's, so called custom or retailer-specific merchandising, in order to differentiate from competitors. Lowe's will request merchandising tools and support for the higher percentage female shopper. Note that such costs are absorbed by the manufacturer.

For a recent line review, Intermatic submitted custom packaging and merchandising for it's timers to Lowe's. The strategy helped to displace a competitor and secure the contract, but the packaging cannot be supplied to other retailers. On the following page is an example of Intermatic's custom packaging for Lowe's from Construction Marketing Advisors. Note lifestyle imagery, color coding and simplified icons with application information.

///CMA

For outdoor lighting, Lowe's considered sourcing and proprietary branding, but in yet another twist, opted for custom branding from electrical products brand Intermatic, with a brand extension Malibu Manchester, coupled with unique fixtures and packaging. Lowe's continually evolves its merchandising strategy and is widely emulated in the industry. Lowe's merchandising options for manufacturers are becoming increasingly stringent.

Uncooperative Co-Ops

The largest co-op hardware network, Ace, uses a similar strategy to Home Depot, typically pairing a national brand with an Ace-branded product. Ace corporate offers margin incentives and promotional assistance for stocking Ace brands. Like Home Depot, Ace employs a buying office in China, and aggressively promotes Ace- branded products.

Manufacturers Must Be Proactive

To succeed in today's power retailer environment, manufacturers must be proactive, and continually build their brands, deliver new innovations, while maintaining 98% fill rates and steady margins.

Manufacturers must work closely with power retailers, and actively participate in category management initiatives. At point-of-sale, the most visible aspects of branding are packaging and merchandising. Only effective brands will stave the threat of retailer proprietary or sponsored brands.

Marketing Architectural/Engineering/Construction (A/E/C) Services

Architectural, engineering and/or construction (A/E/C) firm's marketing is very different than other types of marketing—it certainly does not have much in common with distributor channel marketing or home improvement retail marketing.

How? First, A/E/C marketers target owners or managers of public or private construction projects. The focus of marketing is lead generation and winning projects. Relationships and reputation are critical in A/E/C marketing as the financial risk of construction projects is great.

No question, A/E/C marketing is becoming more competitive with lower construction activity, and new (competitor) entrants. A/E/C marketing includes all aspects of marketing, with different emphasis than other industries. This chapter will share the results of a national survey conducted by the Construction Marketing Association, along with information on two important aspects of A/E/C marketing: using construction lead services and leveraging associations for networking. Finally, to summarize, a Top 10 A/E/C Marketing Best Practices is presented.

Survey Says
1. What types of marketing does your A/E/C firm use?
2. What marketing initiatives are most effective?
3. What marketing initiatives are least effective?
4. How do you measure marketing?

Types of Marketing Used

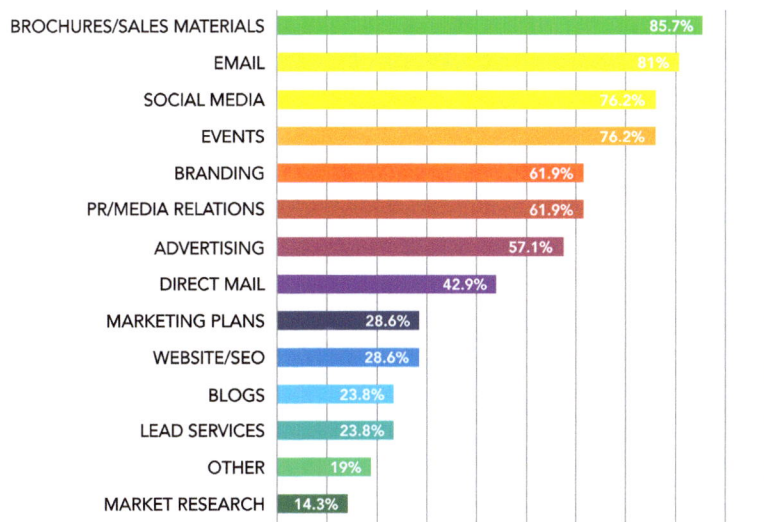

Type	Percentage
BROCHURES/SALES MATERIALS	85.7%
EMAIL	81%
SOCIAL MEDIA	76.2%
EVENTS	76.2%
BRANDING	61.9%
PR/MEDIA RELATIONS	61.9%
ADVERTISING	57.1%
DIRECT MAIL	42.9%
MARKETING PLANS	28.6%
WEBSITE/SEO	28.6%
BLOGS	23.8%
LEAD SERVICES	23.8%
OTHER	19%
MARKET RESEARCH	14.3%

Most Effective Initiatives

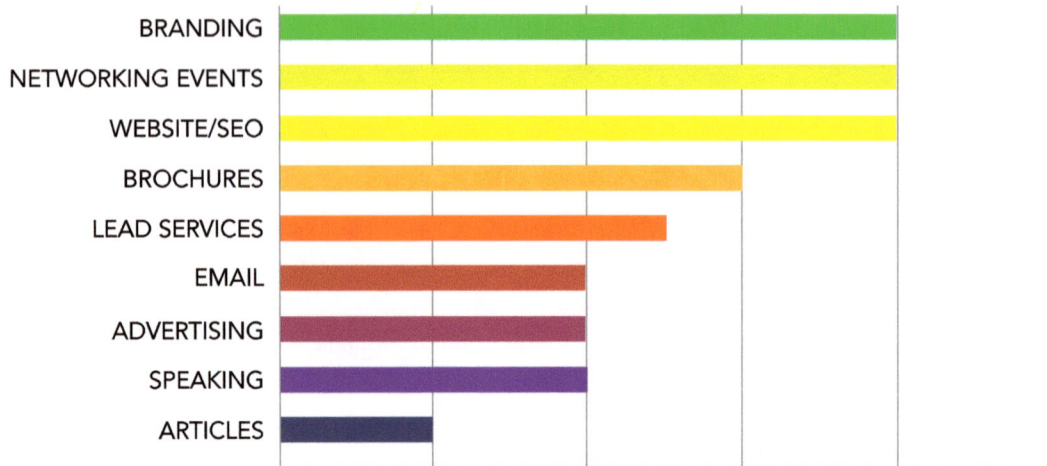

Initiative	
BRANDING	
NETWORKING EVENTS	
WEBSITE/SEO	
BROCHURES	
LEAD SERVICES	
EMAIL	
ADVERTISING	
SPEAKING	
ARTICLES	

Least Effective Initiatives

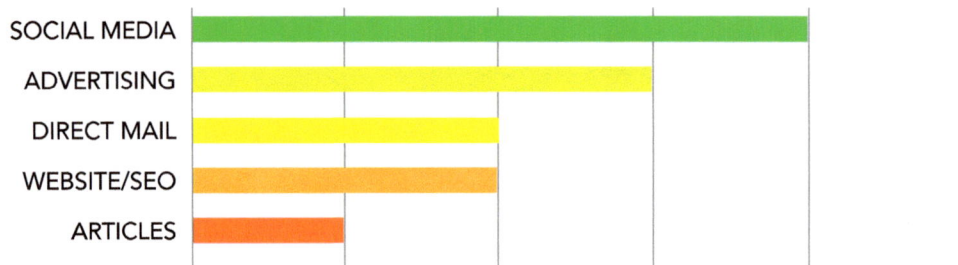

Initiative	
SOCIAL MEDIA	
ADVERTISING	
DIRECT MAIL	
WEBSITE/SEO	
ARTICLES	

How Do You Measure Marketing?

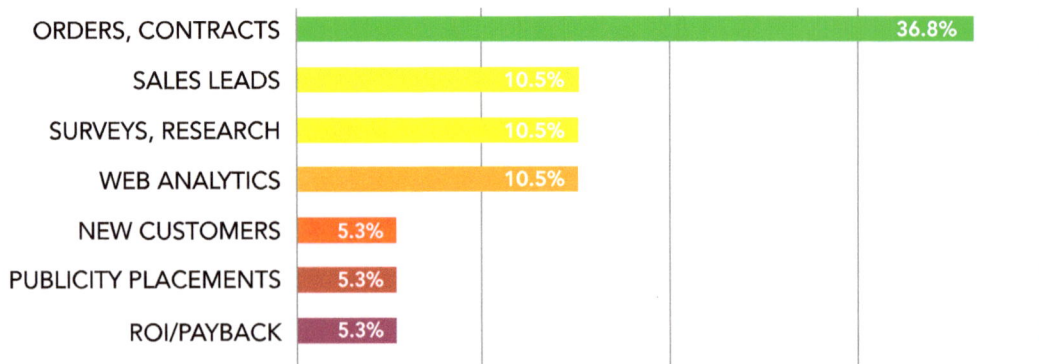

Measure	Percentage
ORDERS, CONTRACTS	36.8%
SALES LEADS	10.5%
SURVEYS, RESEARCH	10.5%
WEB ANALYTICS	10.5%
NEW CUSTOMERS	5.3%
PUBLICITY PLACEMENTS	5.3%
ROI/PAYBACK	5.3%

LEAD GENERATION IS TOP PRIORITY

With both commercial and residential construction down by 50% in many markets from pre-recession highs, sales lead generation has never been more important to marketers targeting construction decision makers, whether construction firms or building product manufacturers. This fact is reinforced by a recent Construction Marketing Association survey—2011 Construction Marketing Outlook—which ranked Lead Generation as one of the top priorities for next year.

So to understand where construction marketers are with lead generation—a baseline—we conducted another survey and share the results here, along with some checklists of key lead generation types.

Next, we evaluate the two largest lead services in the construction market—McGraw-Hill Dodge Reports and Reed Construction Data. Finally, we identify several other construction lead sources that tend to specialize in regions or types of construction project or service offerings.

Survey Says

A recent (November 2010) survey about lead generation in construction conducted by the Construction Marketing Association via SurveyMonkey posed the following questions:

1. *What lead generation techniques or sources do you use in marketing to the construction industry?*
2. *Which lead generation technique/source has shown the best results for your company?*
3. *Which lead generation technique/source has shown the worst results for your company?*
4. *Which lead generation technique/source do you foresee using more in the future?*
5. *What type of company are you?*

Lead Generation Techniques

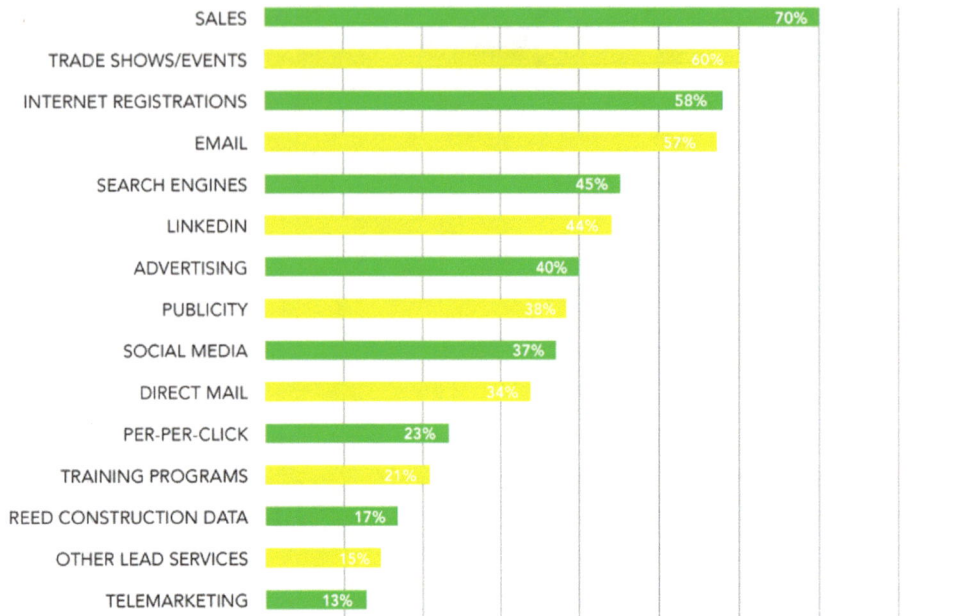

Technique	Percentage
SALES	70%
TRADE SHOWS/EVENTS	60%
INTERNET REGISTRATIONS	58%
EMAIL	57%
SEARCH ENGINES	45%
LINKEDIN	44%
ADVERTISING	40%
PUBLICITY	38%
SOCIAL MEDIA	37%
DIRECT MAIL	34%
PER-PER-CLICK	23%
TRAINING PROGRAMS	21%
REED CONSTRUCTION DATA	17%
OTHER LEAD SERVICES	15%
TELEMARKETING	13%

Regarding the types of lead generation techniques/sources used, Sales Prospecting ranked highest with 70% of respondents using, followed by Trade Shows/Events (60%), Internet Registrations (58%), Email (57%), Search Engines (45%), LinkedIn (44%), Advertising (40%), Publicity (38%), Social Media (37%), Direct Mail (34%), Per-Per-Click (PPC, 23%), Training Programs (21%), Reed Construction Data (17%), other Lead Services (15%), and Telemarketing (13%). Dodge Reports, Networking via associations and Referrals tied at 11%. Specification services like ARCAT, CSI and e-specs were used by 4% of respondents.

Best Results – Lead Generation

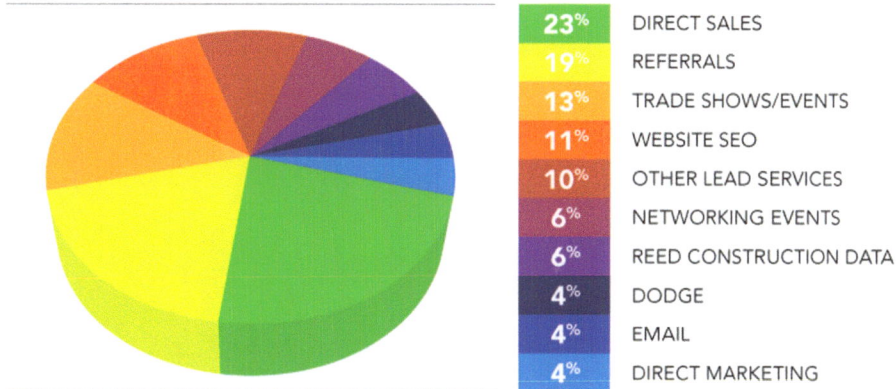

23%	DIRECT SALES
19%	REFERRALS
13%	TRADE SHOWS/EVENTS
11%	WEBSITE SEO
10%	OTHER LEAD SERVICES
6%	NETWORKING EVENTS
6%	REED CONSTRUCTION DATA
4%	DODGE
4%	EMAIL
4%	DIRECT MARKETING

Regarding which lead generation technique/source has shown the best results for your company, Direct Sales ranked highest at 23%, followed by Referrals (19%), Trade Shows (13%), and Website SEO (11%). Networking events and Reed Construction Data tied at 6%, followed by Dodge, other Lead Services, Email and Direct Marketing at 4%. Other mentions included Telemarketing, PPC, Jobsite Visits, LinkedIn and Channel Promotions at 2%.

Worst Results – Lead Generation

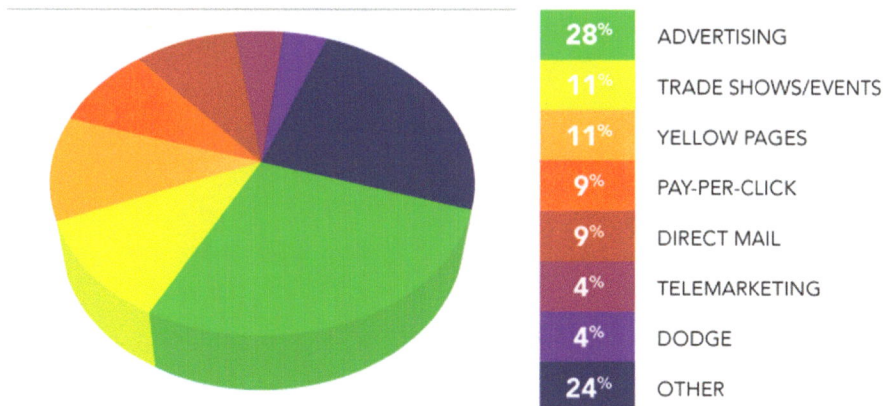

28%	ADVERTISING
11%	TRADE SHOWS/EVENTS
11%	YELLOW PAGES
9%	PAY-PER-CLICK
9%	DIRECT MAIL
4%	TELEMARKETING
4%	DODGE
24%	OTHER

Regarding which lead generation technique/source has shown the worst results for your company, Advertising led all at 28%, followed by Trade Shows and Yellow Pages at 11%; Pay-Per-Click and Direct Mail at 9%. Telemarketing and Dodge Reports followed with 4% of mentions.

Use More – Lead Generation

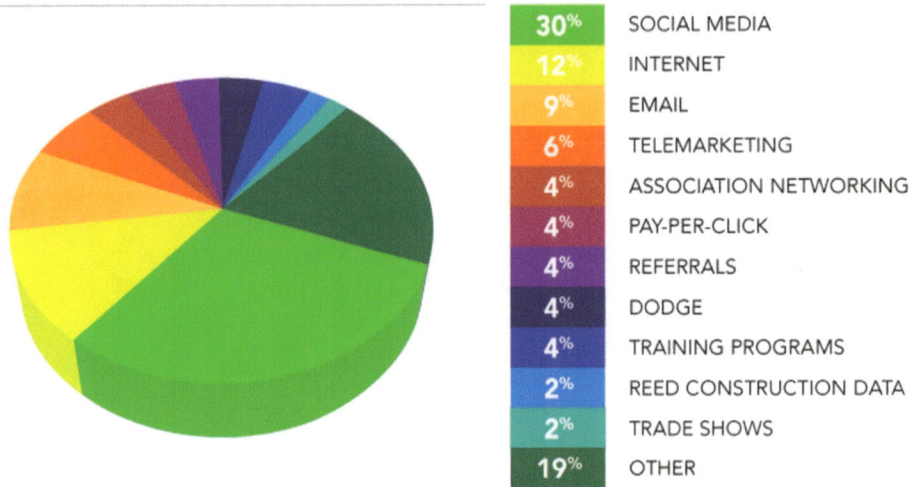

%	Category
30%	SOCIAL MEDIA
12%	INTERNET
9%	EMAIL
6%	TELEMARKETING
4%	ASSOCIATION NETWORKING
4%	PAY-PER-CLICK
4%	REFERRALS
4%	DODGE
4%	TRAINING PROGRAMS
2%	REED CONSTRUCTION DATA
2%	TRADE SHOWS
19%	OTHER

Regarding which lead generation technique/source do you foresee using more in the future, not surprisingly Social Media led all at 30%, followed by Internet (12%), Email (9%), Telemarketing (6%); Association Networking, PPC, Referrals, Dodge, and Training Programs and tied at 4% each. Reed Construction Data and Trade Shows follow at 2%.

Industry Classification

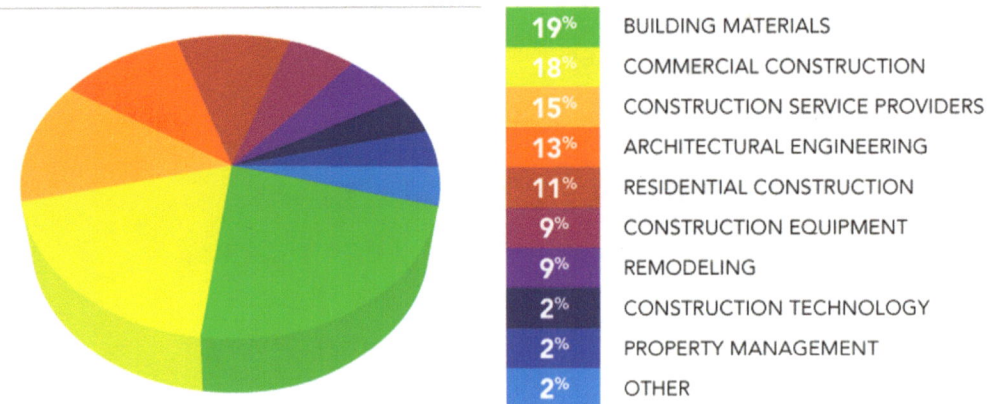

%	Category
19%	BUILDING MATERIALS
18%	COMMERCIAL CONSTRUCTION
15%	CONSTRUCTION SERVICE PROVIDERS
13%	ARCHITECTURAL ENGINEERING
11%	RESIDENTIAL CONSTRUCTION
9%	CONSTRUCTION EQUIPMENT
9%	REMODELING
2%	CONSTRUCTION TECHNOLOGY
2%	PROPERTY MANAGEMENT
2%	OTHER

Regarding type of company, 19% of respondents were building materials (manufacturers or suppliers), followed by 18% commercial construction, 15% construction service providers, 13% architectural engineering, 11% residential construction, 9% for both construction equipment and remodeling, and 2% construction technology or property management.

SO MANY LEADS, SO LITTLE TIME

So what are the sources and types of sales leads? A 2011 Construction Marketing Association webcast, Measuring Marketing Results – Best Practices for Construction identified over 70 types of marketing measures, many of which are sources or types of leads that fall into such categories as traditional, internet and social media. Following are many sources of leads by category.

Traditional Lead Sources

Direct mail/Email lists
Online databases (e.g. D&B)
Customer service telephone surveys
Outbound telemarketing
CRM systems
Customer database entries
Trade show card readers
Trade show registration lists
Association member lists
Association events
Trade print advertising reader response
Secondary market research (published, publicly available, e.g., internet)
Primary market research
Syndicated market research (similar to Lead Services)

Internet Lead Sources

Website registrations
Contact/Conversion Forms
RSS registrations (typically email address)
Pay-Per-Click (PPC, SEM, e.g., Google Adwords)
Web Reverse IP Address Services (Lead Advantage, Leadlander)
Google Alerts
Urchin Tracking Modules (UTMs)
Email service provider reports

Social Media Lead Sources

LinkedIn Connections (email addresses, InMail)
LinkedIn Groups (post discussions, offers)
LinkedIn Companies
Facebook Friends, Fans, Groups, Likes
Twitter Followers
YouTube Subscribers
WeFollow.com
URL Shortener (e.g. Bit.ly offers tracking)
Bookmarking (e.g. Digg, Delicious, StumbleUpon)
Radian6 (identify bloggers, etc)

///CMA

CONSTRUCTION-SPECIFIC LEAD SERVICES
The Big Dog Lead Generators: McGraw-Hill Construction Dodge Reports and Reed Construction Data

By Paul Deffenbaugh

I recently investigated the project lead generation programs of two service providers for a large manufacturer in the northern Midwest. The company wants to provide leads to its sales force so that its product can be specified in commercial construction projects at an earlier stage. The goal is to get in at the planning, not bid stage to take the competitor out of the equation. I thought I would share what I learned about McGraw-Hill Construction Dodge Reports (Dodge) and Reed Construction Data (RCD), the two largest lead generators in this area. Most of this information is readily available from their websites or by talking with sales representatives, but I also interviewed a couple of people who had used both systems. It's hard to assess these services because access to the databases is highly restricted – and rightly so.

During my research, I found that surprisingly, there was an incredible lack of real information about these providers. With most products or services, you can go online and find someone has done a comparative review and other users have posted comments to flesh out the information. The only real source of information about these services are from Dodge (dodge.construction. com) and RCD (reedconstructiondata.com) themselves. For any person doing an analysis, those are hardly reliable sources of information. I have heard, however, of individual companies that have done extensive testing of both services. One company completed a 200-page analysis for its internal use. The manufacturer I represented may choose to take that next step.

First, a disclaimer. I worked at Reed Business Information, which owns RCD, as editorial director for the residential construction media. During a few months of my tenure, my group reported up to RCD. I sat in on meetings with RCD, but I can honestly state that no information I learned from those meetings – if I could even remember it – is included in this report.

How they work.

The most difficult aspect of generating my report was identifying true points of differentiation. For the most part, Dodge and RCD operate in the same manner and provide the same services, although they compete quite viciously. (More on this later. See the subhead, "Tough Competitors.)

Both providers pull much of their data from public sources. By law, public projects and many private projects must be advertised. With that information, the services can identify architects, building owners, municipalities, engineering firms, planners and other groups that are planning or putting out to bid commercial projects. The quality of the data is entirely dependent on the relationship with those people preparing the work. Both Dodge and RCD offer incentives to their providers to make it worth their effort to report the data, such as giving them free access to the database.

Dodge has a long-term relationship with Associated General Contractors (AGC), which enables their reporting. RCD has a new partnership with American Institute of Architects (AIA) and leverages the work it's subsidiary, RSMeans, does in gathering cost information.

The companies gather this information by employing phone banks of researchers who call their sources to get updates on projects, secure plans, and identify new projects coming down the pipeline. All that data, combined with plans, goes into a massive database, which is organized by project. The database is highly searchable and deep with information. Here are some of the kinds of data that are included in these projects.

- *Planning stage, such as proposed, architect selection, schematics, bid stage, etc.*
- *Category, such as commercial, industrial, etc.; both of those will have subcategories; for commercial it may include medical offices, retail,parking garages, etc.*
- *Type of work, such as new construction or addition*
- *Contract type*
- *Location*
- *Company information for planners, general contractors, major trades, etc.*
- *Materials specified including company names and models if appropriate*
- *Value of the project and often value of major subcontracts*

Both companies provide an online interface that gives users access to the databases so they can query for their particular needs. And both companies provide written reports based on selection criteria that are delivered to your company. Pricing is the major motivation for restricting selections, since few companies can afford the cost of full access -- or have the need for all the leads. Generally, leads can be coordinated in one of three ways.

1. *Both Dodge and RCD will link the leads they provide with a proprietary customer relationship management (CRM) software for an individual company*
2. *Deliver the leads to a lead manager*
3. *Distribute leads directly to sales people*

In addition, both Dodge and RCD are leveraging the strength of these services to build other businesses, such as consulting, costing data, economic data, and more. For our purposes, we are looking only at lead generation services for building product manufacturers.

Vital Statistics, Differentiation and Pricing
It should be clear by this point that the differentiation between Dodge and RCD is obscure at best, especially to outsiders. In conversation with sales representatives for both companies and users, I asked this very specific question.

Both companies provide deep information on a great breadth of projects. My user sources tell me that the differentiation often comes within particular material areas. One service may be better for interior decorative products while the other has a stronger electrical product information base. The type of differences may vary from the types of products to the company names included, which would be essential if you are searching for competitors.
McGraw Hill Dodge Reports Reed Construction Data

Vital Statistics

Company Name	McGraw Hill Dodge Reports	Reed Construction Data
Year Founded	1903	1975
Markets Served	US and Canada	US and Canada
Headquarters	New York	Norcross, Ga.
Online Interface	McGraw-Hill Construction Network	Reed Connect
Print Reports	Dodge Reports	Reed Bulletin

RCD claims to have a stronger group of reporters on private projects. Their claimed strength is built on the back of RSMeans, which is a company that gathers unit costs for building product materials all around the world and has significant interaction with architects who specify those products. RCD uses that information and those relationships to update their information on the harder-to-identify private construction projects.

Both companies quietly admit that their civil and public databases are nearly redundant. The reason is simple. Because, by law those projects must be advertised, finding them is quite simple. In addition, the companies are close on their pricing, which is loosely based on a cost per lead. The best example for pricing that I could find was that RCD's fully-loaded database would run a company about $60,000 per year. (I'm sure that could go higher if the company were to download more leads, but the governing factor may be not how many leads you can capture, but how many you can handle.)

RCD recently debuted a new interactive program called SmartSpecs (www.smartprojectnews.com), which aims to make the interface for a company more focused and deliver leads quicker and more easily. The same company with this lead program could see a fee of approximately $12,000 per year. Entry fee for the service comes in at $110 per month. Dodge does the same kind of thing through their hands-on customer service, which they claim as a huge differentiator. By using what they call TargetLeads to pinpoint references and carefully selected keywords, they can bring the costs of lead generation down considerably. As a rule, of course, the cost per lead remains constant. The savings comes in the number of leads and their quality.

Dodge also prices reports on a 10 and 20-pack basis. For $59 per month, you can get 10 reports covering 2 geographic regions that provide the main details of a project. The 20-pack version costs $79 per month.

RCD has similar kinds of reports at similar costs. These should not be compared to having access to the database, which you can query. That is a much more robust approach that gives greater control and deeper information to the user.

Tough Competitors

RCD and Dodge have been fighting head to head since 1975, when RCD was founded. (The company was originally called Construction Market Data, but Reed Business Information purchased it in May 2000 and changed the name.) Recently, the battle on the commerce field moved to the court system.

In October 2009, RCD filed suit in federal court, accusing Dodge of 11 counts of misconduct, which includes corporate espionage. The basis for the suit is the claim that Dodge used subterfuge and false companies to steal RCD's trade secrets.

In October 2010, RCD put out a press release stating Dodge admitted in court that it paid others to access the RCD database, which is supposed to be available only to customers. The company also claims Dodge shared what it learned with its sales staff. Dodge responded by denying it has unlawfully accessed RCD's trade secrets or shared them. They counterclaim that RCD itself hired a consultant to access the Dodge database.

This is pretty good spectator sport, and the stakes are high. In October, a judge dismissed three of the counts, but 8 remain. At this writing, the suit has not gone to trial, and the outcome is still up in the air.

Final Word on the Big Dogs

For manufacturers looking to increase their leads in this tough economy, Dodge and RCD provide great services. Selecting between them is difficult. From the outside, their services are more similar than dissimilar and border on being commodities. When you differentiate yourself on the quality of your reports and the level of your service, which is easily duplicated by a well-funded competitor, you find yourself battling for inches rather than acreage.

On the inside, the user experience will be different for each company. Those firms that have signed on to one service, without testing the other, are doing themselves a disservice. The other might be better suited to your needs, but you won't know until you try it. And that's the problem.

Would you really want to switch lead generating services (or add a duplicate service) at a time when you're desperately trying to control costs? The company I'm working with will now step in and do individual trials with each service to see which is the best suited for them.

Other National Lead Services

BidClerk.com
http://www.bidclerk.com/index.html

Free listing; $69.95/month for all leads ($59.95 for 12 months); public project focus although list private and residential; limited project detail

TheBlueBook.com
http://thebluebook.com/

Free listing; covers top metros; various advertising levels determines lead invites; integrated bidding services; affiliated with Dodge Reports

ConstructionWire.com
http://www.constructionwire.com/

BuildCentral brand name; claim 194,000 projects with focus on private and commercial

NationalContractors.com
http://www.nationalcontractors.com/membership.htm

Commercial and residential, Federal and State; starting at $24.99/month; directory

Regional Lead Services

CDCnews.com
http://cdcnews.com/

Construction Data Corporation; commercial project focus; Eastern (US) seaboard, Texas, Michigan; offers free trial

Construction Information Systems
http://www.cisleads.com/

Northeast focus (NY, NJ, CT, PA, DE); public and private sectors; source directory

ConstructionJournal.com
http://constructionjournal.com/

Eastern seaboard; public and private projects; offers free trial

ConstructionLeadJournal.com
http://www.constructionleadjournal.com/

Western US incl. CA, AZ, NV, CO, UT, WA, OR; weekly project list from $84/month for county or metro

iSqFt.com
http://isqft.com/

Partner with AGC (Associated General Contractors of America) for local coverage; SupplyLink LEADS for BPMs; regions incl. North Central, Southwest region, Rocky Mountain region, Oklahoma; integrated bidding and project management

AECleads.com
http://www.aecleads.com/

California; public projects

CNCnewsonline.com
http://www.cncnewsonline.com/

Michigan and Ohio; planning room, CSI specs

Tools of the Trade: Modern Marketing for Construction Brands

Residential Contractor/Remodeler/Handyman Lead Services

ServiceMagic.com
http://www.servicemagic.com/

$99 enrollment fee; $7-55 per lead depend on size; non-exclusive distribution

HandyAmerican.com
http://www.handyamerican.com/

Free listing; $29.95/month all leads with bid capabilities; consumer reviews

ConstructionWork.com
http://www.constructionwork.com/

Free listing; $39-$399/month lead reports; directory; banner ads, RFQs, etc.

Yodle.com
http://www.yodle.com/

Manage websites and online marketing for small contractors; $69 monthly fee with $447 website set-up; advertising options

ContractorLeads.com
http://www.contractorleads.com/

Residential construction and remodeling; manage internet, direct mail and advertising for monthly fee

Angie's List
http://www.angieslist.com/angieslist/

Consumers pay membership fee; ratings of home services rank high in search; paid advertising options

Government Projects

Onvia.com
http://www.onvia.com/

Database of government projects in US and Canada for 89,000 agencies; industry solutions for architectural engineering and construction supplies

BidSync.com
http://www.bidsync.com/

Electronic bidding software; claim 70,000 public government agencies

FBO.gov
http://www.fbo.gov/

Federal Business Opportunities including construction projects

Other Lead Services

Equipment Data Associates
http://www.edadata.com/

Equipment lease database of UCC filings; used by construction equipment and capital equipment manufacturers and suppliers

ARCAT.com
http://www.arcat.com/

Manufacturers directory and architectural product specifications; target architects and engineers

Sweets Network
http://products.construction.com/

Catalog and directory of architectural products and specifications from McGraw-Hill Construction

Leads Smeads. What Should I Do Now?

Sales Leads in the construction category are no simple tactic. There are many options for generating sales leads or purchasing sales leads from one or more services. Construction firms tend toward the latter (purchase), and may integrate with bidding and related services. Building product manufacturers will likely use a combination of sources, from traditional, Internet and social, to purchased leads if their products are specified by architects or engineers. With construction project activity at historical lows, there is no question the sales lead generation is more important than ever. Likewise, what you do with sales leads, lead management and measurement, becomes just as important. The holy grail is tracing a sales lead to a sale and measuring financial return on investment, which can be difficult due to long sales cycles, or channels of distribution.

ABOUT PAUL DEFFENBAUGH

Paul Deffenbaugh is Chief Content Officer of Deep Brook Media, which develops content and strategies for leading construction brands. With more than 20 years in the residential construction, his background includes editorial director for the Residential Construction Group at Reed Business Information for Professional Builder, Professional Remodeler, Custom Builder, Housing Giants, and HousingZone.com. In addition, Paul was co-founder of the Remodeler's Guild, a national remodeling company. Deffenbaugh has appeared on CNBC, Wall Street Reports, and CBS This Morning. He is a three-time winner and five-time finalist of the coveted Jesse H. Neal Award for editorial excellence, and has been recognized by the American Society of Business Publication Editors and the National Association of Real Estate Editors. Paul earned a degree in Philosophy from Wabash College in Crawfordsville, Ind. and has a Master of Fine Arts in creative writing from George Mason University in Fairfax, VA.

LEVERAGING ASSOCIATIONS FOR NETWORKING

By Deborah J. Hodges

Networking and relationship-building are of paramount importance in the architectural, engineering, and construction (A/E/C) industry. And not many industries offer as many opportunities for networking through associations, unions, trade shows and continuing education events.

The advantages of networking are pronounced: getting introductions to decision-makers, building relationships, access to research, hearing about new projects and getting referrals.

One of the most fundamental and traditional ways to build client relationships is networking through associations. The construction industry has thousands of associations. By identifying a few core associations in your marketing plans that hold the key decision makers of your targeted market(s), you can build a network to share your thought-leadership and become a resource to the industry. Most importantly, networks allow us to check information, gather leads for projects, and win work.

Since each market has unique characteristics, fit-testing your company and its services are vital in the marketplace for effective networking.

Research Market and Clients

In the A/E/C industry, it is traditional to identify if your firm is a market-driven or client-driven firm in the marketing planning process. In either case, research is part of the process. If your company has a distinctive market or service(s), then clearly define it. Analyzing business is one of the first keys to success. It is hard to deliver good results if you are not prepared and targeting the wrong people. Also, look at establishing criteria such as high utility, future spending, regulatory drivers, decision-makers, and needs to produce successful market and client development. By covering these issues, you are raising the benchmark and prepared to be an excellent resource to your network.

Today, technology and the Internet are the primary tools used to evaluate potential contacts, companies, and associations for your networking and lead development. Develop consensus on expected returns with your team if pursuing an association or contact group. This will ensure greater participation from them and help build a richer relationship for all parties involved in networking. Don't forget to build your own database of contacts from your networking efforts. This information will go a long way in building a long-term network of industry contacts and prospects.

Building a Network

Most often, A/E/C marketers are searching for leads for projects to promote their firms and services; however, building a network is valuable for client development. The essential reasons for networking are to know about projects coming up and stay current on issues in the industry. This requires knowing a lot of people-real estate brokers, bankers, real estate lawyers, facilities engineers, owners, equipment manufacturers, and public agency officials. It is also important to network with other architects, engineers, and construction professionals.

///CMA

"Selling the invisible," A/E/C services, requires building a network of key contacts who think distinctively. It is common to look at industry or trade associations for building a network. The key is to build a network with an association to gather information to be a more informed thought-leader, share leads on projects, and meet with decision-makers. You can ferret out information—fact versus opinion with a qualified network. This saves time and is a true example of "fit-testing" your prospects. It is very important to ask good questions to gather leads and begin relationships.

Improve Your Networking and Leads

A successful and effective networking approach is proven or judged in "outcomes." The bottom line is –was your company selected as part of the building design team or awarded a project? That is what your company is going to use as a measuring stick. Is your networking leading to more opportunities and projects? It is highly recommended to "fit-test" your prospects and your company prior to networking.

A marketing SWOT Analysis is a great tool to use for marketing and positioning your company with contacts and associations. Map or define your services and their benefits in writing before networking. Know and internalize those facts. It will help you build more business faster and developer longer client relationships because you selected your network carefully and did your homework. Keep in mind, the prospective client wants to know why your company and services are of value to them. You will be prepared for their questions and comments.

Also, think realistically about contact time and capture time. Will it take one month or one year before your company has a project opportunity with the contact(s)? Knowing this or evaluating this question is important. You can produce faster returns on your leads and produce better results by evaluating your services and benefits against your potential contact, network, or association. Keep in mind-it is important to make it a "living reality."

When networking, try to determine if a short meeting over coffee could be helpful to exchange information. Always remember that sharing information is vital to keep the network healthy and moving forward. If you share information, it may lead to a longer face-to-face meeting with a decision-maker for a project. Keeping in contact, with periodic telephone calls, meetings, and by attending association meetings, is an essential business practice. If you don't contribute or stay in contact, then you will not be part of the network for very long. If there is not a good fit, ask for referral or lead to another source—that's networking.

As with any good marketing campaign, keep your targets, tactics, and timeline defined and your networking will be tuned up. These three T's should be used to your advantage here. Don't be caught without them to avoid "pursuit fatigue" or "networking fatigue." Changing directions to meet needs, tight schedules, and expectations can often take us off-track of our goals.

In summary, networking is an important tool in today's competitive world. The lower construction activity is making it more difficult to identify leads and projects. Be a strategic thinker when developing your networking plan with contacts, associations and public agencies. By networking to build client relationships, your chances of success are greater.

ABOUT DEBORAH HODGES

Deborah is President of Golden Square LLC, an association management firm, and Executive Director of the Construction Writers Association (CWA). Prior to CWA Deborah served in marketing roles with Bovis Lend Lease, OWP/P (Cannon Design), Nova Environmental Services and more. In addition, she served as President of the Society for Marketing Professional Services (SMPS) for 19 years, and is on the Board of Directors for the Construction Marketing Association (CMA). Deborah earned a MA Business Administration from DePaul University, a BA Organizational Communications from North Central College, along with advanced studies at the University of Notre Dame.

To summarize A/E/C Marketing Best Practices from the 2011 CMA webcast, following are the Top 10:

Top 10 A/E/C Marketing Best Practices

1 Understand your perception, position, segmentation, SWOT.

2 Develop a marketing plan with objectives, action calendar and measures.

3 Search optimize your website (Website Grader 90+, reviews, PPC?)

4 Aggressive networking with associations (local/regional, AGC, ASA, BOMA, AIA, etc).

5 Develop/manage lead generation (project leads, customers, targets, contacts, emails).

6 Build awareness through publishing, PR, speaking.

7 Ongoing communications to contacts, titles, verticals, etc.

8 Leverage blogs and social media to communicate company and industry content.

9 Experiment with new markets, example geographic, government, etc.

10 Leverage free publicity, wire distribution, editor lists.

Tools of the Trade: Modern Marketing for Construction Brands

Unit IV: Practical Marketing Considerations

FINDING MODERN MARKETING TALENT

By now, you have learned about the new marketing mix, new rules for measuring marketing, and that the need for content is transforming marketing departments and managers into authors and publishers. Terms like Marketing Technologist, and Marketing Quants (for quantitative) are gaining popularity. Marketing is changing—rapidly! Surely the skills required to manage this marketing revolution are different.

The implications for recruiting, training and managing this new breed of marketer are pronounced. Are traditional marketing skills obsolete? Do educational curriculums support new marketing? Can senior marketing executives manage young managers without understanding new media and marketing?

To be sure, there are marketing skills and experience that transcend traditional and new media. In specialized construction segments, market and product knowledge will always be important. Understanding of planning, forecasting, budgeting and market research are required skills for certain levels of marketing management. Project management skills, writing skills, and the ability to generate creative ideas, or at least brief, guide and manage other creative staff or agencies are all typical marketing roles. On the construction service side, proposal writing and bid management take priority in marketing. On the retail-side, expertise in merchandising and packaging take prominence.

No question, specialists can be hired to manage certain aspects of new marketing including website programming, search engine optimization, social media, marketing automation or database marketing. While traditional marketers come from educational backgrounds in business, communications, journalism, liberal arts, and yes, engineering; increasingly these specialists and other new marketing talent may come from computer science, IT or math programs.

Higher education curriculums are catching up slowly. Community colleges have moved aggressively into interactive media, including certificate programs. Traditional bachelor degree programs and some graduate programs are adding interactive courses, even complete programs.

Marketing associations are certainly focused on new marketing skills. There are hundreds of seminars and training programs about all types of social media and interactive marketing. The American Marketing Association (AMA), Business Marketing Association (BMA), and Construction Marketing Association (CMA) each offer extensive training programs and resources regarding new types of marketing and media.

///CMA

Human resource departments and marketing job-seekers must embrace new marketing skills and requirements. Specialized recruiters, job boards and directories will take share from generalist recruitment options. The Construction Marketing Association offers a Career Center using the million-record JobTarget database for both job-seekers and employers seeking specialized marketing talent.

Our Construction Marketing Association has been successful in hiring interns in marketing, and training them on both traditional and new media. Newly-minted college graduates, not surprisingly, bring excellent social media skills (especially Facebook) that can be leveraged into new and interactive media.

Kevin Enke, Marketing Director for Robert Bosch Corporation, and CMA Board member looks for marketing talent with trade association experience including the American Marketing Association, PR Society of America, or certified project managers from the construction trades. He reinforces that importance of the Internet, with construction firms increasingly using search engines to source products and services. Bosch focuses marketing resources on both professional contractor channels and retail home improvement channels, specifically Home Depot and Lowe's. In retail, traditional category management is transitioning to "shopper marketing" which encompasses in-store, online, and all communications pre- and post-purchase. He adds, "With the rate of change in the marketing mix, you are either driving that change are being swept up by it."

Selecting Marketing Partners: 3 Steps to Find a Great Marketing Agency

Finding and selecting a great marketing, advertising, creative, Internet or social media agency partner is one of the most important decisions you can make as a marketer. Finding an agency that can generate great ideas, as well as manage and implement projects expertly and efficiently. And perhaps most important, a partner that can help you be successful with measurable marketing results. Shouldn't be too hard, right? After all, there are hundreds of agencies out there begging for your business. Many of them are fantastic. Some just will not be a good fit. Still others will be disasters-in-the-making.

Entering into a union with a bad agency partner may not only end in divorce, but can also be expensive, embarrassing, or even get you fired. Yet, it happens all the time. What are some of the straws that break the agency partnership's back? A recent survey by the Construction Marketing Association (CMA) identified the following:

Reasons for firing an agency:

1. Poor marketing or sales results
2. Agency advice is weak (marketing, strategy, creative), or responsiveness is poor
3. Agency fees are excessive or disputed
4. Agency is not in tune with new media (SEO, social, blogging, etc)
5. Agency hired by prior management

And conversely….

Reasons for hiring an agency:

1. Need a specialist for a specific marketing project
2. Get new ideas for marketing
3. Want a new partner that can achieve results
4. New managers/management not tied to old partners

As in everything, due diligence can help prevent the former scenario and make the latter a success. There are several avenues that will lead you to potential agencies. One of the best is through referral/networking. Searching online can net a lot of agency candidates, but narrow the lists down by reviewing results-oriented case studies on agency sites. Or, if you have the budget, you can hire an agency search firm to help you. But before you do anything, determine key drivers.

Phase I: Establish Selection Criteria

- *Realistically assess your budget vs. agency size*
- *Decide if category or industry expertise is critical, and if so, make this a criterion*
- *Determine if specific marketing skills are important (creative, internet, social, PR, etc)*
- *Consider geography—will there be frequent on-site meetings?*
- *If you have an in-house marketing department, think about how an agency will work with it and augment it*
- *Do a mini SWOT analysis to determine what your new agency can leverage and/or improve*

Phase II: Identify Potential Agency Candidates

- *Depending on the scale of your marketing program, narrow down to 5-10 or more agency candidates that fit your criteria and review their websites thoroughly (per above, agency size vs. your budget is key, you don't want to be the largest or smallest client)*
- *Next, make contact with the most promising candidates and set-up phone interviews*
- *Send a written request for proposal (RFP) to agency candidates who did well in the phone interviews*
- *Conduct on-site visits and/or request agency presentations from a shortlist of agency candidates that did well with RFP responses*
- *Request the team that will be working on your account be in the presentation—know the players!*
- *Do ask for budget parameters for the types of marketing projects and programs you will be assigning*
- *Recruit a internal selection committee that, depending on program scale, is at least two and no more than 5 managers*
- *Use a scorecard or ranking on 5-10 criteria to add objectivity, but also consider your "gut" instincts*

Phase III: Choose Your Agency!

At this stage, be sure to have internal discussions with your selection committee. While committee members should rank or score agency candidates individually to avoid a dominant personality imposing his or her will, committee members should openly share their results and reasoning.

This group meeting and process should deliver the clear winner. However, if it's down to two viable choices, invite them to duke it out by executing the same test project. Then, evaluate them based on responsiveness, strategy and ideas, creative execution, project management and fees.

May the best agency win! Now, all that's left is to deliver the good news.

Marketing Automation: What It Is and Why You Need It

Credit to Josh Stailey of The Pursuit Group, Inc. and The Business Marketing Institute

Marketing automation is the secret engine behind effective lead generation, nurturing and management. For several good reasons, marketing automation is among the most significant initiatives in the marketing profession today. Yet, there remains considerable confusion about what marketing automation is and how to make it work.

In its original incarnation a few years ago, marketing automation was seen as a way to make enterprise marketing departments more efficient. The toolset usually included a database for managing digital assets (content, art, logos, etc.), a system for managing asset production and approvals, collaboration tools, a campaign calendar application and some e-mail and web content management software.

But since then, buyers of almost everything—from consumer products to business-to-business equipment and services—have participated in a revolution that has forced marketers to address things like:

> *Potential buyers no longer reveal themselves or invite personal interaction with vendors until they have researched and determined a solution*

> *The need to understand and respond to "digital body language", the online behavior of customers and prospects*

> *The rise of social media as a tool for prospects to learn about solutions and customers to grade their own vendor experiences*

"The term "marketing automation" is perhaps one of the most widely used, ill-defined and ambiguous terms in the marketing and sales technology landscape", states industry analyst Ian Michiels. Now—especially for SMB (small- and medium-sized businesses) and B2B companies – the term "marketing automation" revolves around what Michiels calls "marketing engagement automation," which focuses on how prospects and customers interact with the array of online and offline communications channels. In his own words, new marketing automation "might include setting up an email campaign, sending it out, and tracking performance; or creating a new landing page with a form capture element; or more importantly, managing communication with a prospect across multiple channels (email, the Web site, microsites), and tracking their behavior to identify the relative propensity to purchase."

That's close enough to ease the confusion. Now, the most important issue…

WHY YOUR COMPANY NEEDS MARKETING AUTOMATION

Almost every business-to-business company out there has a leaky sales funnel. In many, only the hottest prospects and the clearly unqualified leads get the proper treatment; the rest of the funnel leaks like a sieve. The qualified—but not yet sales-ready—leads are routinely deferred, forgotten or ignored until they fade away. Yet, it is this last class of prospects that often defines whether your company is just getting by or going to the next level. For example, in high technology, several studies have shown that over half of the people who demonstrated initial interest actually purchased a product in that category within two years. But in many cases the initial supplier they reached out to didn't nurture them, so they ended up buying from another vendor.

The new marketing automation tools enable your company to accomplish two major goals:

1. *Stop the leaky funnel by nurturing qualified prospects until they are ready to buy, and do it without involving valuable sales talent in the process;*

2. *Recognize the new "stealth" buyers by their online behavior, track their interactions, provide necessary information, then respond quickly when their behavior signals they are ready to buy*

Even if this were all an automated marketing/sales funnel could do, it would be valuable to most companies. But that's just the start; the role of marketing automation is to not only prevent prospects from falling through the cracks, but to:

- *Increase success ratios by tailoring and managing outbound interactions and content to each prospect's specific situation and need;*

- *Use inbound marketing to generate and nurture potential buyers not reached by outbound lead generation efforts;*

- *Score leads and prospects based on both their "fit" (e.g., industry, size, etc.) and behavior (e.g., online and offline activities);*

- *Develop, then maintain, a seamless flow of information between marketing and sales;*

- *Provide in-depth, real-time reporting on all leads, prospects, activities and communications between you and potential buyers;*

Sound like a silver bullet for marketers? Could be…but it doesn't come easily.

MARKETING AUTOMATION IS NOT A SET-AND-FORGET TOOL

Even though marketing automation is a popular and fast-growing concept, some industry observers have already issued warnings about the "CRM effect." That's the old (at least in Internet years) problem in which companies rushed to embrace CRM as the "silver bullet" for sales automation without having appropriate processes in place throughout their sales force. The result: some two-thirds of all CRM initiatives "failed" to reach stated goals. And some multi-million dollar investments in CRM were abandoned altogether.

CRM has proven to be a valuable tool, when launched and sustained with appropriate sales processes, training and motivation. But memories are short and the same risk holds for marketing automation. Four ingredients must be in place for marketing automation to succeed:

> 1. *Marketing processes defined and tested*
>
> 2. *The ability to comprehensively capture prospect interactions on your website (and with every other form of digital interaction—e-mail landing pages, etc.—as well)*
>
> 3. *A library of content that can be applied to every possible interaction. This includes content customized by product, geography, buying cycle stage, or other relevant filters*
>
> 4. *The ability to hand sales-ready prospects over to your sales force at the right time (and get them back for further nurturing if they do not buy)*

That's a handful. But we think it's worth the effort. Consider the research from Aberdeen Group that shows companies with the highest performance in annual revenue and return on marketing investment were four times more likely than peers to automate customer engagement with a marketing automation solution.

Marketing automation helps marketers increase the number of leads and prospects moved through the funnel, manage both outbound and inbound marketing efforts simultaneously, and deliver only sales-ready leads to your sales pros. In addition, real-time visibility into the pipeline enables marketers to focus on channels that drive the highest conversion rates, calculate customer acquisition rates/costs by marketing channel, and identify when campaigns or initiatives drive above average close rates.

And the results extend far beyond marketing metrics; marketing automation can shorten the time for prospects to convert to revenue, reduce bottlenecks in the sales cycle, and help forecast sales growth more accurately by identifying realistic and achievable targets.

On the unlikely chance that you haven't heard of marketing funnel automation until now, you will in 2011. The concept is no longer a novelty, but a proven boost to marketing effectiveness and a rational and accountable way to—finally —close the gap between marketing and sales.

THE FOUR PILLARS OF MARKETING AUTOMATION SUCCESS

Getting marketing automation right starts with a wider definition than simply an investment in new technology. In fact, technology is just one leg of a four-pillar foundation: technology, process, content and connectivity. Here's an overview of the other three pillars:

> *Process is an efficient routine for every step and stage in the marketing/sales cycle; technology schedules and oversees the actions and reactions in a pre-designed workflow*

> *Content is the substance of every outbound and inbound communications between you and your prospects; technology houses and deploys the right communications at the right time*

> *Connectivity ensures that all possible touch points—e-mail, landing pages, each page on a website—are wired together; technology provides that complex, real-time interlink*

Neglect just one of these and your marketing automation system cannot deliver full value. Neglect more than one and your implementation is likely to fail.

PRE-AUTOMATION—PREPARING FOR TECHNOLOGY

Prior to buying a marketing automation solution, or even looking for one, review your marketing/sales assets. Determine which of your assets can be integrated and which need to be created or replaced. Here's a beginning checklist:

1) **Lists** – *You probably have more lists than you think. That's par for the course in marketing and sales, where efforts are often dispersed, disjointed, or even dysfunctional. How are the lists you have in each of these categories?*

> • *Leads – Most organizations get leads from a variety of sources: trade media, the company website, tradeshows, sales people, etc. Are yours organized with separate fields for first name, last name, phone, and postal address? Do you have email addresses for your leads? What qualifying information do you have about them and is each information element in an individual field?*

> • *Prospects - Also known as qualified leads. Because most companies don't have a nurture cycle for qualified-but-not-ready-to-buy prospects, these tend to be neglected, if not abandoned outright. What do you know about your interaction with them? These may be your greatest source for future sales.*

> • *Customers – Because they often disappear from the marketing radar once they come on board, these will also be a major source of new marketing opportunity. What information do you have about them (revenue, purchase cycles, types of products, services, etc.) and their people? Is it organized effectively?*

Don't worry about what to do with these lists just yet. At this point, you need to know they're there, and how to get them organized properly.

2) Links – *Identify every place your company maintains a digital presence, as each will be a link that needs to be captured and poured into your marketing automation system. This is far more than the "contact us" page on your website:*

> • *Every single page on your website should be able to capture visitor activity, especially if you want to track individual online behavior and use that to automatically customize the next step in the process (e.g., send a particular type of content or alert a sales rep)*

> • *Landing pages from various campaigns should be "track-able", as well as the web browsing done after*

> • *Web forms, where visitors register to download white papers or other information. These are perfect tools for automated data capture*

> • *E-mails, including corporate campaigns and the ones your sales reps run on their own Chances are, your company has dozens, if not hundreds, of links to identify and move into the marketing automation system.*

3) Content – *Thanks to the Web and Google, buyers today want at least part of their connection to you to be electronic, web-based and self serve. Which makes content the fuel that keeps the marketing automation engine running.*

Most companies have a ton of content that can be sliced up, repurposed and repackaged in a way that prospects want to absorb throughout their buying cycle. So expect to assemble lots of articles, reviews, independent tests, white papers, configurators, technical sheets and the like. And that's just for your website for reading or downloading. Then add in:

> • *E-mails and attachments for long-term nurture campaigns (think one contact every two weeks for a buying cycle that extends over 18 months and branches by segmentation)*

> • *Landing pages*

> • *Videos and presentations*

> • *Social media posts, including company and individual blogs*

So inventory your content. In our experience, more companies underestimate the content they will need than any other of the marketing automation "pillars." This sales-nurture content will be the hardest to acquire or create…and the most valuable in your future nurture cycles.

> **4) Workflow** - *This is the sharp edge of the process, the way you get marketing automation to integrate links, lists and content into a coherent selling cycle. Leading vendors have built robust workflow creation tools into their software, and good workflow strategists can leverage internal resources twenty-fold with automated—instead of manual—steps in the cycle.*
>
> *Your pre-technology challenge is to audit your current workflows (if you have them), or, if not, to document how marketing goes about landing, qualifying and nurturing leads, and what criteria they use to determine when a lead is ready to buy. A good way to do that is by using flowcharting and process mapping to show how a lead moves through your funnel and becomes a customer (or not).*

Here's a high-level workflow sample:

The boxes represent activities you take in marketing to leads and prospects: sending e-mails, creating landing pages and web forms, loading and making content available via links. The diamonds represent the options that a targeted lead or prospect has…opening an e-mail (or not), visiting a landing page (or not), completing and submitting a web form (or not), etc. Each of those yes/no decisions yields new boxes in the workflow, which yields new decisions. And so on, until the target buys, opts out, or you decide that enough is enough. For your salespeople, the most important boxes in a workflow are the notifications or alerts, when the prospect is ready to buy and needs person-to-person contact.

The marketing automation system you select will integrate this seething mass of people, process and content into a unified, effective nurture marketing flow—but only if you tell it to. And in order to do that, you need to go through all of this.

This is not meant to be discouraging. But it's easy to underestimate what it takes to design, provision and implement an effective automated nurture process. And while marketing automation can yield enormous return on investment, there's no magic potion that makes it easy.

Unit V: Marketing Resources

Effective marketing requires information and resources. The purpose of this TOOLS OF THE TRADE book is to support your ongoing needs for information about all aspects of strategic and tactical marketing. To this end, the Resources unit identifies publications, websites and associations, beginning with marketing and then presented in the order of chapters. Do you have suggestions for future resources? Please email the author: neil@ConstructionMarketingAssociation.org.

MARKETING

Publications:

> *Marketing News (www.marketingpower.com/AboutAMA/Pages/AMA%20Publications/ Marketing%20News/MarketingNews.aspx*

> *BtoB (Marketing) magazine (www.btobonline.com)*

> *Marketing Today magazine (www.MarketingToday.com)*

Associations:

> *American Marketing Association (www.MarketingPower.org)*

> *Business Marketing Association (www.Marketing.org)*

> *Construction Marketing Association (www.ConstructionMarketingAssociation.org)*

> *Society of Marketing Professional Services (www.SMPS.org)*

BRANDING

Publications:

> *Branding Best Practices: A Guide to Effective Business and Product Naming (Lulu.com, ISBN # 978-0-615-22146-5)*

Websites:

> *All About Branding (Articles, www.AllAboutBranding.com)*

> *Best Brands of the World (Logo database, free downloads, www.BrandsOfTheWorld.com)*

> *Brand Channel by Interbrand (www.BrandChannel.com)*

> *Best Global Brands (Interbrand annual study, www.Interbrand.com)*

> *Internic Whols Database (Identifies website domain owners, www.Internic.com)*

> *United States Patent and Trade Office (Search U.S. trademarks, www.USPTO.gov)*

> *International Trademark Association (www.INTA.org)*

MARKET RESEARCH

Publications:

> Journal of Marketing Research (www.marketingpower.com/AboutAMA/Pages/AMA%20Publications/AMA%20Journals/Journal%20of%20Marketing%20Research/JournalofMarketingResearch.aspx)

> International Journal of Market Research (www.IJMR.com)

Websites:

> Syndicated Market Research Directory (www.MarketResearch.com)

> Survey Monkey Free Online Surveys (www.SurveyMonkey.com)

> Zoomerang Free Online Surveys (www.Zoomerang.com)

Construction Lead Services:

> Reed Construction Data (www.ReedConstructionData.com)

> McGraw-Hill Dodge Reports (www.Dodge.Construction.com)

> Blue Book (www.BlueBook.org)

Associations:

> American Marketing Association (www.MarketingPower.com)

> Market Research Association (www.MRA-Net.org)

CONTENT

Publications:

> Chief Content Officer (www.ContentMarketingInstitute.com/chief-content-officer/)

> B2B Content Marketing Benchmarks, Budgets & Trends   (www.ContentMarketingInstitute.com/2010/09/b2b-content-marketing/)

Associations:

> Content Marketing Institute (www.ContentMarketingInstitute.com)

Websites:

> Top Content Marketing Blogs (www.Junta42.com/community/top-42-content-marketing-blogs.aspx)

> Content Vendor Directory (www.junta42.com/content-marketing-directory.aspx)

> Top 50 Article Submission Sites (www.Vretoolbar.com/articles/directories.php)

> Content Marketing World (Event, www.ContentMarketingWorld.com)

INTERNET

Websites:

> *Google Analytics (www.Google.com/analytics)*

> *Google Website Optimizer (www.Services.Google.com/websiteoptimizer)*

> *Google Adwords, Traffic Estimator (www.Adwords.Google.com)*

> *Internic Whols Database (Identifies website domain owners, www.Internic.com)*

> *Hubspot's Marketing Grader (Free SEO score, www.MarketingGrader.com)*

Associations:

> *Internet Marketing Association (www.IMAnetwork.org)*

> *Web Marketing Association (www.WebMarketingAssociation.org)*

> *Search Engine Marketing Professional Organization (SEMPO, www.sempo.org)*

Whitepapers:

> *SEO Must-Know Basics (Marketing Profs, www.marketingprofs.com/articles/2011/4573/seo-must-know-basics-the-hows-and-whats)*

> *Learning SEO: A Step by Step Guide (Hubspot, http://www.hubspot.com/learning-seo-from-lexperts-guide)*

> *An Introductory Guide to Paid Search (Hubspot, www.hubspot.com/marketing-ebook /introductory-guide-to-paid-search/)*

SOCIAL MEDIA

Publications:

> *Social Media Marketing Magazine (www.smmmagazine.com)*

> *The Social Media Marketing Book (www.TheSocialMediaMarketingBook.com)*

Websites:

> *Radian 6 Social Media Monitoring (www.Radian6.com)*

> *Sysomos Social Media Monitoring (www.Sysomos.com)*

> *Social Media Search (www.SocialMention.com)*

> *Facebook (www.Facebook.com)*

> *YouTube (www.YouTube.com)*

> *Twitter (www.Twitter.com)*

> *LinkedIn (www.LinkedIn.com)*

> *Hubspot (www.Hubspot.com)*

> *Marketing Profs (www.MarketingProfs.com)*

> *Social Media Logue (www.SocialMediaLogue.com)*

> *Social Media Examiner (www.SocialMediaExaminer.com)*

Associations:

> *American Marketing Association (www.MarketingPower.org)*

ADVERTISING

Publications:

> *Advertising Age (www.AdAge.com)*

> *Adweek (www.Adweek.com)*

> *MediaPost (www.MediaPost.com)*

> *Communication Arts (www.CommArts.com)*

> *SmartBrief (www.SmartBrief.com)*

Associations:

> *American Association or Advertising Agencies (4A's, www.AAAA.org)*

> *Association of National Advertisers (www.ANA.net)*

> *Advertising Education Foundation (www.AEF.com)*

> *Internet Advertising Bureau (www.IAB.net)*

> *International Advertising Association (www.iaaglobal.org)*

PR

Publications:

> *PR Week (www.PRweek.com)*

> *Public Relations Magazine (www.PlatformMagazine.com)*

> *O'Dwyer's PR News (www.OdwyerPR.com)*

> *Publicity Insider (www.PublicityInsider.com)*

Associations:

> *Public Relations Society of America (www.PRSA.org)*

> *The International Association of Business Communicators (www.IABC.com)*

> *Communications Media Management Association (www.CMMA.org)*

TRADE SHOWS

Publications:

> *Exhibitor Magazine (www.ExhibitorOnline.com)*

> *Trade Show Executive (www.TradeShowExecutive.com)*

> *Meetings & Conventions Magazine (www.Meetings-Conventions.com)*

Associations:

> *Trade Show Exhibitors Association (www.TSEA.org)*

Websites:

> *EXPO (www.EXPOweb.com)*

> *Conventions.net (www.Conventions.net)*

DIRECT MARKETING

Publications:

> Direct Marketing News (www.dmnews.com)

> Direct (www.directmag.com)

Associations:

> Direct Marketing Association (www.The-DMA.org)

> Email Marketing Institute (www.EmailInstitute.com)

NEW PRODUCT DEVELOPMENT

Publications:

> New Product Development for Dummies (ISBN# 978-0470117705)

> PDMA Handbook of New Product Development (ISBN# 978-0471485247)

> Journal of Product Innovation Management (www.pdma.org/view_webpage.cfm?pk_webpage=231)

Associations:

> Product Development & Management Association (www.PDMA.org)

> Product Development Institute (www.Prod-Dev.com)

> New Product Development Certification (www.pdma.org/view_webpage.cfm?pk_webpage=231)

> International Association for Product Development (www.IAPDonline.com)

Whitepapers:

> The Four Pillars of Successful Product Launches (www.marketingprofs.com/articles/2007/2240/the-four-pillars-of-successful-product-launches)

PRICING

Associations:

> Professional Pricing Society (www.PricingSociety.com)

> Product Development Institute (www.Prod-Dev.com)

Publications:

> Pricing Solutions (www.PricingSolutions.com)

CHANNEL MARKETING

Publications:

> Journal of Marketing Channels (www.tandfonline.com/loi/wjmc20)

> The Handbook of Channel Marketing (www.elew.com/Handbook%20of%20Channel%20Marketing.pdf)

Websites:

> Channel Management Solutions (www.ChannelManagement.com)

HOME IMPROVEMENT RETAIL

Publications:

> *Hardware Retailing (www.nrha.org/v2/Hardware_Retailing/)*

> *Home Channel News (www.HomeChannelNews.com/)*

> *LBM Journal (www.LBMjournal.com)*

Associations/Websites:

> *North American Retail Hardware Association (NRHA, www.nrha.org)*

> *Home Improvement Research Institute (www.hiri.org)*

> *Path To Purchase Institute (www.P2Pi.org)*

> *Top 500 Retail Scoreboard (www.HomeChannelNews.com)*

> *Golden Hammer Awards (www.GoldHammerAwards.com)*

> *Home Depot Supplier Resources (www.Suppliercenter.HomeDepot.com)*

> *Lowe's Supplier Resources: (www.LowesLink.com)*

Events:

> *National Hardware Show (May 1-3, 2012, www.NationalHardwareShow.com)*

A/E/C MARKETING

Websites:

> *Reed Construction Data (www.ReedConstructionData.com)*

> *McGraw-Hill Dodge Reports (www.Dodge.Construction.com)*

> *McGraw-Hill Sweets (www.Products.Construction.com)*

Associations:

> *The Construction Specifications Institute (www.CSInet.org)*

> *Society for Marketing Professional Services (SMPS, www.smps.org/Resources/I-am-a-Marketer/)*

> *Construction Marketing Association (CMA, www.ConstructionMarketingAssociation.org)*

Whitepapers:

> *Funnel Government Funds to Your Clients' Projects: Five Components of a Strong Government Affairs Program (http://www.smps.org/Foundation/Research-and-White-Papers/)*

ABOUT NEIL M. BROWN

Neil M. Brown is Chairman of the Construction Marketing Association, and Chief Marketing Officer (CMO) of Construction Marketing Advisors. Prior to these roles, Brown was CEO of numerous marketing consulting and creative agencies for the past 15 years, managing some of the biggest brands in the construction sector. Prior to the agency-side, Brown was a brand manager at electrical products manufacturer IDEAL Industries, and later CMO of an architectural metals manufacturer. Neil earned an MBA from Northern Illinois University, and a BS-Marketing Cum Laude from Southern Illinois University. Neil is a frequent author and contributor to *Advertising Age*, *BtoB magazine* (formerly *Business Marketing*), *Marketing News* and other publications. He is author of two books, *Tools of the Trade: Modern Marketing for Construction Brands*, and *Branding Best Practices: A Guide to Effective Business and Product Naming*.

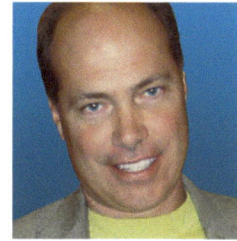

ABOUT THE CONSTRUCTION MARKETING ASSOCIATION

The Construction Marketing Association (CMA) provides professional development and certification, marketing training, resources and information, networking and recognition. CMA sponsors the Construction Marketing STAR™ Awards, and Construction Marketer of the Year™ Awards. And CMA produces the Certified Construction Marketing Professional (CCMP) program. Full information is available at ConstructionMarketingAssociation.org. The site links to the Construction Marketing Blog with marketing news, resources and related content, and the association's Twitter, Facebook, YouTube and LinkedIn pages.

Questions? Contact Neil Brown at neil@constructionmarketingassociation.org

NOTES

_____

_____

_____

_____

_____

_____

_____

_____

_____

_____

_____

_____

_____

_____

_____

Tools of the Trade: Modern Marketing for Construction Brands

///CMA